"As online channels have grown in influence and span, new pathways for career development have opened up. *Social Networking for Business Success* is a useful guide for navigating these opportunities, offering clear, cost-effective ways to use online channels to grow your personal brand, expertise, and audience. More than just a primer, *Social Networking for Business Success* provides concrete tactics and tools for developing a social media following, optimizing for search and paid ads responsibly, and setting goals for your business."

—MEGHAN ANDERSON, inbound marketing manager,
HubSpot; on Deloitte's list of top ten fastest-growing
technology companies

"*Social Networking for Business Success* is a fantastic book that summarizes a lot of the lessons I learned the hard way when I started my own business. Miriam and Hannah realize that time is precious, so this book doesn't have any fluff. It's full of tons of immediately actionable, practical tips. As a bonus, it was really easy and fun to read. It's a great investment in your business success."

—PETE KISTLER, co-founder, Brandyourself.com,
an *Entrepreneur* magazine top five collegiate start-up

"Miriam and Hannah have combined forces to bring us a guide to leveraging social networking and online media that is as broad in its scope as it is deep in its wisdom. If you're looking for advice on how to get started or rev up your existing online business, this is the first book you should be reading."

—NEAL SCHAFFER, author of *Maximize Your Social:
A One-Stop Guide to Building a Social Media Strategy
for Marketing and Business Success*

"In today's economy, everyone should think about how to market themselves as if they were a business or brand. *Social Networking for Business Success* simplifies this process for new entrepreneurs and for business owners who know they need to ramp up their online presence to stay competitive. This book provides a soup-to-nuts education on how to launch a business online. Read it and you won't waste any time figuring out how to get started."

—DAVID RIKLAN, founder, SelfGrowth.com,
1 self improvement website on the Internet

"As a real estate and mobility expert, I know the value of relationships and growing and maintaining a strong network to succeed. *Social Networking for Business Success* provides exactly the information small business owners need now to be successful in this competitive marketplace. I highly recommend it."　　　　　　　　　　　—**JILL HEINECK**, Heineck Relocation Partners

"Starting and running a business is hard work, but never in history has it been so easy to connect with an audience, find a customer, or market your brand. Social media allows anyone to connect with the entire world given a little work and very little money. This book shows you how to do it right.

Whether you are starting a side business, going out on your own, or even running an established business this book can help you leverage social media to advertise and market your product or service. I found it very informative for my consulting business and have implemented many of its recommendations. I highly suggest you do the same!"

—**DAVID LINTON**, founder,
Arobase Group–An Apple Consultant Company

"I'm the MOXIE Miriam and Hannah describe in this book—a full-time employee with a flourishing business on the side for nearly nine years, and I've found lots of helpful tips in this book. When I began my business, social media was in its infancy, and I've been teaching myself along the way. This book offers 'one-stop shopping' for the basics and more. It will allow me to tune up my efforts!"　　　—**MEGAN CARTIER**, owner, Flow Yoga,
and senior vice president, marketing, Wells Fargo

"Social media can feel like a blur to some business owners or entrepreneurs and a waste of time to others. The smart folks, however, understand the tremendous opportunity to use these tools—they just don't know how to do so effectively. Lucky for them that *Social Networking for Business Success* has arrived. It's a practical and smart guide to the effective use of social media today for business. And well worth the investment."

—**TIM TYRELL-SMITH**, marketing consultant,
branding and business strategy at Fix, Build and Drive

100 Conversations for Career Success
Miriam Salpeter and Laura M. Labovich

Social Networking for Career Success
Miriam Salpeter

SOCIAL NETWORKING FOR BUSINESS SUCCESS

MIRIAM SALPETER AND
HANNAH MORGAN

NEW YORK

Library of Congress Cataloging-in-Publication Data

Salpeter, Miriam.
   Social networking for business success / Miriam Salpeter and Hannah Morgan.
     pages cm
   ISBN 978-1-57685-928-5
   1. Business enterprises—Computer networks. 2. Social networks. 3. Success in
business. I. Morgan, Hannah. II. Title.
   HD30.37.S245 2013
   658.8'72—dc23
                                    2013023027

ISBN 978-1-57685-928-5

Printed in the United States of America

9 8 7 6 5 4 3 2 1

For information or to place an order, contact LearningExpress at:
   80 Broad Street
   Suite 400
   New York, NY 10004

About the Authors

Miriam Salpeter M.A., is owner of Keppie Careers, a coaching and consulting firm helping entrepreneurs and job seekers leverage social media and traditional tools to achieve their business goals. Miriam is in-demand as a social media and job search strategist, consultant, and speaker. She has two other highly acclaimed and award-winning books published by LearningExpress, LLC: *Social Networking for Career Success*, and *100 Conversations for Career Success*. Traditional media outlets, such as *The Wall Street Journal*, *The New York Times*, and Forbes.com, frequently cite Miriam's advice regarding how to leverage social media; CNN named her to its list of "Top 10 Job Tweeters You Should Be Following." Miriam contributes weekly to *U.S. News & World Report* and to AOL Jobs.com, and shares cutting-edge strategies for business owners and job seekers via her own site, KeppieCareers.com.

A vice president for a Wall Street firm before earning a master's degree from Columbia University, Miriam headed the Career Action Center at the Rollins School of Public Health of Emory University before launching her own business. She has been helping to empower job seekers and small business owners for more than 17 years. Learn more via her website and blog: http://www.keppie careers.com and on Twitter: @Keppie_Careers.

Hannah Morgan founded CareerSherpa.net three years ago as a part-time venture to dispense actionable advice on topics such as personal reputation management, networking, personal branding, and social media. By following many of the principles outlined in this book, she seamlessly transitioned her business to a full-time endeavor.

Hannah is now a sought-after speaker and trainer, respected for her insights about how anyone, from a job seeker to a small business owner, can use social media to build an online presence, create brand recognition, and grow a supportive community.

Nationally and locally recognized for her expertise, she has been listed in Monster.com's "The Monster 11 for 2011: Career Experts Who Can Help Your Job Search," YouTern's "Top 50 Blogs for Young Careerists," and The Daily Muse's "15 Career Experts Not to Miss on Twitter." Hannah writes for CareerSherpa.net as well as *U.S. News & World Report*, sharing modern methods for standing out in today's competitive world. Learn more via her website and blog; http://careersherpa.net, and on Twitter: @CareerSherpa.

CONTENTS ▶

CONTENTS

Acknowledgments

We are grateful for our in-person and online colleagues and friends who generously share information and ideas and inspire us to do the same. It never ceases to amaze us how much useful data fills our social media feeds. Often, when we were looking for a particular resource, all we'd need to do is check Twitter, and someone would have shared exactly what we needed. This supportive and informative community is one reason we were so excited about writing this book. A special thank you goes to the LearningExpress team, especially the Director of Book Publishing, Sheryl Posnick, who enthusiastically encouraged us to take on this project and provided useful and enriching feedback.

FROM MIRIAM
I could never accomplish my business goals without the love and support of my wonderful husband, Mike. I am so proud to dedicate this book to you. Thank you for everything—from listening to me read chapters aloud, to adeptly managing things on the home front after working all day yourself, so I could tweak a chapter or tackle

another project. I am so lucky to have you as my partner in everything that matters.

Every day, I try to be a positive role model for my three sons and to teach them by example that you can own a business and have a life. Some days are better than others. I appreciate their patience, understanding, and the fact that they think I am a famous author!

Hannah—thanks for agreeing to jump in with both feet and co-author this book with me! It's been so much fun working with you, brainstorming ideas, and sharing resources. I love that our friendship started online and has taken so many steps since then. I'm lucky to have you as a colleague, friend, and collaborator.

FROM HANNAH

I dedicate this book to Pop, for giving me roots and wings, and for serving as the ultimate role model for entrepreneurial spirit, nurturing relationships, and building an unforgettable reputation.

Due to the love, understanding, and support of my family, I was provided the time to write this book. I am extremely grateful! Rich, Chase, and Elliott: I love you all so much.

To my friends who let me tap into their wisdom and share their experiences, thank you.

And, most importantly, thank you Miriam, for inviting me to be a part of this project! I learned so much by collaborating with you. It has been an incredible journey!

Introduction

This is the book we would have liked to have read when we started our businesses. We wrote it to be useful whether you are just thinking of starting a business "on the side," or if you have a company that's doing well, but you are ready to launch it to the next level. As entrepreneurs ourselves (Hannah started her business while working full-time, and Miriam launched hers after leaving her previous job), we both experience the benefits of using social media every day. In this book, we teach you how to demonstrate your expertise, grow your network of potential customers and clients, and learn new things that can make the difference between having a hobby and having a successful, thriving company.

Lucky for all of us, social networks have leveled the playing field:

- If you want to be a consultant, coach, or market other services, and you have the expertise, you can create a business and connect with clients online. In the online world, introverts can compete just as well as extroverts; you don't need to be gregarious to display what you know; you just need to have the skills your clients expect.
- If you have products to sell, you can learn how to highlight their features, advertise how they can make a difference to customers, and garner a community of friends and fans who

will serve as a funnel for customers—all from the comfort of your home or office, or on-the-go via mobile devices. (How awesome is that?)

Having your own business is about taking action, trying new things, making mistakes and learning from them, and most importantly, building new connections.

You can do it! Using social media does not require you to be a rocket scientist or a technology specialist. With the right tools and focused expertise that you'll learn from our book, you'll be able to move ahead with confidence. And, guess what? While this book has a lot of information, we promise we have only included what we think you need to know without the fluff.

So, let's get started. We hope you'll agree that using online tools to start or grow your business is an incredible experience. Take some risks, develop a few new skills and have fun. We're glad to be along for the ride!

To your success!

—*Miriam and Hannah*

1

Why Starting Your Own Business Makes Sense: Times (and the workforce), They Are a-Changin'

I n the old days, having a job meant working in one place, often for decades at a time. You probably only searched for a new position if you were unhappy at your current job, or if a better opportunity came along. Today, however, it's unusual to find someone loyal to one company for an extended time.

More businesses are hiring contingent workers, otherwise known as temporary or contractors, instead of full-time employees. Tammy Erikson of *Harvard Business Review* wrote, "Temporary placement service provider Adecco predicts the growth rate for contingent workers will be three to four times the growth rate among traditional workforces." Adecco predicts temporary workers will eventually comprise about 25 percent of the global workforce. As a result, finding traditional jobs will continue to be highly competitive. Employers will replace many jobs with contract workers.

THE NEW INDEPENDENT WORKFORCE

According to the website Mavenlink, the number of self-employed, independent service firms, solopreneurs (independent business owners), and temporary workers grew by an estimated 4.3 million workers between 1995 and 2012. They expect the contingent workforce to grow to 40 percent, or 64.9 million workers by 2020. If these come true, 40 percent of American workers, or nearly 65 million people, will not be working in what we know as "traditional" jobs by 2020.

These data suggest income security is unlikely to come from working in one organization for the long haul. Instead, many professionals are turning to entrepreneurism as an anecdote to the tough job market; they are creating their own "jobs" by becoming business owners in their own right.

If you're considering this path, you are not only in good company; you're a smart cookie! For years, futurists have been predicting the end of jobs as we know them, suggesting that, increasingly, companies will turn to independent contractors instead of full-time employees to accomplish key tasks.

When the times are changing, you need to change, too. Whether you are considering launching a full-fledged business, or just want to do a little consulting on the side, consider this a wake-up call to delve into social media for your career or business, if you have not already done so. Knowing how to use these tools will make a huge difference to your success, because using them well will help market your skills, products, and services.

The "Gig" Economy

We used to think of temporary work being the purview of short-term administrative support people, seasonal retail positions, and accountants before tax day. Now, the temporary workforce includes not only people who work for temp agencies, but also those engaging in what has become known as the "gig economy." This workforce includes independent contractors, freelancers, and entrepreneurs who hang a literal or virtual "shingle," and launch their own small businesses.

Luckily, while the tide is changing in favor of a contingent, or temporary, workforce, there are fewer barriers to starting a business now than ever before. Years ago, you needed to invest money or secure a loan to launch a business. You probably would have rented a brick and mortar office or store, and paid for ads in the Yellow Pages, print journals, and magazines. If you were a service business, you may have limited your clientele to local prospects; a national (or international) audience was beyond the reach of most contractors or small businesses.

Is Having a Business For You?

Maybe you're not sure if business ownership is for you. If you plan and use your time well (and use the information we provide in this book), you can test the waters, and start your business on the side while you keep your full-time job.

Keep in mind: social media and online tools allow you to create side businesses providing multiple streams of revenue. Even if you are not ready to commit to being a full-time business owner, we believe you should begin to envision side revenue streams, no matter how safe you believe your job to be. Think about how to diversify your portfolio of income opportunities. One way to do this is to use social networks to demonstrate your expertise, and create new contacts who can help lead to new income opportunities.

Create a Side Hustle—Be Someone With MOXIE

In the "new economy," having multiple income streams provides a layer of security you cannot expect from an employer. You may see people refer to this moonlighting phenomenon as having a *side hustle*. We think the term "hustle" has negative connotations. (One definition is "to obtain by aggressive or illicit means.") We want to define and use a new term to describe someone who starts a business on the side while working.

The word "moxie" refers to someone who has "courage, nerve, or vigor." According to Dictionary.com, a non-alcoholic drink named moxie popularized the term because the company touted it as helping people "build up nerve." We polled our networks, and everyone agreed *moxie* conjured up positive connotations, so we thought it would be a great term and acronym for people who are:

Managing
Other (secondary)
X-tra
Income
Engagements

In our book, when we refer to a MOXIE, we are talking about someone who is earning income on the side, while still working in a traditional job. Some MOXIEs may want to transition to working in their "extra engagements" full time at some point, while others just want extra, new income streams.

Don't Let Your MOXIE Gig Interfere With Your Main Job

If you do start a business on the side, be careful not to put your day job in jeopardy. Make sure your employer doesn't have rules against moonlighting—you may have agreed to policies by signing documents when you started your job and not remember it.

Some rules of thumb:

- Don't do work for your side gigs while you are on the clock at your full-time job.
- Don't use your company's computer, phone, or any supplies for your side job.

- Don't compete with your current company for clients.
- Never use or share any proprietary information from your current company.

Evaluate the pros and cons of telling your boss about your MOXIE gigs. If there is no policy against having a second job, and it will not affect your current job, you may decide to keep your side job to yourself. If you think your side job puts your full-time position in danger, make sure you are ready to face those consequences.

In this book, we'll show you what tools are best to use when you launch or ramp up your business, whether it's a full-time

A MOXIE SUCCESS STORY

Dan Schawbel, managing partner for Millenial Branding, LLC is a Gen-Y workplace and consumer expert, and author of *Me 2.0* (Kaplan Publishing, 2009). Dan is a great example of a MOXIE. He was a marketing specialist at EMC when he was inspired to start a blog about personal branding. The blog led him to create the Personal Brand Awards, which was a recognition program for people who were building successful brands using social media. Dan then launched Personal Branding TV, which is an online video series, with him as the host, giving personal branding tips, helping students, and interviewing CEOs about how they built their brands over the course of their careers.

When he authored an article about personal branding for About.com, it was a launching pad for other opportunities to write for new audiences, including American Marketing Association, *Brandweek Magazine*, and *BusinessWeek*.

While still employed full time, Dan wrote a book proposal about personal branding for students and young professionals, and shopped it around to 70 agents before finally signing a contract with Kaplan Publishing. During that time, he came home from his full-time job to start working on the book, and wrote during the weekend.

Due to his diligent networking and publicity efforts, *Me 2.0* launched to much acclaim, and Dan received an invitation to speak at Google after they read his profile in *Fast Company*.

continued from page 5

This was when Dan's employer found out about his hobby. They received a Google alert about his book. This led to Dan creating the first social media position at EMC, which he did while continuing his writing and publicity efforts on the side. After three years, it was clear to Dan that he didn't need a full-time job anymore. He resigned his job at EMC, and launched Millennial Branding, LLC. Even better? He later signed EMC as a client!

engagement or you are a MOXIE. Even though many online resources are free and relatively easy to use, there are best practices to help you make the most of them—and to do so efficiently, as you may start your business on the side while you are still working full time.

We'll teach you how to highlight what you have to offer in a way that will appeal to your audience, and showcase your best skills and accomplishments for the people who need to know about you.

Get It Done

Things to do:

- Evaluate your job or business prospects.
- Look around—is there writing on the wall you should be reading? Should you be planning for a change?
- If you are thinking of starting a MOXIE gig, be sure to learn about your current company's policies, and decide if you might be risking your current job.
- If there's no policy preventing you from starting a job on the side, weigh the pros and cons of talking to your boss about your plans.

2

Traits and Characteristics of Successful Business Owners: How Do You Rank?

Y ou are convinced that this is a good time to start a business, at least in theory. However, not everyone is well-suited to the work and lifestyle of an entrepreneur, whether you're a full-time business owner or someone with MOXIE who runs (or plans to run) a business on the side using "courage, nerve, or vigor."

Your Expertise—You have to Bring It

Sometimes, books about starting a business gloss over the fact that you need to actually have expertise—specific skills and abilities—in order to succeed. In an effort to prove that anyone can be an entrepreneur, these books often share stories where people seem to earn money based on being in the right place at the right time.

Throughout this book, you can expect straight talk from us, including a list of practical "Get It Done" action items at the end of every chapter. This straight talk starts with a philosophical underpinning we hope you will embrace: nothing is going to help you achieve your business goals more than your own sweat equity.

Social media is a wonderful platform to connect with people, but it is not a magic wand. While there are many practical and logistical concerns when starting a business, which we address throughout this book, one of the most important questions to ask yourself before you get started is: What are my skills? What am I good at doing? Are there people who will pay for what I offer or sell?

In Chapter 13, we will outline how to explore the nitty-gritty of business building. In the meantime, consider the more day-to-day concerns of running your own business. For example, are you willing to stick with your idea even if you do not experience immediate success? Can you tolerate failure?

Evaluate Your Personality

Before you embark on an entrepreneurial adventure, stop to recognize and identify specific personality traits you have or lack that may influence your success. Face it—if you can't balance your own checkbook or send an email, you probably need a little remediation before starting a business on your own, or alternatively, you may need to find some business partners to pick up the slack. Before starting or growing a business, learn about your personality and identify potential weak spots and areas for improvement.

In their book, *Heart, Smarts, Guts and Luck: What it Takes to be an Entrepreneur and Build a Great Business* (Harvard Business Review Press, 2012), authors Anthony Tjan, Richard Harrington, and Tsun-Yan Hsieh interviewed many successful business owners and entrepreneurs to identify entrepreneurial personality traits. They determined that self-awareness, even more than having a high IQ, helps business builders succeed. In other words, you don't need to be brilliant to succeed in business, but you do need to be able to recognize what you're good at and understand your limitations. For example, if you fail to realize you lack the time, interest, and patience to build a useful website, and you build one anyway, your business may fail.

The book's title showcases what the authors believe are the four key traits to entrepreneurial success: heart, smarts, guts, and luck. They offer a free Entrepreneurial Aptitude Test via their website (HSGL.com), which they explain is "a brief survey designed to identify your unique make-up of key "'entrepreneurial DNA' traits." The test is based on research collected from the top 200 business founders and builders around the world. While the results may not be surprising to you, you should take the test to make sure you are aware of your personality type, strengths, and weaknesses. This awareness is one big step toward business building success. Other well-known personality assessments, such as the Myers-Briggs Type Indicator (MBTI), may help you decide if you have the skills necessary to start a business. You can find a free assessment link to the MBTI on our website under "resources" or contact a certified examiner to take a test.

After taking these tests, you may ask what you should look for in your results. While there is no fixed rule about which personality traits predict a successful career as a business owner, there is research to indicate what traits are most useful. For example, a post in the *Harvard Business Review* suggested the key skills for entrepreneurs include persuasion, leadership, personal accountability—such as demonstrating initiative, self-confidence, resiliency, and a willingness to take responsibility for personal actions—goal orientation, and interpersonal skills.

The Guardian Life Small Business Research Institute identified the following personality traits as key for small business success based on surveying more than 1,100 small businesses.

- **Collaborative**—These entrepreneurs know how to delegate as necessary, with a focus on creating opportunities for other people.

- **Self-fulfilled**—These business owners value personal fulfillment and are focused on doing something for a living that they love to do.
- **Future-focused**—These business owners focus on cash flow and business plans. They know what they want to do, both day-to-day and into the future.
- **Curious**—These business owners always want to learn (including learning about how other people run their businesses); they seek out best practices and innovative approaches.
- **Tech-savvy**—These entrepreneurs rely on technology to help pursue their business goals.
- **Action-oriented**—These business owners are proactive and show initiative when building their businesses, with a focus on how to take their business to the next level and differentiate from competitors.

⤳ TIP

One very important point: when you have a strong and well-developed online network, business building is more manageable. When you are active and engaged online, it's easier to follow what is going on in your field, collaborate, focus on the future, quench your curiosity, maintain up-to-date information about technology, get answers about how to use that technology more efficiently, and take action that differentiates you from others.

Although the key traits for successful business owners vary from field to field, other important qualities to have include being well-organized, persistent, able to manage risk, make decisions, and function on little sleep. Unlike a traditional corporate job, when you run your own business, you won't have someone standing by to troubleshoot your technology issues, fix the printer, type a letter, or suggest best approaches to overcome client issues. Unless you partner or hire people immediately, you will initially be the administrative assistant, accountant, marketing director, content creator, and everything else for your business.

There are many other important considerations to evaluate in addition to your personality when it comes to running a successful business. We will explore these topics in more depth later on.

What Do You Enjoy?

Since we all know it's possible to be good at things we don't necessarily enjoy, ask yourself these key questions: What do I love to do? Can I envision sacrificing other things I enjoy in favor of working on this business? What are my hobbies? Marci Alboher, a vice president for Encore.org and an authority on careers and workplace, coined the word "slasher," in her book, *One Person/Multiple Careers: A New Model for Work/Life Success* (Business Plus, 2007), to describe someone who cannot describe his or her profession by using a simple word or phrase. Maybe you are an architect/photographer or an accountant/novelist. Look at the different sides of your "slash" career and decide if you may be able to earn an income from the "recessive" side of your slash.

AN ENTREPRENEUR FOLLOWS HIS PASSIONS

John Youngblood, owner of Guts and Glory Tennis (http://www. gutsandglorytennis.com), a full-service tennis stringing and products business, spent 15 years as a student services professional, where he held various leadership roles at a university. He explains how his passions led to his career transition:

"In order to be happy in your working life, there is no choice but to choose an area that gets you jazzed to wake up and go to work each morning. For me, I had spent the first 15 years of my professional life involved in a career that allowed me to help people in a variety of ways. I loved what I was doing and could not believe they actually paid me to do it! Then, as often happens when working in

continued from page 11

larger organizations, good work was rewarded with increasing responsibility. With the responsibility came more administration, greater hours, and slowly being drawn away from the elements of the profession from which passion was derived. Burn out and organizational politics extinguished the passion, and without the passion, it was time to move on. The next move, for me, was a radical change. For a conservative, non-risk taker, starting a business was a scary proposition. However, I had motivation, drive, and a record of success so I decided to follow my 'real world' passion and make a career out of one of my favorite hobbies."

John saved enough money to allow him to live for a year, or even two years, before he began to turn a profit, which he notes was "critical," as he "would have been in deep trouble without these financial reserves." John explains,

"I began my business working out of my home via the Internet and the actual cash start-up costs were reasonable at a few thousand dollars. The biggest expense was that I was no longer pulling in a salary and was forced to live off of financial reserves during the start-up phase of my business"

It took John at least 72 hours per week to launch his business, but, like many in his situation, he explains,

"The hours were from the comfort of my home with the company of my beloved dog, so in a sense, the hours were quite reasonable. Being able to turn commuting time into productive hours was a huge plus for me as was the flexibility that working from home and for myself provided. I still work crazy hours, but that is my own doing as I choose to continue to run my business as the sole employee and with that choice comes significant hours."

One factor in his success is that he tries "not to be like anyone else." John explains,

"I am not afraid to deliver services that are different and I am not afraid to take chances on new products that I believe have the potential to succeed. I have a business plan and have experienced growth each year in a difficult economy. I continue to expand products and services, but I do so carefully and am not afraid to vary from

continued from page 12

my plan if an opportunity arises and I need to re-evaluate and change direction. My company is lean, nimble, innovative, and flexible. These characteristics have helped to build our success to date."

His advice to others looking to start their own businesses is,

"I would have invested more heavily in some of my initial product offerings. My conservative nature prolonged the growth of my business. In retrospect, I needed to believe more and just go for it. Not in a reckless way, but certainly not as conservatively as I started."

John would recommend,

"Do what you love. If you do not have a passion for what you are going to do, the chances of success are slim. Owning a business takes a lot of time, hard work, and sacrifice. The rewards have to be something that touch your heart as well as your bank account."

Getting a new business off the ground is not an easy endeavor. Whether you do it as an extra engagement/MOXIE or full time, you will spend many hours toiling, researching, connecting with potential clients, responding to inquires, and getting the word out about what you offer. Our advice is to do your best to choose a business you really enjoy so you don't mind the many hours you will be putting into growing it and making it successful.

Your Time-Management Skills

While there are many important skills for entrepreneurs, one that we think deserves its own category is time management. Depending on what type of business you plan, be aware that you may be giving up your weekends for a long time (especially if you're starting something new in addition to your full-time job). Most people, however, love their side gig work so much that the time it takes to grow their business doesn't phase them. If you can no longer attend that weekly jam session or play on the softball league, prepare your friends and family in advance and try to get them excited about what you are doing for your career.

Tips to Manage Your Time

Plan what you need to do in advance. Never sit down in front of your computer without a plan and a to-do list, even for seemingly small tasks. Even though we are big fans of social media, we recognize how easy it is to become distracted by Facebook, Twitter, or LinkedIn. Before you know it, you spent two hours on the computer and have no tangible result to show for it.

On the other hand, if you schedule and plan your social media engagement, you can accomplish a lot. The difference is that your two hours of planned time with specific goals is more valuable than aimlessly clicking through social media profiles.

Set a schedule. Choose whatever calendar program or system works for you. Block out your business time and identify what needs to get done in that time. Track and review how much time you are spending and be sure to evaluate and make adjustments as needed. If it really takes you two hours to get something done and you are allowing one hour, that's not realistic and you need to reflect the change on your calendar.

YOU CAN BE A MOXIE—IT JUST TAKES COMMITMENT

If you're thinking, "I can't be a MOXIE, I have a lot of responsibilities outside of work," then you'll want to know Hannah's story. She was working 40 or more hours a week at her day job when Rochester Institute of Technology invited her to share her expertise with their eMBA graduates. She thought, "I need to build some authority outside of what I'm doing at work to substantiate my credibility and expertise." So Hannah taught herself to blog during the only time she

continued from page 14

had to commit to this outside endeavor—4 a.m. to 6 a.m., before her family responsibilities kicked in for the day. Eventually, she left that full-time job and now runs a successful business doing what she enjoys, but on her own terms.

Hire people. If you know it will take you longer to do something than you have time for, consider outsourcing that work, even to a high school or college student if possible. Recognize that maybe it's not worth your time to spend months figuring out how to create a website yourself. You may be better off finding an expert in that area so you can get exactly what you want. Make sure to do an analysis when you consider big projects and decide when it makes sense to bring in team members or helpers to assist.

Work in blocks and automate where possible. While we are not huge fans of automating all of your social media interactions, such as setting up systems to automatically tweet or re-tweet information or pre-scheduling updates on social networks, you should dabble with some scheduling tools (we'll elaborate in Chapter 20 about tools to help automate some tasks). Just be sure you aren't going to get into trouble at your day job when they notice you seem to be tweeting throughout the day. You'll need to be prepared to explain your automated tools and make sure you don't inadvertently respond to someone while on someone else's company time. See Chapter 22 for resources to help you manage your time.

Ask people to help and find advisors. Save time by relying on your network. If you create or join a supportive online group (this book will teach you how to do that), you may find it becomes easier to ask a quick question via Twitter, in a LinkedIn group, via email or to a listserv, and receive numerous suggestions and replies. Be sure to contribute to these forums as well, and you'll be rewarded with answers and just-in-time assistance. (Learn more about how to leverage an advisory board in Chapter 18.)

Get It Done

Assess yourself and your skills to decide if having a business, or being a MOXIE, is right for you:

- Recognize that your personality affects your ability to be successful at a business and consider some assessments so you'll be more self-aware, an important business trait in and of itself. Consider taking the Entrepreneurial Aptitude Test and the Myers-Briggs Type Indicator to hone in on your skills and weaknesses.
- Think about what you are good at, what you want to do, and how you'd enjoy spending your time. Know what you are willing to sacrifice to get your business off the ground.
- Think about the skills you don't have (for example, web design), and think about who you can contact to get the help you need.
- Focus on time management issues. Identify if any of the resources or applications included here or in Chapter 22 will be useful to you and start learning how they work.

3

What Social Media Does For Your Business

Whether you're currently running a business or planning to start something on the side, social media tools will help you move things to the next level. When people can easily see from your social networking efforts that you are an expert in your field, it's much easier for them to invest their trust (and money) in you. Why? Because social media tools allow you to:

- Demonstrate your expertise, so people know what (and how much) you know and how you can help them solve their problems. When you do this well, you inspire trust in potential clients and customers, which is important if you want them to part with their hard-earned money.
- Meet new people and expand your network beyond what you could ever achieve with in-person networking alone.
- Learn what thought leaders in your industry are thinking and writing about.
- Be discoverable, so you can benefit from a "pull" marketing approach, where you make it easy for people to identify and

contact you, instead of constantly relying on a "push" approach, which requires you to constantly seek new business. When you set up your social networking profiles well, they act as magnets, helping attract clients and customers.

In Chapter 7, we'll outline which networks are best for each of these social networking underpinnings. In this chapter, we give you some ideas to help you wrap your mind around how you can accomplish all of these goals online.

How to Demonstrate Your Expertise and Inspire Trust Online

When you are planning your online activities, the first thing to keep in mind is how you can showcase what you know. For some people, there's a fine line between telling people about your expertise and being too self-promotional. If you have a tendency toward over-promotion, be sure to ask a friend if your posts appear too forward once you get your social media campaign launched. If done correctly, you will be able to use the various networks and online tools to illustrate that you are up-to-date with what is going on in your area of expertise and that you can contribute to the conversation.

What Should I Say to Demonstrate Expertise?

One common question about social media is "How will I know what to say?" It is a lot easier than you may think. The key is to post updates relevant to the audience you want to reach. Get people thinking, "I need to keep up with her updates, because she sends a consistent stream of information I need to know."

In their book, *100 Conversations for Career Success,* Miriam and co-author Laura Labovich suggest you consider the following to showcase your expertise online.

Comment on the News of the Day as it Relates to Your Industry

For example, if you are selling organic food products or have a line of chemical-free drinking containers, you might share this update via any social network (Facebook, Twitter, Google+, etc):

> *FDA bans bisphenol A (BPA), an estrogen-mimicking chemical from baby bottles and children's drinking cups [include link to article]*

Another newsworthy update related to a pet business may be:

> *Ingredient in many pet food brands is now recalled [include link].*

Tips like these can be the easiest updates to share because they come directly from the news. Keep up-to-date by tracking several reputable national and local news sources. For example, your local newspaper probably has a Twitter feed or a Facebook page, or both. The same goes for your local television news station, where you can sometimes learn useful data relevant to your business or your field. National and cable news sources all run Twitter feeds pointing you to up-to-the-minute and "breaking" news. A quick search in any network will allow you to easily identify and follow this information to keep you in-the-loop.

Read and Remark About Books

Make a list of popular books relevant to your field and showcase them in your updates. Comment on the content and invite discussion. For example, you may post:

> *I just finished reading Seth Godin's The Dip—an oldie, but a goodie! I'd recommend it to anyone who wants to learn something about life and marketing.*

Ask and Answer Questions

Find questions other business owners post to solicit opinions and suggestions via LinkedIn's groups (we explain this feature in Chapter 9). You can certainly answer the questions there, but there is no rule against using questions from one network to pose in another. Either ask or reply to the question via your favorite platform. If you are using Google+ or Facebook, you can create a more extensive comment than you can post on Twitter. For example, on Twitter, you may ask:

What is your favorite email marketing platform?

On Google+ or Facebook, you can include more details in your question:

I'm looking for an email system that is easy to use, handles auto-responders, and can connect with Paypal. Ideally, I'd like to pay less than $10/month. Phone support is a bonus! Any suggestions welcomed.

(Learn more about how to ask questions on different platforms in chapter 16.)

Create a Blog on Your Business Site

A blog is your best online resource. You'll want to update it frequently with posts that will help potential clients understand that you know your stuff. What should you write? Provide advice and tips—just enough to showcase your knowledge and expertise, but not enough that they won't need to hire you for the services you offer.

"Blogging is a big part of our customer acquisition strategy. As our business is focused on helping entrepreneurs and small business owners, so too is our blog. A key piece of our blog strategy is publishing guest blog posts from entrepreneurs providing advice and personal experience. We think this is a good way to provide value to readers without our blog being all about us, all the time."

—Nick Barron, co-founder of Swapel.com

"Ultimately, as a blogger, I am providing helpful knowledge to busy entrepreneurs and business professionals, which, in turn, creates a trust factor between us. Eventually, my blog readers and social networks will think of me when they need my services or when someone they know needs my services. And if they like me and have what I call a 'social crush' on me, then I get hired more often than not, thus growing my business."

—Lori Gama, Social Media Strategist

"I use and recommend businesses use a blog as part of digital marketing strategy. This includes hiring someone to write blog posts. I'm doing it now for an outdoor furniture store, and have done it with authors, publishers, RV sales and rental, as well as supplements."

—Ricardo Angulo

Read Blogs and Respond Via Your Updates and Comments

It's a good idea to identify and spend time reading blogs about your field. When you do, you'll have an unending stream of information to share with your online community, and be one step closer to creating alliances with thought leaders in your industry. Remember, you want to be considered in that list of names!

BE STRATEGIC WITH YOUR BLOGGING

Todd Schnick, Intrepid Marketing Strategist and Business Talk Radio Host, blogs at intrepid-llc.com. He explains the intention behind his posts:

"I write blog posts that are intended for one person, usually a prospect or a client. Frankly, I cannot write an essay for my blog that is for everyone. In my opinion, it can't be done. Or certainly, cannot be done well. You see, when you do this, you muddle up the message, and water it down, and then it becomes truly boring and ordinary, and not unlike 1,000 other blog posts you've seen somewhere on the Internet.

No, you need to be strategic with your writing.

Let's say you are working a business opportunity with a specific prospect. And they present a challenge or roadblock that is preventing them from moving forward with the deal. You could address the challenge privately to them over the phone or email. But why?

Why not write a blog post that addresses the issue publicly on your blog? Keep in mind, focus INTENTLY on the prospect, write specifically for him or her. That gives your writing important focus. When the post is finished, you can forward the post link directly to the prospect and say 'Great question. In fact, I recently wrote an article that addresses that very question. You might find some value in it!'

Here's the secret: You know darn well your prospect isn't the only one with that question or concern. And now you've created content that not only serves your prospect, but will help many others."

You can simply tweet or post links to the blogs you like, or you can comment on the posts in your updates. For example:

I agreed with #1 & 2 in this post about best management styles; stay tuned for my post responding to the others. [include link].

While you may be reading blogs to give you fodder to post on your profiles, commenting on blog posts individually is a wonderful way to communicate your expertise. Avoid banal, uninteresting comments, such as "I really agree with what you are saying here." Instead, add some insight and offer your expertise.

HOW TO IDENTIFY BLOGS TO READ

When you hone in on key contacts, browse their LinkedIn profiles to see if they also write a blog. Anyone serious about blogging will include a link to the blog in his or her LinkedIn profile.

Using social media exposes you to a lot of different contacts who probably also blog. For example, just perusing Google+ or Twitter feeds will help you identify new bloggers you may enjoy following. Once you have a good list of blogs, it will be much easier to create valuable and useful updates for your online communities, even if you choose not to blog yourself. If you use Google+, you can click through to Sparks, or the What's Hot feature, and then insert a search term to see recent updates about the topic. This allows you to find blogs written about topics you want to know more about.

The following resources are useful for finding relevant blogs to read for your business:

- **Alltop.com:** A magazine rack of blogs. This site categorizes numerous topics and provides easy access to blogs in your targeted niche.
- **Google Blog Search (blogsearch.google.com):** A site that provides millions of relevant search results from feed-enabled blogs.
- **Google Alerts:** Google allows you to track subjects or keywords and receive email alerts when it indexes something relevant. Go to www.google.com/alerts to set up alerts that will no doubt include content from many blogs.
- **Twitter:** Many people who tweet also maintain blogs. Follow the link from a person's Twitter profile to learn about their blogs. Many of the links your Twitter friends share could belong to blogs you may find useful.
- **Google:** Enter {best blogs, topic} in Google, where the topic is your area of expertise. For example, {best blogs, accounting} yields several results, including the top 50 blogs for accountants.

continued from page 23

- **Technorati.com:** Select *Blog* instead of *Post* at the top, and type your search term topic. Technorati provides a list of results ordered by authority, a measure of a blog's standing and influence in the blogosphere.
- **StumbleUpon.com:** This site uses a ratings system to create a collaborative opinion about a site's value. StumbleUpon provides a list of almost 500 topics, and you can select your interests and potentially be matched with other people's suggestions.

How to Meet New People and Extend Your Network

It's not hard to see how demonstrating your expertise and simply engaging online by posting updates about your niche would also result in you meeting new people. Let's face it—if you hope to have a business that stretches beyond your local area, you're going to have to do something to help people outside of your immediate circle and your city's limits get to know you. Sharing your expertise, as described above, is one way, but you'll also want to make efforts to engage directly with people you identify as being good networking contacts.

Find New Contacts on LinkedIn

It couldn't be easier to find new people to join your network on LinkedIn. The site offers numerous ways to get to know people you would otherwise never meet. The trick is to reach out to these strangers in a way that appeals to and intrigues them, not by generically requesting a connection.

Use Existing Contacts to Grow New Connections

There's no better way to expand your network than by going to your existing network. Visit the LinkedIn pages of well-connected colleagues or people in your industry. Most of the time, you will be

HOW TO ASK FOR A CONNECTION ON LINKEDIN

If someone you're connected to on LinkedIn is connected to a person you'd like to know, you can click the "Get introduced" link on your desired contact's profile. If there is more than one person connecting you to your target, LinkedIn will ask you to choose who should make the introduction. Pick the person who knows you and the third party well enough to persuade him or her to respond.

Include a subject line and write a message explaining why your contact should initiate the connection. Be specific, and consider including information about how you might be a good resource for the contact, in addition to why you want to connect to the person. Be aware that the new contact may see the message you write.

allowed to click through in their profiles to see their connections (Use the link right under "Recommendations" on their profile page.) While some people make their connections private, you should be able to link through and see a list of potentially good contacts for you. If you come across people you want to know, you can ask your mutual connection for an introduction.

Grow Your Connections via Groups

Search for Groups that may interest you and join some active industry conversations. Once you identify the leaders, make a point to ask to connect. Use LinkedIn's "Insightful Statistics on this Group" feature to evaluate groups and decide which groups are most worth your time. Just scroll down the webpage while clicked into a LinkedIn group's page. You will be able to review how many group members there are, where they are from, their seniority levels, and how many discussions and comments there are. Be sure to join groups where you'll get the most mileage for your posts and updates.

Use LinkedIn Skills and Expertise to Expand Your Network

Buried under the "More" tab, this section makes it easy to see who else is out there with specific skills you want to search. You'll be able to search for other people who rank well for the search terms you use, and even which companies rely on people with the searched skill. Once you narrow down some people, you can look for ways to connect with them, either by visiting their other social networks (such as Twitter, which is linked on many LinkedIn users' profiles) or blogs. You may know people in common or share groups with them, which means you can reach out with individual messages via LinkedIn.

Use News Updates in LinkedIn Signal to Meet New People

LinkedIn Signal allows you to search updates posted in LinkedIn. When you use this tool (located under the "News" tab), you may find people you didn't know who are industry experts or actively posting information that interests you.

Tap into Advanced Search

The "Advanced Search" option is on LinkedIn's top toolbar. This is a great way to help narrow a search for any type of person. You can even narrow the search by geography or by where people used to work.

LinkedIn Today

Found under the "News" tab on LinkedIn's toolbar, this service allows you to customize the news you want to follow and then provides quick links directly via your computer or mobile phone. It's a great way to learn new things without doing a lot of direct research.

Find People to Follow on Twitter

Twitter is an open network, which means you can find, follow, and interact with people without any introductions or intermediaries.

The most important thing you can do to extend your network is to find people who are tweeting about topics that interest you. These contacts will help connect you to people who will be interested in hiring you or purchasing your products.

Your Contacts

Once you follow a few good contacts, you can easily go to their Twitter pages and click through to see who they are following and follow those same people. Keep an eye on the people your favorite Twitter contacts mention in their Twitter streams—those might be good contacts for you to have in your network, too.

See if your contacts follow any lists (by clicking through to "Lists" on his or her Twitter page). This is another easy way to find interesting new people to add to your network.

Review Third-Party Twitter Lists

A variety of online tools exist that make it easy to identify key players in your field.

- **http://listorious.com:** This website conducts searches using key words of interest to you. You can then follow individuals from the resulting lists.
- **http://twibes.com:** This website offers categorized lists of people.
- **http://wefollow.com:** On this site, you can search for terms and topics (or people) of interest and follow them.
- **http://www.twellow.com:** Twellow, also known as the Twitter Yellow Pages.
- **http://justtweetit.com:** A directory to help you find other Twitter users.

Use Twitter's "Who to Follow" Tools

Twitter isn't always on target when it comes to suggestions, but you should keep an eye on these suggestions anyway, as they may include prominent people in your field. If so, you'll want to connect and interact with them.

Use and Follow Hashtags

- People on Twitter use hashtags (denoted by the # symbol) to make tweets more easily searchable. You may be able to identify and follow tweets about industry conferences, jobs, and general topics of interest. Either click on any term beginning with a # (for example, #smallbiz), or use the following tools to try to identify common hashtags:
- **http://www.whatthetrend.com:** lists short blurbs about popular hashtags.
- **http://hashtags.org:** plots hashtags on a graph and shows tweets containing that tag.
- **http://tagal.us:** an online dictionary for hashtags.

Track Information from Conferences via Hashtags

Depending on your field and how savvy your industry is, you may be able to find and follow a hashtag from a conference and watch live tweets showcasing key points from events you cannot attend. The hashtag is the # symbol with a previously decided word or acronym, such as #AMA13 for the American Medical Association's conference in 2013.

Find People Tweeting from Your Local Area

Twitter is an international community, but sometimes, it is nice to identify Twitter friends you could potentially meet in real life. Use tools such as the following for this purpose:

- **http://twitter.com/geofollow:** a location directory to help you find people in your area.
- **http://www.happn.in:** discover the most discussed topics in your area.

- **http://search.twitter.com/advanced**: search for tweets near your location.

Participate in a Twitter Chat

Chats are great ways to meet and network with people you might otherwise never know who have similar interests. People organize a time to get together on Twitter for discussions about their mutual interests. They use a hashtag (#) to designate the conversation, and everyone is invited to participate.

Google "{Twitter chat schedule, Keppie Careers}" to find a list of moderated chats.

Hop on Twitter at the designated time and use one of these tools to track the hashtag for the chat:

- http://tweetchat.com
- http://tweetgrid.com
- http://twubs.com
- http://wthashtag.com
- http://monitter.com
- http://tweetree.com
- http://www.tweetdeck.com

Be sure all of your tweets directed to the chat include the hashtag. Be sure to network and follow up with people you meet on the chat after it is over. That's the point of the chat!

Search Twitter Bios

People include information in their bios that will help you decide if they are good contacts. Searching bios for keywords can help you identify new colleagues, contacts, and even potential employers. Use http://followerwonk.com to search for keywords, such as industry name, title, etc.

How to Meet People on Facebook

Even though people traditionally use Facebook to connect with people they already know, you can still use it to expand your network.

Expand Your Network by Finding and "Liking" Company Pages

If you're hoping to do some subcontracting with specific companies, it can't hurt to become a member of their Facebook communities. Search for the company names that interest you, and "Like" their company via your personal Facebook page. It's easy to search for company pages with Facebook's search toolbar, or to find pages linked directly from the company's website. Be sure to keep an eye on their posts and make sure you contribute to the conversation on their pages.

Join and Become Active in Facebook Groups

Groups on Facebook are similar to LinkedIn groups; they are places to share stories, ask questions, discuss events, or post news on a particular topic. You can also learn about the culture, conversation, and internal news at your target companies. You can add value to the group by joining in or starting discussions, posting links and resources to the wall, moderating or managing sections of the group, and so on.

Find Facebook groups by typing "Groups" into the top toolbar. Use the specific search options to identify public groups to join. Once you find some groups, get active and have online conversations with people you want to meet.

How to Expand Your Contacts on Google+

Similar to Twitter, Google+ is a completely open network—you can find and follow anyone who interests you, and you can comment and interact with people without needing third-party introductions.

To find people you may want to get to know, use the top toolbar's search engine in Google+; the dropdown tab allows you to select what you'd like to search, including people, posts, pages, etc. Don't miss this useful way to identify who is using Google+ and who may be a good business contact.

Find and Connect with People in Your Contacts' Circles

Just like on Twitter, if you already identified someone you enjoy following via Google+, you can also look to see who is in their circles.

View Other People's Circles

Visit someone's Google+ profile page and look on the right—you can view the complete list by clicking on "View All" when scrolling over their circles.

Review Events to Meet New People

Google+ has an events tab, too. Here, you can search public events you may want to attend and view who may be coming once you are on the Events page.

Use Google+'s Explore Tool

On the left side of your screen, check out the "Explore" tab to see if you may find anyone interesting!

Use Google+'s Communities

Google+ hosts groups called "Communities," which are segmented by interests. Follow the Communities icon on the left of your screen to find out if there are any useful groups that interest you. You can ask to join if the group isn't public. You can also start private communities, plan events, start hangouts, and share information.

Search Applications for Google+

Below are tools to help you find people on Google+ who share your interests.

- **http://findpeopleonplus.com:** Indexes millions of users (and counting) and has interesting statistics.
- **http://www.gpeep.com:** Register on this service to help other people find you. Click "Add Yourself Now" in the upper left hand corner of the page. Include all of your information, especially the Category/Industry and Profession sections and tag yourself with any details people (recruiters) may use to try to find you.
- **http://www.recommendedusers.com:** Suggests people in niche topics to circle.
- **http://www.googleplussearchengine.com:** Use keywords to find people.
- **http://socialstatistics.com:** Tracks over 45,000 users and popular posts.
- **http://www.group.as:** Helps you group your Google+ contacts. "Google+ grouping made simple. Add to existing groups, create your own or just find interesting people to follow."

Find New Contacts on Pinterest

Pinterest is a relatively new, but fast-growing site that allows you to "pin" information you like on virtual pinboards. It is different from most of the other big networks we cover because it is heavily focused on visuals—you pin pictures, which then link to URLs for more information.

You can use Pinterest to grow your network by searching the site for keywords, such as "easy recipes" if you are a food blogger. You can search by pins, boards, or people. You can find Pinterest contacts who post using keywords related to your interests.

Once you find boards, you can "follow" the ones cultivated by people who interest you. You should repin, share, and comment on the boards, which can result in new contacts and possible business partnerships.

Finally, be sure to share content on your own boards as well. Include items that you liked or repinned from other people's boards, or visually engaging content you added yourself. Examples include photos of your products (fashion, furniture, food, visually attractive items you create and sell), pictures from events you attend or host, books relevant to your industry, photos of people you respect, videos, infographics (visual representation of information), and quotes.

CREATE YOUR OWN VISUAL CONTENT

Did you know you can create your own infographics? Try Visuall.ly, Easel.ly, and google.com/publicdata/directory to produce aesthetic, sharable content on Pinterest. You may find your information going viral!

If you're on Facebook, you've probably seen contacts sharing visual representations of quotes. People love these! You can create a sharable quote by building a quote to look visually attractive as a PowerPoint slide, saving it as a JPEG and sharing it to Pinterest or other networks.

Be careful not to use images that are copyrighted or protected. Always list the image owner and the person who said the quote.

YOU NEVER KNOW WHEN PINTEREST WILL HELP EXPAND YOUR NETWORK

Miriam has a great story about Pinterest. Recently, a woman from a company contacted her with an opportunity. During their conversation, Miriam asked how the woman had found her, assuming it would be from some of the channels she frequents most often, such as Twitter, or possibly via her blogs or books. The woman responded, "I found you on Pinterest. I am an art history major, and I enjoy searching where there are visual results. I liked the boards you created."

The moral of this story: you never know what network will make the difference for you, so don't rule anything out.

Google Alerts

Although not specifically a social network, we'd be remiss if we didn't mention how easy it is to track what's been said about a topic, keyword, or person through Google Alerts. Google will deliver a note to your email every time it indexes something about a topic you choose. Search {Google Alert} to learn how to set these up. Be sure to also track your own name and your company's name to find out what people are saying about you online.

How to Be Found

Ultimately, everything you do via social media can contribute to helping someone find you.

Google+

Do not leave Google+ out of the mix. Why? If you connect with people through a business page or personal profile on Google+, and a connected individual conducts a Google search about a topic relevant to you or your keywords while signed in to his or her Google account, your information is much more likely to come up as a response to that inquiry because of your connection.

How does that help? For example, let's say you meet someone at a conference or event, and she connects with you on Google+ because she is interested in knowing more writers or editors. Six months later, she forgot about meeting you, but needs to contract with an editor for a new project. If she Googles {editor}, she is more likely to see a result from your Google+ stream or from you because you are connected through Google+. You land near the top of her search results without spending a single penny on Google AdWords!

YourName.com or YourBusinessName.com

We cannot overemphasize how important it is to run a website optimized to benefit from search engine traffic. When you create your business website, we recommend you build or have the site built on a blog platform such as WordPress. Why? Because WordPress is set up to allow you to create and publish content easily that search engines will find. This well established and popular platform, used by the likes of the *New York Times*, eBay, *NBC Sports*, CNN.com, UPS, and Yahoo!, contains built-in tools to engage and interact with search engines. This back-end optimization helps people find you! (We share information about how to use SEO techniques and how to make it as easy as possible for people to learn about you online in Chapter 10.)

Create Strong Social Media Profiles

Every detailed, well-optimized profile you write about yourself will help people find you. This includes your profiles on all the big networks (LinkedIn, Twitter, Facebook, and Google+), as well as any other relevant network. For example, if you have a visual-focused business, your Pinterest, Instagram, and Flickr profiles will be important.

Look at Chapter 4 about keywords to learn more about how to make yourself a top result when people search the networks and Google.

FIND AND OWN YOUR NAME ONLINE

Even if you don't want to build out complete profiles on every existing network, you may want to own your name or business name on networks you may consider in the future. Two tools to help you manage this project include:

- KnowEm.com "allows you to check for the use of your brand, product, personal name, or username instantly on over 575 popular and emerging social media websites." You may want to consider and secure your brand before someone else does.
- Namechk.com allows you to "check to see if your desired username or vanity URL is still available at dozens of popular social networking and social bookmarking websites."

Having strong profiles connected to your "home base" of a website will make it much easier for people to find you and to learn about your services or products.

Get It Done

What are your action steps for this chapter?

Recognize how important social media tools are to help you:

1. **Demonstrate Your Expertise**
   - Figure out what you can say on the various networks to showcase your expertise. Get ideas by reading other people's content, including their tweets, updates, and blogs.
   - Read and remark about books. Make a list of popular books relevant to your field and highlight them in your updates. Comment on the content and invite discussion.
   - Ask and answer questions through various networks: LinkedIn Groups, Quora.com, Twitter, Google+, and other online networks.
   - Create a blog on your business site. Update it with content demonstrating you are an expert in your field.
   - Read blogs and respond via your updates and comments. Use the advice and resources in this chapter to identify the best blogs for you to read.
2. **Meet New People and Extend Your Network**
   Decide on which networks you would like to start and begin finding contacts. Use the suggestions in this chapter for each big network to mine for contacts you already know and those you have yet to meet.

   Don't forget, you need to make it as easy as possible for people to find you, too. When you reach out and connect, be sure to have your online profiles optimized and your bios filled in so people will be interested in reciprocating your interest. (See Chapter 5 for details about how to create optimized profiles.)

3. **Learn New Things via Social Media**

   You'll never know what you are missing online until you jump in and see what you can learn. Keep an open mind. You can learn everything from specific details about local industry events, to information that will help you move forward with your business, like trends, news events, and what people think about subjects relevant to you and your work.

4. **Be Found**

   Google+ is an important tool to make sure it's as easy as possible to find you, but all of the social networks will help people find you if you become active on them. Your website should be the number one result when people look for you online, so be sure to follow the suggestions throughout this book on how to create and maintain a strong and interesting website.

   Consider capturing your name and/or your business name on the various social networks using a tool such as KnowEm.com or Namechk.com. Remember, having strong profiles connected to your "home base" of a website will make it much easier for people to find you and to learn about your services or products.

How to Identify and Use Keywords

Targeting is King

In order to use social media tools successfully, you must focus on how to target your message so you can speak directly to your audience. It is crucial to know what you offer, but even more so, it's important to understand how your skills fit into what your audience needs from you. If you fail to identify *how* your customers and clients are looking for you, you will miss many opportunities to connect with them.

WHAT IS A KEYWORD?

AboutUs.com has a great definition of a keyword:

"A keyword is a single word or phrase defining a topic, subject area, or concept. When people refer to keywords in websites and search engines, they're talking about the words and phrases that tell search engines what a website is about . . . Your keywords are the words and phrases you want to rank for in search engines."

continued from page 39

In other words, keywords are the words and phrases people will use to look for a business like yours when they use online search engines. For example, if you sell cupcakes in Detroit, one of your keyword phrases may be {cupcakes, Detroit}. "Rank" refers to how easy it will be for people to find your business via the keyword search. If you rank on page one of Google's results for {cupcakes, Detroit}, it's much easier for people to find you than if you rank on page three or four of the search. Most people won't scroll through pages and pages of results.

Using complex algorithms, search engines such as Google find the keywords on your website and blog and categorize your information based on what they find. Keywords appear in technical places, such as in your alt text, meta descriptions, and title tags in your website's design. (You only need to understand this technical information if you plan to create your own website.) It's important to make sure you design your blog (or hire someone to do it) to include these important clues for search engines.

Before you can include keywords in your websites, you need to select the best words to use. If you don't target, you may spend a lot of time spinning your wheels. Just as you wouldn't want to show up at a party on the wrong night, mistargeting leaves you alone in a virtual room. Make sure you know the keyword equivalent of where your people are partying to achieve the most success.

As you define and refine how to market your business online, you must articulate how your products or services benefit customers. While we want you to do your research and prepare, do not be fooled into thinking you must identify everything your customers might need, or outline *all* the services and products you want to offer. The perfect is the enemy of the good—if you try to perfect your ideas before you get started, you may never start. Call your first efforts a test, beta, or trial to get out of the gate.

How to Evaluate Your Ideas

Chris Brogan is President of Human Business Works and author of *Trust Agents* (Wiley, 2010). In one of his posts on ChrisBrogan.com, he recommends answering these questions:

1. Does it help someone else?
2. Can that someone else pay for it?
3. If not, who will pay for it?

If the answer to questions 2 and 3 are "no" and "no idea," here's a hint: wrong answer.

These questions force you to assess your idea in simple terms. One of the most important questions in that list is "Who will pay for it?" You may want to start or grow a business based on your passions, but if there is no market for your product or service, you will not want to rely on that business to support you financially.

Who is Your Customer or Client?

When you evaluate your idea, it may help to envision an imaginary target customer. When you close your eyes and get a little creative, who do you see visiting your site and buying your products or services? We want you to begin thinking like your customers as you begin to strategize how to present you and your business as a solution to their problems.

DEFINE CUSTOMER DEMOGRAPHICS

Fill out a complete inventory about your target client. Adology.com lists these topics for you to consider when envisioning your customers or clients:

Geographics. Where are your customers? Are you targeting only local areas, or is your client base much larger?

continued from page 41

Demographics. What are the demographics of your customers or prospects?

- Age
- Gender
- Income level
- Do they have children at home?
- What do they do for a living?

Psychographics. What are your customers and prospects interested in? What do they value most?

- Lifestyle interests
- What causes and charities do they support?
- What are their attitudes about shopping?
- What are their personal goals?
- What motivates customers to buy what you sell?

Shopographics. How much and how often do your most valuable customers make purchases?

- What are their big ticket purchase intentions?
- What are their big ticket purchase frequencies?
- What are their annual household spending budgets?

For example, the food blogger we introduced in Chapter 3 may answer the questions as follows:

Geographics: Customer base is not local. Potential target audience is any English-speaking reader.

Demographics: What are the demographics of your customers or prospects?

- Age: Most likely early 20s to early 50s
- Gender: Probably female
- Income level: Lower income to middle-class families
- Do they have children at home? Yes
- What do they do for a living? Probably employed in service businesses

Psychographics: What are your customers and prospects interested in? What do they value most?

- Lifestyle interests: Family-oriented activities
- What causes and charities do they support? Schools, religious institutions, etc.

continued from page 42

- What are their attitudes about shopping? They like to get a bargain
- What are their personal goals? To successfully provide for their families on a budget
- What motivates customers to buy what you sell? They may buy something that they think will save them time, more likely if it might save them money

Shopographics. How much and how often do your most valuable customers buy?

- Big ticket purchase intentions: Never
- Big ticket purchase frequency: Never
- Annual household spending: Covers the basics

Why is it important to go through this exercise? It will help you understand your audience's needs, wants, and desires, and allow you to customize and differentiate what you deliver and how you will market to them. This is an important exercise as you begin thinking about identifying your keywords. Additionally, while it may seem your business should try to serve the most people possible, research suggests most businesses will be more successful if they narrow their focus and target a specific audience.

With all of this in mind, your first step to keyword optimization is to brainstorm and strategize. Narrow your focus and ask yourself:

- How are people most likely to be searching for a business like mine?
- What keywords will they use?
- Where will they look?
- When they seek information, what do they expect to find? For example, a short, detailed blog post? A long, involved article? A bullet point?

Your goal is to be the answer that Google or any search engine delivers to potential clients' and customers' queries. In this chapter, we'll describe how to choose your best keywords. Keep in mind the following objectives:

1. You want Google to provide your website as a result when people search for your keywords (we'll discuss this later in the chapter). This, objectively, may be difficult without paying a consultant and spending a lot of money on Google AdWords.

2. You want to use the power of social networks to influence what Google knows about your business. You'll need to create an online name for your business or brand by using relevant keywords on your website and through social media tools.

In Chapter 5, we dive into search engine optimization (SEO) for your website. In this chapter, however, we'll give you the groundwork you need to try to understand how to lay the foundation for an SEO site.

Before delving into keyword research, recognize that this is a fluid exercise—you aren't going to choose keywords once and wash your hands of the issue. Instead, successful entrepreneurs will tweak and refine keywords as they build and grow their businesses. When you start with in-depth keyword research, you will be off on the right foot. The most analytical approach is to begin with these steps:

1. Identify customers or clients. How are they likely to try to find you? (We will talk more about identifying your customer in Chapter 13.)

2. Identify the keywords your customers will use to find you. (We discuss tools to help you do so in this chapter.)

Choose Words So You Can Rank High in Searches

When you pick your keywords and test them, keep in mind that it is easier to rank high in keyword searches if you use words that generate fewer results. For example, if you test a keyword using Google, and there are ten million results, it is going to take an astronomical effort to rank well for that keyword. Don't let it frustrate you; instead, see if a more specific word or phrase exists that you can use to try to earn a higher rank via Google. Try to choose phrases where there are 100,000 results or fewer.

While more people will find you when you try to rank for keywords with fewer hits, you also want to consider how many people are searching for the keywords you choose. The perfect balance you're seeking is a keyword with many people looking for it and the fewest results.

WHAT'S IN A NAME?

One important place to try to include keywords is in your business's name and URL (website address). Ideally, your business name will include words people will use to search for someone like you, and your URL will include keywords. Cute or clever names are fun, but if you can incorporate keywords, it will eventually help you to rank in search results for your keywords. For example, we profiled John Youngblood and his business, Guts and Glory Tennis, in Chapter 2. Had he named his business No Guts, No Glory, it would have been an example of a business being clever (since "guts" references tennis strings), but it would not have included the important keyword: tennis. Be sure to read Chapter 8 for more suggestions about naming (or renaming) your business.

How to Select Keywords

Once you identify several keywords or keyword phrases, you (or your web designer) will build them into the infrastructure of your blog. You'll also use them in your blog posts, social media profile bios, and social media updates.

Before checking into the analytics and the research, start by brainstorming words and phrases related to your business.

Consider a small business owner who manages a blog and whose goal is to win sponsorships from food manufacturers and companies that offer discounts on healthy food. She targets readers who are interested in saving money on their food bills while providing interesting, tasty, and healthy meals to their families. She provides various products, including eBooks, on her site, to help people narrow down their grocery choices.

As a result, she may brainstorm the following list of keywords:

- Food blogger
- Best recipes
- Save money on meals
- Feed your family for less
- Cook inexpensively
- Cook for less
- Cooking for less
- Best meals for less money
- Healthy food for your family
- Organic food for less
- Fast meals for less
- Healthy meals for dinner

She may have even more keywords on an initial list. You should consider general as well as specific terms to help narrow down your targets, but always focus on your audience and what you provide that interests them.

Google AdWords

A good next step toward increasing your search rank is to use the Google AdWords tool (google.com/adwords) to shorten your key words list to several words or phrases. We recommend you choose three to five. There is no technical limit, but you do want to be sure your words are specific and relevant. Having a list of 100 keywords and phrases will be overwhelming and unmanageable. Remember, your goal is to find frequently searched terms or phrases with low competition. Entering {healthy cheap meals} in the tool results in hundreds of other suggestions, including:

- Recipe (an overly general keyword)—101,000,000 global searches
- Cheap and tasty meals—720 monthly global searches

Sometimes, being more specific helps, but it depends on how you phrase it:

- Healthy chicken meals—5,400 monthly global searches
- Healthy recipes with chicken—110,000 monthly global searches

When you start to use the Google AdWords tool to select new keywords, you should expect to spend some time trying different combinations of keywords.

Continuing with our example, the food blogger may find that cost-related terms do not seem to be frequently searched topics, regardless of how they're paired. There is not a lot of search traffic for terms containing "inexpensive," "cheap," and "healthy."

In this case, our food blogger may be better off choosing keywords relating to another area of her blogging focus. For example, they might choose "simple and easy recipes," which has 2,720,000 monthly searches, or "easy easy recipes," which yields 3,350,000 global monthly searches. Sometimes it can be surprising what terms people use to search!

Assuming the business owner in our example chose to focus on "simple recipes," there is a variety of possible good keywords with medium or low competition:

- Simple recipes
- Simple and easy recipes
- Easy easy recipes
- Easy recipes

If the blogger focuses on a particular type of recipe, such as "beef recipes" (1,830,000 searches) or "vegetarian recipes" (1,500,000 searches), those keywords have lower competition, and may be good additions to a list focusing on "simple and easy."

Keep in mind, you don't want to choose words if they are irrelevant to your product or business. If you only write about chicken recipes occasionally, then any traffic seeking information about cooking chicken will be short-lived and likely not useful for you.

Additionally, if you are hoping to attract customers from a certain location or geographical area, make sure you incorporate that information into your keywords.

You may want to create a chart. Google's AdWords Reference Guide suggests tracking each word, how many searches it has, and how many results they yield. You will also want to group keywords into categories. For example, keywords focused on location may go on one list. You can also rank them according to how much competition or searches exist for the word. Remember, your ideal keyword has little competition—which may mean only 200,000 results instead of 1,000,000—and a high number of people searching for it.

Once you have a big list, maybe 100 keywords and phrases, start narrowing it down. Eliminate words that are too vague, for example, "menus." Delete words that have too much competition or too few people searching for them. Once you've whittled away at your list, you will be able to pick the words that describe your business and what makes you unique.

Consider Phrases: Long-Tail Keywords

Consider how you search online for what you need. You probably don't search for keywords or phrases. Instead, you probably include long-tail keywords such as, "simple and easy recipes for vegetarians." Long-tail keywords typically include three to five words and target specific search traffic that tends to be more focused, even though it may not be as plentiful. In other words, there may be fewer overall searches for "simple and easy recipes for vegetarians," but once someone with that need lands on your site optimized for that phrase, it's a quality lead. (Learn more about long-tail keywords in Chapter 5.)

Tools to Help Choose Keywords

Remember, you are always going to do better with niche keywords, so focus on what is unique and special about you or your business. This is also known as your "unique value proposition."

There are many online tools to help you choose keywords. Some that you may want to try include:

- **google.com/adwords:** As mentioned earlier, the Google AdWords tool allows you to check your keywords to find out how much competition there is (via Google), and to see how many monthly searches there are for that term. Ideally, you want keywords with low competition and a high number of searches.
- **Wordtracker.com:** This is a paid tool, but there is a free trial.
- **Scribecontent.com:** This is a paid tool with a free trial and some supportive webinars to help you make the most of the site's features. It includes a keyword research tool and a tool to help analyze your online content (for a blog), as well as resources to help you build links to other sites. (Read more about link building in Chapter 20.)

The following are tools marketing professionals use to help them identify keywords for their campaigns. Investigate these to see if they may be useful for you.

Smart Blogs on Soical Media suggests:
- http://keyworddiscovery.com
- socialmention.com (social search and analysis)

John Jantsch, via American Express/openforum, suggests:
- http://topsy.com (real-time search for the social web)
- https://ads.youtube.com/keyword_tool
- http://www.kurrently.com (real-time search for Facebook and Twitter)
- http://48ers.com (real-time social search)
- freekeywords.wordtracker.com/keyword-questions (find out what questions people are asking in your niche, as noted by John Jantsch in *American Express/Open Forum*)

Where to Incorporate Your Keywords in Social Media Tools

When you have great information to share, take steps to try to expand the number of people who are interested in what you have to say and who will share it with the people they know. One way to do that is via social networks. When you create content people want to read and share through social media, you may be surprised how your business and influence may grow. We are both great examples: both of us have built our businesses, in part, on being found online.

Incorporate Keywords in Your LinkedIn Profile
You'll want to take advantage of tools within LinkedIn to help tweak your keywords. Start by finding the Skills and Expertise section located under the "More" tab on the LinkedIn toolbar. Start typing the keyword you think you would like to use.

For example, a graphics designer who specializes in logos and graphic work for dental offices and clinics might enter the most obvious keyword, "graphic designer." LinkedIn will provide a series of related terms, such as motion graphics, graphic arts, computer graphics, and graphic art. Consider the relevant suggestions as possible keywords for LinkedIn and your other profiles.

When you choose "graphic designer," LinkedIn provides resources and information relevant to that skill, including an excerpt from Wikipedia, an entire list of related skills, and the skill's projected growth potential. It also provides related companies who hire people with that skill, and suggests relevant groups. These are all fantastic tools to have at your fingertips when selecting keywords for your profile.

There are so many opportunities to use your keywords on LinkedIn. When incorporating your keywords, focus first on any bold headers on your profile to make sure they include words people will use to find you.

Headline: 120 Characters (Including Spaces)

Your headline is the best and easiest place to include your keywords because it is all about you! This is the place to include your pitch, and your pitch should focus on your keywords. For our graphics designer specializing in dental logos, a headline may be:

Graphics Designer/Digital Design/Web Support Graphics Expert/Specialize in Logos/Graphics for Dentists.

Your Titles

If you are making a major shift—for example, from student services at a university to a tennis-related business—it's possible you won't be able to incorporate keywords in your previous titles because your new keywords would not be relevant to those past experiences. However, if your shift was not so drastic, and you can use your keywords to describe your actual titles, it can help you to be found more often via searches in LinkedIn. For example, instead of:

Graphic Designer (your actual title), augment it with keywords accurately describing your work:

Graphic Designer | Logo Designer and Digital Illustrator

A LinkedIn title that is more descriptive than your actual title is generally acceptable, as long as you don't try to give yourself a promotion. For example, if you were a Graphic Design Assistant, use that title before your descriptive add-on; do not change it to Graphic Designer.

Your Summary

Fill your summary with enough keywords to make sure LinkedIn's search engines know about your expertise. Incorporate useful information here, and a story that will make people want to learn more about you. Here is an example of a short summary followed by a lot of keyword focused details, inspired by Maria Hancock, senior graphic designer at The BOSS Group in Atlanta, GA:

> I can bring your visual needs to life, from a drawing on a paper napkin to final print production. Known for my ability to execute on-deadline, dynamic visuals with minimal client direction; if you need a strong conceptual thinker who can develop designs from idea to market—you've found one! With a portfolio of customized visual solutions that effectively interpret clients' corporate branding, experience, and expertise, I'm the artistic partner you need to help accomplish your strategic business goals.
>
> Develop dynamic, creative visuals: print marketing collateral, web media, multimedia designs.
>
> Effective communication skills: exceptional listener, facilitate verbal and written co-worker interaction, engage with customers.
>
> Social media development & maintenance expert.

Mentor team members on new tools.

Oversee cross-project management.

Adapt schedule to effectively prioritize concurrent projects, fluctu-ate project goals to achieve deadlines.

Identify and execute innovative solutions to complex marketing problems.

Proficient in Adobe Applications [Photoshop, Illustrator, InDe-sign, Bridge, Acrobat, Framemaker, Flash] and Quark. MS Office Suite [Word, Excel, PowerPoint, SharePoint, CRM and Outlook.

Your Skills

Be sure you also incorporate your keywords in some of the 50 skills you can include in your LinkedIn profile. (There should be a bar in your LinkedIn profile when you edit it, allowing you to link though to your Skills section if you do not already have one set up, or you may see an option to add skills on the right side of your screen when you edit your profile.)

Your Status Update

Since your status update is searchable, don't forget to include key-words in your updates. For example:

> *Just completed new graphic design and branding for Dental Office of Houston [link].*

Experience

Every job description is another opportunity to display those key words. Even if you are not looking for a traditional job, recognize that people search LinkedIn when they want to hire someone for their expertise. Make sure you clearly outline that expertise via the descriptions of your experience, and incorporate the keywords you chose for your LinkedIn profile in the descriptions.

Use Your Keywords in Twitter

If you favor the "quick and dirty," Twitter is for you. Write a targeted, 160-character or less Twitter bio full of keywords, and it will be easier for other Twitter users to search for and find you there. For example:

> *Graphic Designer/Digital/Web Designer. Create Branded Logos and Online Art for Dentists and Dental Professionals*

Your Updates

It helps to consistently incorporate your keywords in your updates, too. In fact, if you have keywords that you can turn into hashtags, that's even better. Remember, a hashtag is a term on Twitter designated by a # sign. For example, we may post updates with the hashtag #smallbiz. This makes our posts easier to find if someone wants to search Twitter for information relevant to small business owners.

Don't go overboard, but identify a few key terms you want to be known for and incorporate them as hashtags in your tweets. For example:

> #design, # graphicdesign, #branding, #dentists, #dentalpros

FIND INFLUENCERS ONLINE

Klout (www.klout.com), a service that attempts to rank how influential people are online, plays right into your keywords. You will have more "Klout" in your target areas if you tweet about and use hashtags for the words that describe what you do well. Sign up for Klout and connect your online profiles so it can identify you as an influencer.

Peerindex.com is another service that "measures interactions across the web to help you understand your impact in social media." They note, "We want you to learn about the people you influence and see who influences you." While not as well known as Klout, this is another tool to add to your information-gathering arsenal.

Add Keywords in Google+

All of your public updates on Google+ will be indexed and findable on Google, so don't waste this opportunity to influence how people find you online. Sprinkle your keywords liberally in your Google+ profile.

Introduction

Target your audience and incorporate keywords you want people to use when they are searching for you, which will "teach" Google search about your areas of expertise. Borrow from your LinkedIn Summary section to complete this section.

Occupation and Employment

You should have a tagline to describe what you do, so consider using it in the Occupation and Employment sections. Google+ uses your recent employment as your tagline; this information appears under your name and is the first thing people will see when they find you on Google+. Instead of just listing your business or employer name, expand the description of your current employment to include accolades or useful information. You can use your LinkedIn headline in this space.

Your Updates

Since Google indexes every public update, be sure many of your updates include your keywords. Try to write updates that naturally include the keywords (but not excessively, because it may appear that you are posting useless updates just because you want to add your keywords). It should not be hard to include at least one of your keywords in many of the posts you share and write.

For example, a graphic designer may write an update such as:

> *Read what this graphic designer has to say about branded logos and online art. As a designer myself, I agree with most of her points, but I would argue with #5. What do you think?*

Possible keywords in this update include: graphic designer, branded logos, and online art.

Use Keywords in Your Facebook Page

Be sure you use your keywords in your "Work and Education" section and your "About Me" in your personal Facebook page. In your business Facebook, be sure to fill out your "About," "Mission," and "General Information." Depending on how you set your privacy settings on your personal page, these can help you be found via search.

Luckily, it's easy to transfer what you created in your LinkedIn and Twitter profiles to use in your Facebook section. Don't repeat everything word-for-word, but use your strong keywords to populate each profile.

Use Keywords in YouTube

As a fast-growing and successful search engine, YouTube—the second largest search engine behind Google—is an important network. You can upload a video related to your business that highlights your expertise. For example, you could create a "How To" or "Tips and Tricks" video highlighting how you can help solve your audience's problems. You can even have a series of "shows" where you conduct interviews, interpret the news relating to your field of expertise, or actually respond to client questions.

How do your keywords play into this strategy? In Miriam's book, *Social Networking for Career Success*, social media consultant Katrina Kibben (http://katrinakibben.com) explains that the easiest way to attract people to your YouTube video is to transcribe the content into the video description verbatim. She explains,

> *"The description I am referring to is available for editing after you upload the video (not the description that is shown while the upload is processing). There is no character limit so feel free to include all of the content available.*
>
> *"When you transcribe these videos, you earn search traffic to your YouTube channel by making it easy for search engines to "read" your content. Plus, with the new annotation tools and*

custom backgrounds, you can showcase your brand while the videos are viewed."

She warns, "Now remember, one video will not drive millions of hits to your YouTube channel or to your website. Create a series of quick 30 to 45-second videos on a certain topic then create a playlist of those videos with a keyword relevant title."

Use keywords in your transcription and when you "tag" your video, and you'll have another place where people can easily find you.

Check Your Keywords: Search for Yourself

Once you set up your profiles with your keywords, be sure to test your strategy by searching for your keywords. Search each of the networks and search engines.

It's possible to see immediate results when you tweak your LinkedIn profile. For example, if you are not showing up in results for a particular word or phrase and you add it to your profile, a new search may show an immediate increase in your rank on LinkedIn. It is a lot harder to influence your overall Google or search engine results—that is more of a long-term proposition.

FIND YOUR ONLINE MENTIONS

Google Alerts—This useful tool from Google allows you to monitor when someone mentions you or your business name online. To set up alerts, just Google {Google alerts} and select the term you want Google to monitor. You'll get an email whenever Google indexes the term or terms you select.

Socialmention.com—This website is similar to Google Alerts, but it monitors social mentions. For example, if someone mentions you or your business on Twitter or another social network. You can receive free daily email alerts to track your brand, company, CEO, marketing campaign, or even a developing news story, a competitor, or the latest on a celebrity.

Get It Done

Having carefully selected keywords is important, and using them in your website (more about how to do that in Chapter 5) and via social networks is one way to get the word out about you and your expertise. It is not an overnight strategy—this is more of a "get started on the right foot so you won't be sorry later" strategy. You are likely to see most of your results down the road.

Finding keywords isn't a "once and done" project, so remember to always consider how to tweak and update your keywords. Here are your "Get It Done" steps to get started:

1. Be targeted. Know what you offer, but even more so, understand how your skills fit into what your audience needs from you. Brainstorm and strategize. Ask yourself:
   - What are the demographics, psychographics, and shopographics of your target audience?
   - How are people most likely to be searching for a business like mine?
   - What keywords will they use?
   - Where will they look?
   - When they seek information, what do they expect to find? For example, a short, detailed blog post? A long, involved article? A bullet point?
2. Identify customers or clients. How are they likely to try to find you?
3. Identify the keywords that customers will use to find you.
4. Use social media tools to make sure you promote yourself as an expert service or product provider relevant to your keywords.
5. Brainstorm keywords you believe describe you and would be likely keywords for people to use in search toolbars.
6. Use tools mentioned in this chapter to select keywords you can rank high for in search. Google AdWords will be helpful, even if you don't plan to purchase ads on Google.

Keep this in mind if you want to incorporate location-based words.

7. Consider long-tail keywords or phrases as part of your research. Many people search by asking a question or inputting a series of words.

8. Once you select your keywords, start to incorporate them into your social media profiles.

LinkedIn

Update your headline, job titles, summary, and status with keywords, as all of these are searchable. Sprinkle keywords in your Experience section, and be sure to fill out the Skills section, too.

Twitter

Your bio and your updates need to be optimized for search. You don't have a long bio, so make every word count! Use relevant hashtags (#) to identify terms people can use to search Twitter and find you.

Google+

Google owns search, so don't waste the opportunity to be found when you use Google+. Pack your introduction, occupation and employment, tagline, and updates with keywords.

Facebook

Be sure you use your keywords in your "Work and Education" section and your "About Me." Depending on how you set your privacy settings, and if you use a business or a personal Facebook page (both can help you), you want that information to be available in search.

YouTube

Use keywords in your transcriptions and when you "tag" your videos, and you'll have another place where people can easily find you.

9. Search for yourself. Once you set up your profiles with your keywords, be sure to test out your strategy by searching for your keywords. It's easy to make changes and re-check your search results in social networks such as LinkedIn. Unlike results for your website, you can influence immediate changes.

10. Find out if someone mentions you online. Set Google Alerts and monitor online mentions with a tool such as Socialmention.com. Keep an eye out for people mentioning your information online, as they may not always use your name or business name when recommending your information. When you keep a careful eye out for mentions, you have a chance to connect with people who care enough to mention your work, but aren't savvy or interested enough to include specific details.

CHAPTER 5

Search Engine Optimization (SEO) for the Non-Technical

Search Engine Optimization (SEO) happens when you used the keywords your customers are most likely to search for on your site. Remember, your goal is for customers to find your site on the first page of Google results when they search for your keywords. We're not SEO gurus, but you don't need to be one either to create a successful, SEO-optimized site for your business. However, whether you decide to create your own site or contract a website developer, it is important to have basic knowledge of how SEO works. This knowledge will enable you to be strategic and consistent in how you present and market your new business. From your "About" page to your blog posts and social profiles, getting top rankings on search engines matters.

This chapter focuses on the things you should know about to affect your "find-ability" on the web. Revisit these SEO tips regularly to ensure your SEO is up to snuff.

The most important thing to remember: the best way to improve your authority and relevance on the Web is by *continuously* creating new content (blog posts, pictures, images, videos, podcasts, etc.). It's also important to keep your site's user experience in mind. The experience your customer has on your site, including how long the pages take to load, is important. If your potential customer can't figure out how to find what they are looking for on your site, they'll leave and probably not come back.

How SEO Works

The Internet is like a big database of information. Search engines read information on the web and prioritize the relevant or important results. When you structure your site well and use smart SEO strategies, you can influence rankings as they pertain to "relevance" and "importance." Many factors determine relevance, for example, direct keyword matches, results from previous searches, your content's popularity, and Google's "search plus your world," where Google provides results based on who is connected to you online.

When you create web content, you can influence how the search engine will rank it by how you label the information. As you start your business, you will develop and post new content online. If you don't use the right keywords, it can take time and sometimes even money to make it right. There are many different strategies for maximizing your site's ranking, and as a result, many experts who claim they can help (for a fee). The clean-up process can be lengthy and, once finished, there is no guarantee that the fixes will work. All this can confuse even the most seasoned business owner.

The search engines have different algorithms, or formulas, which they use to identify and rank pages found online, and these change frequently. We don't recommend you try to game the system; in fact, that can get your site into trouble. When we asked you to identify keywords associated with your business idea in Chapter 4, there was a reason. Using the right keywords in context will help you win authority and direct traffic to your site.

These are two resources we use for SEO help:

- Hubspot.com
- SeoMoz.com

Your Customers Find Their Answers Online

Years ago, all you needed was a shingle and a Yellow Pages listing to market your business. Today, consumers get their information differently—they go online. According to a 2012 comScore, Inc. study, there were 17.1 billion searches conducted in just one month in the United States, and that number will continue to rise due to mobile device usage.

As you probably know from first-hand experience, when people have a question or a problem, they turn to the Internet. Data from a Pew study suggests that 92 percent of adults online use search engines to find information on the Web, including 59 percent who do so on a typical day. No matter which search engine they use, if you and your business can provide answers to their questions, you will attract potential customers, generate leads, and ideally convert them into paying customers.

You Want to Be #1

As explained in Chapter 4, identifying keywords and setting up your website and social media profiles with the right words will make it easier for potential customers and clients to find you. You should also know that where you rank in search engine results pages (known as SERP) is very important. You not only want to be on the first page, you also want to be in the #1 position, because being one of the first 10 search results listed translates into an average click through rate of 52 percent for Google and 26 percent for Bing, according to a Slingshot SEO study. This should be your goal, and it is not a once-and-done activity. Just as you will always be tweaking your keywords, focusing on SEO is also ongoing.

Two Kinds of SEO You Need to Care About

On-site SEO, the content contained within your website, is very important. In addition, using social media will greatly enhance your site's reach—this is known as off-site SEO.

On-Site SEO: Managing How Your Page Ranks
Each search engine uses a different complex algorithm to rank content. However, there are some reliable guidelines you can follow to help search engines find your site, and rank it as authoritative.

> ↪ **TIP**
>
> Take a baseline of where your site ranks today when you search for it. Test it on different search engines by searching for your site's name and keywords. Be sure to clear your browser's cache for subsequent searches.

Use Words on Your Site
A jazzy website with photos, moving objects, and graphics (technically referred to as Java and Flash) looks nice, but unless it is set up properly, search engines won't detect it. Search engines search or "crawl" HTML content, the programming language used to create websites. When search engines crawl and evaluate the content on

your website, you want them to find everything. If your site uses pictures, icons, buttons, logos, and images, be sure you give them an ALT tag, tagged and labeled with appropriate keywords in order for the engines to read them. (This is easy to do in WordPress. When you upload a new picture, you'll have the option to tag it.) If you hire a web designer, be sure to ask him/her about tagging images and fancy moving objects.

Name Your Webpages Properly

In WordPress, you can choose what is known as a permalink, which determines the makeup of the URL (web address) for your pages. In the back end of your WordPress site, visit Settings/Permalinks. Select the option known as "Post Name." When you do, each page within your website should have a URL that looks something like this: www.yourcompanyname.com/about.

RECOMMENDED WEBSITE PAGES

Besides an "About" page, there other pages your site should include for better user experience and search engine crawling such as:

- Home
- Services
- Products
- Testimonials
- Contact
- Privacy Policy
- Publicity and Press Coverage
- Portfolio
- FAQ

Use Keywords in Context

According to SEOmoz's Beginners Guide to SEO, "One of the best ways to 'optimize' a page's rankings is to ensure that keywords are prominently used in titles, and text." Additionally, having keywords used at the top of the page and in context makes for better results.

> **⤳ TIP**
>
> Remember, your keywords are not just your business' name. They are the terms and phrases your target customer uses when searching for someone like you.

These keywords will naturally be included on your webpage and blog content—that is, if you selected the right keywords for your field and your audience. In order for your keywords to have maximum impact with readers and search engines, try to include them in the names of pages or titles of blog posts. Also, use keywords in your headers. (In WordPress, select "Heading" when you create these subtitles. This is important because search engines prioritize these headers over regular content.)

An example for our food blogger, based on the keywords selected in chapter 4, might be:

> **Ideas for Simple and Easy Vegetarian Meals** as the heading for one of her pages. She may then have a series of blog posts with variations of this:
>
> **10 Easy Easy Meals for Summer**
> **The Best Vegetarian Meals on a Budget**
>
> Within the post, she would have a main header, which introduces the content under the post title. Those may look like this:
>
> Title: **10 Easy Easy Meals for Summer**
> Head 1: ***How to Cook Simple Meals***

Title: **Best Vegetarian Meals on a Budget**
Head 1: *Healthy Recipes on a Budget*

It's easy to select subtitles in WordPress. You will see a drop-down menu when you edit a page or post.

Long-Tail Keywords

As you learned in Chapter 4, a long-tail keyword is a specific search phrase that contains three or more words. It often contains a main term, which is a more generic search term, one or two words long. According to SEOmoz, long-tail search comprises 70 percent of search traffic. According to HubSpot, there are many reasons to use long-tail keywords:

- **They produce higher quality traffic and increased conversion rates.**
- **They are often less competitive than individual keywords.**
- **They help you rank for difficult terms.**
- **Long-tail search is the most popular type of search.**

A keyword for a massage therapist would be "massage therapy." We used the Google AdWords tool to find long-tail keywords. Some medium-ranked results that would make for good long-tail keywords are "massage therapy benefits" and "health benefits of massage therapy." Use these terms to create titles for pages or blog posts. They would also be good words to include in content shared on social networks like Facebook and Twitter.

An example of a Facebook update or tweet with a link to your blog might be:

> *Do you wonder what the benefits of massage therapy are? Your questions answered here* [include link to your blog].

You can also find long-tail keyword suggestions by going to Google's search box. Begin typing in a keyword and see what additional words Google suggests. These are long-tail keywords you will want to pay attention to and consider adding to your site.

For example, when you begin entering "photography" these options appear:

> Photography careers
> Photography classes
> Photography news

If relevant, these keyword phrases could help you build content for your site.

Update Content Regularly

We both maintain blogs, and for good reason. When you regularly update content on your site, the search engines index the new content, which helps to build authority. Every blog post you write allows you to use keywords that support your business. Format your blog post by using keywords in the title of the post, as headers in the post, and within the actual content. The truth is, this comes naturally when you are writing about the problems and solutions for your customers. You don't need to overthink it, just be aware that keywords should be a part of your ongoing content.

A Well-Linked Site Equals a Well-Liked Site

As you add new pages to your site, it is important to link them to existing pages or posts already on your own site. Find a way to link to a newly created page from an existing page, or vice versa. Doing so helps keep visitors on your site longer and takes them deeper into your site. As a result, your website gains authority and, ultimately, a higher place among the search engine rankings.

Use Meaningful Anchor Text to Internal Links

One way to link to content on your site and keep your visitors reading and staying longer is to use anchor text. Anchor text refers to the words used to link to additional pages or content on your site. We commonly see it appear like this:

For additional information, <u>click here</u>.

In that example, the anchor text (hyperlinked to another URL) is "click here." However, this isn't the most search-engine-friendly approach to linking. Instead, use related words to include as the anchor text such as:

Read more about <u>how to improve SEO</u>.

In this case, ideally, the anchor text links to another page on your own site describing SEO.

The bottom line is user experience. Make the links useful for the user, so they will follow them intuitively.

Quality External Links Add to Authority

When you conducted research about your competitors, chances are you discovered some with high-ranking Alexa or Google Page Rank status. If you believe in their content and it jibes with the values and messaging of your own business, include their links on your site as a list of additional resources. When you add a link to their site, they receive a notification called a pingback. In some instances, the owners of that business may be interested in checking out you and your business.

Page Load Time Impacts Ranking

KISSmetrics reports that 40 percent of people abandon a website that takes more than three seconds to load. This can be especially true with mobile users. While speed alone may not drastically affect your page ranking, it can boost customer confidence and trust in your site. There are easy ways to prevent your site from loading too slowly.

First, images should be optimized for the web. By optimizing images, you format them in a smarter way so they result in a smaller file size. If you have Photoshop or another photo editing program, you can use that to decrease the size of your image by choosing the "saving for the web" option. Otherwise, you can use a free tool like Yahoo's Smush.It (smushit.com/ysmush.it/) to compress the image and upload a smaller image on your site.

Second, avoid using too many plug-ins on your site. Though they may add fun functionality, consider the trade-off in time added to your site's load time. Remember, we're talking split seconds here—if each plug-in adds even a negligible amount of time, their combined load time can make a big difference to impatient visitors.

Additionally, there are many technical steps you can take to optimize load time; however, you may need to ask your web developer or someone with experience in this area for specific strategies.

Google Analytics allows you to see the load time for your site and the percentage of people abandoning their attempts before your site loads. Whether you use Bing, Google, or other free Webmaster tools, set them up as soon as possible once you launch your site so you, and anyone who ends up working on your site, can see the historical data.

MEASURING SITE SPEED

These are some tools that can measure your site's load time and help you assess what you can do to speed up your website:

- Neustar.biz/
- CloudFlare.com
- Google PageSpeed (https://developers.google.com/speed/pagespeed/insights)
- Iwebtool.com
- Pingdom.com
- Yslow: www.developer.yahoo.com/yslow

OPTIMIZING WORDPRESS FOR SEO

If you are running your site using WordPress, you will want to know about plug-ins. Plug-ins are mini applications that add additional functionality to the website. Here are plug-in recommendations for improving your site's SEO and speed if you are using WordPress (which we highly recommend, and discuss further in Chapter 9):

- WordPress SEO by Yoast
- W3 Total Cache

Add Multimedia (Video and Audio)

Google loves YouTube (this may be because they own it!). Using video is a powerful way to increase your site's ranking as well as its user experience. Though people develop more video content every day, there is still less of it than there is plain text to read—and less means it is easier for you to rank highly. More people of all ages and backgrounds are becoming mobile and watching video. Videos are integral to the success of any SEO strategy. Audio is also popular for its ease of sharing, and the fact that it allows people to multitask.

Have a Sitemap

What is a sitemap? In simple terms, a sitemap is the structure of your website read by web crawlers. It maps out the hierarchy of your site's webpages, like an archive. This file should be easily discoverable by search engines when they crawl your site. Google and Bing provide indexing tools to help you create a sitemap. If you are using a WordPress site, there are plug-in tools that build this for you, such as BWP Google XML Sitemaps or Google XML Sitemaps. Having a sitemap allows the search engines to crawl it more effectively. Search engines should see all the pages that you want them to see, and the more pages they index from your site, the more trust your site gains. It means that your website has more information to offer.

Off-Site SEO: Using Twitter, Facebook, LinkedIn, and Google+ to build Google Juice

Today, you have many options and entire communities of people to help spread the word about your business! The search engines recognize this fact.

Implement Social Sharing Tools

Have you noticed "share" buttons on the top, bottom, or sides of articles? This makes it easy for readers to share content on Facebook, Twitter, Google+, Pinterest or wherever they have friends and contacts. When people visit your site, you want to provide them with options to share your content with their connections. There is also a sort of a "grading scale" inherent in sharing. When many people "like" what you say on Facebook, re-share what you wrote on Twitter, or +1 your links on Google+, they are endorsing your content. Since search engines are looking for relevant and authoritative information, social sharing tools can help build authority and ultimately rank your site higher in search.

These tools make it easy for your readers to share your site's content:

- Addthis.com
- Sharethis.com

Share Your Own Content

Clients often ask which social networking platforms have the biggest bang for the buck. The answer depends on your customers and your goals (as explained in Chapter 9). If you are looking for platforms to start building a stellar community, we recommend Twitter and Facebook based on our own personal experiences and the stories from our colleagues and clients.

Guest Authoring and Posting

Writing articles to post on other sites is a good strategy to improve SEO. How does it help? Your goal is to have content that includes your keywords with links back to your site. These are called "back links." For example, if your keywords include {portrait photographer, Tempe, AZ}, you would want to include those words in your guest post with a link to your website. For example, the bio that appears with your information post may include: If you're looking for a **portrait photographer in Tempe**, call me. The bold words would be a hyperlink to your own site. Review Chapter 17 for more details on guest blogging.

Submit Press Releases about Your Business (Locally and Virtually)

When you have good news to share, it is important to get it out there, right? Once upon a time, you needed to hire a PR firm to manage this for you, but today, you can do this yourself. On one hand, all you need is to sign up (for a fee) with WebPR, which will blast your release to hundreds of outlets. This helps with SEO because it places your content and links to your site on other high-authority sites. Additionally, you can create relationships with reporters for your local or regional newspaper and television stations on Twitter or Google+. You can also sign up for Help a Reporter Out (helpareporter.com). This free service allows you to receive inquiries from reporters who are searching for answers and expertise. It allows you to easily monitor and respond to press requests and potential media opportunities for your company, partners, and clients. (Read more about this in Chapter 17.)

Commenting on Other Notable Websites

Commenting does not guarantee your SEO will improve, but it certainly can't hurt. If you use keywords in your comments and add value to the discussion (and thereby build authority), you could kindle new relationships with the blog's author or other people who comment.

Additional Off-Site Linking Ideas

Michael Johnson of PixelPunk.com provided these creative suggestions for getting off-site links to your site:

- Get listed with a Chamber of Commerce: For a $100 application fee, many will link to your site.
- Sponsor an event or support a charity like Big Brothers Big Sisters, and they may link to your site.
- Interview someone and blog about it: They may Tweet and Facebook the link.
- Write a whitepaper and embed it as a PDF on your site for search engines to pick up.
- Give a lecture at a college or university class: Links ending in .edu are great if they advertise your lecture on their site.
- Pitch yourself to the local media for a story: For example, the local business magazine will link to your site in the online article.
- Join a Board of Directors: They usually have a website and will link to you.
- Ask for rations on UrbanSpoon.com, Foodspotting.com, Yelp.com: These sites offer restaurant and retail ratings.
- Post reviews on Amazon.com.
- Contribute to document sharing sites like Slideshare or Scribd.
- Link to Foursquare.com from your site.
- Post photos in Flickr.com, a photo sharing website.
- Write and distribute press releases: Include embedded links.
- Add your business to Manta.com: This website offers corporate profiles.
- Add your information to Wikis: Explore wikis such as Wikitravel and Wikinews.

Get It Done

- Get a baseline on how your site ranks and continue to monitor your Alexa and Google Page Rank regularly and note any changes (both good and bad).
- Continue to read and learn enough to be knowledgeable about SEO.
- Use keywords on your site.
- Be smart when you name your website and pages.
- Use keywords and long-tail keywords in context. Include them on page titles, blog posts, images, and video labels, and other content you share offline.
- Use keywords as meaningful anchor text to internal links, and link newer pages and content to other pages on your site.
- Acquire and post links from authoritative sites.
- Make sure your page loads as quickly as possible using the tools suggested.
- Add multimedia (video and audio) content.
- Have a sitemap so search engines collect as much content from your site as possible.
- Implement social sharing tools and share your own content.
- Seek out opportunities to submit guest posts.
- Submit press releases about your business.
- Leave comments on other high-ranking, authoritative websites.
- Set goals for yourself—for example, guest post once per month, submit your name to three local and three professional associations, or comment on two blogs per week.

6 Research the Competition

Competition isn't necessarily a bad thing; do not let it deter you. The benefit of doing research is that it helps you differentiate your offerings so you can stand out from the crowd. You may also learn how your potential competition is attracting customers. You can use this information to build a better mousetrap for your own business.

Online Research

Begin searching with Google and Bing for the keywords you identified in Chapter 4. Pretend you're one of your customers and ask questions you predict your customers might ask a search engine. Additionally, identify businesses that offer the same or similar services as you. As we said earlier, in most cases it doesn't matter where the business is located, unless your product or service is truly regional or geographically specific. You can even use those same terms to search companies within LinkedIn's company search section or you may choose to search by industry within LinkedIn.

Industry associations or professional groups are helpful resources to find competitors. Your local librarians should be able to help you research groups where you can canvas competitors, as they have access to research tools not available to the public. When Miriam was researching prices for resume writing before she began her business, she recalls digging out the Yellow Pages and calling local business owners to ask questions. They were reticent to provide details, and this effort took a lot of time. The Internet makes this research easier, but be sure to network in person with members of your industry. You may consider joining the associations you encounter when you research your competitors!

Keep track of companies similar to yours in order to monitor and assess what services they offer and changes they make to their sites. This will help you keep up or adjust your own business services. Bookmark them in your browser, with tools such as Delicious, that let you set up folders by subject, or consider creating a private pin board on Clipix.com. You may also prefer plain old paper or a Word document to track information.

MORE RESEARCH TIPS

An Inc.com article titled "10 Things to Do Before You Start Your Start-Up" provides this helpful suggestion to help you keep an eye on the competition: "Sign up for email alerts about search terms of your choice on Google News, which tracks hundreds of news sources. After you study it, deconstruct it using Fagan Finder, a bare-bones but very useful research site. Plug the address into the search box." You will learn about the other sites that link to it, which may reveal alliances, networks, suppliers, and customers. You may want to pursue business relationships with these potential contacts. Inc. notes, "Business data aggregators such as Dun & Bradstreet and InfoUSA provide detailed company information, including financials, although the services are not cheap. Your aim is to understand what your competition is doing so you can do it better."

Alexa and Google Rankings

Alexa and Google PageRank evaluate, or rank, your site's traffic and importance. Alexa indicates traffic volume to your site. It is not an absolute number, but more of an indicator of approximately how many visitors you get—the lower the Alexa number, the better. You can download an Alexa toolbar to your computer to easily see ranks for most pages you visit. When you use the toolbar, it may actually improve your site's Alexa rank. Google PageRank measures the importance of a particular page. The score ranges from 1 to 10, where 10 is the highest and most important. Your score indicates whether you have a credible, authoritative, and relevant site for your customers.

Tools to Measure Alexa and Google PageRank

- Google PageRank Checker
- PRChecker.info
- Alexa (www. alexa.com/siteinfo): This site is also good for competitive information

There are also tools to help you scope out the keywords competitors use on their websites such as KeywordSpy.com, Spyfu.com, SEOBook.com, and SearchStatus.com. You can use some of your competitors' keywords as your own and try to rank higher, or select a different set of keywords unique to you and your business.

We recommend you scour competitive websites and collect the following information:

- Who are their customers?
- What are their main differentiators/How do they position themselves?
- Where does your business idea overlap?
- What do you like about the look of their sites?
- Have they included pricing?

- How do they ask prospects to contact them (phone, email contact form, other)?
- Do they list what social platforms they are on (Facebook, Twitter, LinkedIn, YouTube, etc.)?
- Do they have blogs?
- Do they have newsletters?
- What are their primary "calls to action" on their sites? What are they asking readers to do?
- What are their Google and Alexa ranks?
- What groups, associations, or memberships do they belong to?
- Do they appear to be successful?
- What do you like and dislike about their sites?

Evaluate Your Idea Against the Research

With your research in hand, begin to decide how you will differentiate yourself and your business from the competition. For example, you could provide faster work and higher quality products, or make it easier for customers to place orders or do business with you. Another differentiating factor could be your level of interest in the service you deliver. Any skilled practitioner can deliver highly effective training. However, when a business owner delivers their training with energy, enthusiasm, and passion, the participants can tell the difference.

Don't focus entirely on price. You probably do not want to offer a product or service that differentiates you based on being the least expensive. You want to price yourself competitively, but the best businesses usually do not start out by aiming to be the cheapest solution. We talk more about setting your fees later in this chapter.

Think creatively. Enlist the help of other people you know by asking them to evaluate your idea. You could even ask your potential customers what they want and how they want it, what they *don't* like about the company they currently use, and what they do like. For example, if you hear potential customers say they seldom get a call back when they leave a message, consider how you could build your business around being responsive. Many successful businesses started by solving a customer problem.

FILLING A CUSTOMER NEED

MyBrands.com, based in Rochester, NY, began because they identified the need to deliver hard-to-find, specialty, or discontinued products to brand loyal customers. Consumers generally cannot buy directly through the manufacturer, and that's where MyBrands comes in. They act as the order-taker for specific manufacturers who want to deliver discontinued products or hard-to-find products around the country. Hefty Baggies was the first brand to sign on with MyBrands back in 2001. MyBrands founder, Suzanne Clarridge, had worked at Hefty when requests from consumers came in for baggies. This business model clearly met an un-addressed problem and provided a win-win for consumers and manufacturers, as well as MyBrands' success.

NICHING IS NICE

You think you want to serve the largest audience possible, so it seems counterintuitive to choose a niche. Think about it: if you broke a bone, do you want to go to just any doctor, or look for an orthopedist? If you want to learn how to play golf, would you prefer to find a pro golfer, or someone who teaches three or four different sports? Of course, you could learn golf from anyone who knows how to play, but you may be willing to pay a little more to work with a professional who focuses only on golf. (Plus, when you target your niche, it's a lot easier to hone in on your keywords, as we discussed in Chapter 4.)

For example, you could be a plain vanilla "consultant," or you could be a consultant who specializes in Search Engine Optimization (SEO) within the sports industry. One of the MOXIEs we interviewed started his

continued from page 81

side job by combining his love of technology with his passion for sports. Doug McSorley, a lacrosse coach and SEO consultant, was a Quality Assurance (QA) Engineer for more than 10 years working for large companies, but he knew he didn't love the work. He decided to do website design and IT consulting on the side, but realized he needed to offer something different due to the economy and competition in these two areas. Since he was a self-taught wiz at SEO, he understood the latest and best algorithms search engines use. Also a sports enthusiast, Doug landed consulting assignments via his coaching and sports connections. Word of his interest and talent in SEO spread within the college and professional sporting industry. What is the thing Doug says differentiates him from others? He was always willing to learn and continue to figure out the latest search engine algorithms as well as how page rankings affected overall analytics. He noted, "I loved this stuff. It totally energized me."

Doug also offers this insight: "Another suggestion I have is never stop learning. I'm currently working on my bachelor's degree in Sports Marketing and Media." Think about what you can do to learn something new and discover a niche service you can add to your business.

The opposite of choosing a niche is trying to be all things to all people. However, taking on the wrong types of clients can be dissatisfying, frustrating, and even costly. Similarly, taking on a client or delivering a service outside of your core strengths can result in less than satisfactory outcomes. It is tempting to accept work you know you shouldn't. You may think, "Some money is always better than none." However, if the client or project is outside of your scope, it may not be worth your time. Ask yourself, "Will it lead to future assignments or business that would be more closely aligned with what I want to do and do well?" Remember, just as a good referral can generate new business, a bad recommendation can affect your reputation.

Where Is Your Customer?

Do you plan to deliver your product or service virtually, in person, or both? Remember, we live in a global economy, so do not limit your marketing and outreach to only local customers. We want you to first consider where you can find potential customers without focusing solely on geographic location. However, sometimes tapping into your existing local network, those who know and trust you, can enable you to nurture your business locally and expand globally. It may be that the product or service you deliver is not available locally or it could be relatively easy to become a local resource and expert. We hope you consider both.

How Will You Deliver Your Product or Service?

In the olden days, people purchased all products from a retail location or storefront. Brick and mortar is expensive, and, in most cases no longer necessary. You can even deliver training via webinar platforms, videos, or eBooks. You can conduct coaching or advising via Skype or other platforms. Technology is leveling the playing field, and increasing opportunities for smaller businesses.

Pricing Your Products and Services

This is tricky! You don't want to over- or underprice your offerings. How you manage this on your site may depend on exactly what you offer. For example, if you provide a service, you may have an hourly rate (for coaching, for example), or your fee may change depending on the complexity of the project. Some sites list prices for all their services. Others may list a base (bottom) rate and ranges, which help avoid tire kickers, or people who cannot afford to hire you. If you sell products, you will probably list prices for each item.

Things to Consider When Developing Prices

As you price your services and products, consider these questions:

- How much do you need/want to make per month?
- How many hours will you invest in your work?

- How many products and services do you need to deliver in order to reach this goal?
- Are these expectations realistic and/or achievable?
- What are your expenses? (This includes phone, Internet, and subscription services, as well as many other things.)
- Will you make a profit after expenses?

If the answer to that last question is "no," you can charge more, decrease your expenses, or get better and faster at your work so it takes you less time to deliver your product or service. Note: All of your time is not billable. You will be investing time to market your business, respond to inquiries, develop new content, and pursue marketing and networking activities.

Don't Be Afraid to Test Your Pricing

As you get started, you may decide to test two or three different price points. Systematically evaluate which of those price points converts into more sales, not just leads. A lower price point may deliver more leads; however, closed business is more important.

Create a Board of Advisors

Very few successful businesses start in a vacuum. The key is identifying your weaknesses to fill the gaps. Identify people you know and respect in different areas and run your business idea by them. Ask detailed questions and ask for specific feedback on your idea to make the data as meaningful as possible. You may even choose to create a formal or informal board of advisors to help you.

Think about the people you know and respect. Perhaps they were past colleagues, managers, or leaders. They may be long-time family friends or college buddies. As you think about people you would want to help advise you and provide honest feedback, also think about your weaker areas and try to pull in expert advice from anyone who can bolster your skills. For example, if you despise selling, ask someone you know who is a super-star closer and top performer to help advise and teach you some of their secrets, or at least point you in the right direction for getting more information.

These might be the key backgrounds or skill sets you want to have represented on your board:

- Operations/process
- Customer service
- Sales
- Accounting
- Marketing
- Another new start-up owner

Having people from different industries on your list is also a good thing. It will provide you with alternative ideas and ways of thinking about how you deliver your product or service. If you choose someone with solid knowledge of your desired business practice, someone who already serves your potential customer, someone with strong financial savvy, someone who can see the big picture, and someone you greatly respect for any other reason, you'll have an amazing advisory team. Be sure you only invite people who will be honest and direct with you.

TAPPING OTHERS FOR IDEAS

Groups and forums for small business owners are helpful resources as well. If you want advice about how to tap into new customer markets, you could pose a question in a LinkedIn group. You could also use Quora.com to find out which software product is best suited for your business. You may even choose to appeal to as large an audience as possible to find your answer. You can do this by crowd sourcing the answer to your question by posting it to your social networks. For example, you may write a blog post about your dilemma, or post the inquiry to an open forum, such as Twitter, Facebook, or Google+.

How to Invite Someone to Join Your Advisory Board

Why would someone want to serve on your board of advisors? Generally, people are flattered when you ask for advice or help. Think about what you can offer them in exchange for their time. It might be tickets to a sporting event or concert, a subscription to their favorite magazine, or even a copy of a book you think they'll enjoy. Show appreciation by promoting their business via your in-person and online networking. When you ask for their help, specify the time commitment you expect from them. Is it a one-time thing or do you want ongoing support? Be honest from the start, and try to make it as easy as possible for your advisors to help you by accommodating their schedules, and by being organized and prepared when you speak to them.

You may find that some of your competitors may become your best advisors. It is possible to identify people who will be willing to share information and advice depending on your field. Camaraderie does exist in some fields, so do not overlook this possibility. Identify people who can serve as an advisory board of sorts for you and your business. These advisors can be people in your field, but they may also be professionals you admire in any industry. Don't limit yourself by only trying to meet those who are doing what you want to do. For example, you may invite a legal expert, someone with a history of marketing expertise, and someone who always seems to have many contacts and is willing to put people in touch with each other (a connector).

Doug Johnston of Impact4Results is a start-up owner who invited his board of advisors to listen to his idea over dinner. He provided them with his business plan, a mock-up of his website, and a financial prospectus in advance. Those who attended knew what was involved and recognized his commitment to making his idea successful. He selected people with expertise in starting a business, someone from a sales and marketing background, someone who would assess the business plan, and someone whom he believed would provide brutally honest feedback. He walked away from this dinner with new ideas and went back to the drawing board to refine his idea. He was incredibly grateful to have learned what he learned before launching his business.

Professional Organizations Who Help Small Businesses

These are organizations that can help you evaluate your ideas:

SCORE
SCORE is a nonprofit association and a business counseling/mentoring organization. They provide free counseling, resources, and advice to people who are in business or want to start a business. They have been doing this for nearly 50 years. They also provide free or low-cost workshops on business topics. Their volunteer counselors are experienced business owners or managers who volunteer their time to help small businesses succeed. Their online resources include business tools, templates, webinars, tips, and a newsletter.

U.S. Small Business Advisory (SBA)
The SBA provides services in the following four areas:

- Access to Capital (Business Financing)
- Entrepreneurial Development (Education, Information, Technical Assistance, and Training)
- Government Contracting (Federal Procurement)
- Advocacy (Voice for Small Business)

Their website is loaded with resources for answering your small business start-up questions.

Hannah met with a SCORE counselor early in her business's development. She had a rough outline of what she wanted to do and was looking for general guidance and recommendations. The SCORE counselor had come highly recommended. What Hannah failed to do was develop specific questions for the counselor. During the meeting, Hannah also discovered the SCORE counselor had little experience with virtual or online businesses. He sent Hannah off with some general questions about her business plan, but it wasn't the help she had been hoping for. Hannah learned that, sometimes, we don't know what questions to ask in order to assess our business idea. Sometimes it takes talking to others who have started similar businesses in order to gain valuable feedback about your ideas and have them share some of the lessons they learned from the school of hard knocks.

Small Business Development Centers (SBDCs)

Small Business Development Centers (SBDCs) are partnerships primarily between the government and colleges/universities administered by the Small Business Administration. Their purpose is to deliver educational services for small business owners and aspiring entrepreneurs at no cost. Some of the services they provide include assisting small businesses with financial, marketing, production, organization, engineering, and technical problems, and feasibility studies. You should also check with your local economic development offices, incubators, or community college.

Take Risk and Action

Just because you have a good idea and you are solving a customer's problem doesn't mean they will be pounding down your door to buy it. People have to know about your business. In future chapters, we will discuss how to build a marketplace to market your product to a community of people who know, like, and trust you. These are the cornerstones of why people buy.

The other important point to note from our own experiences and those of people we've talked with is that your initial business idea may morph and change. You may have initially thought you knew your customer, but upon delivering your service, realized they needed something different. Perhaps advancements in technology have made it easier for you to add services or products that were cost prohibitive before. Writing a book used to be something few could achieve. However, with so many self-publishing options, this may now be a viable option.

An example of someone who redefined his services is Doug Johnston of Impact4Results. He began as a consultant or, as he called it, a contract executive, where he worked on special projects and planning. Doug also had the opportunity to occasionally speak to executives at large companies on communications, leadership, and planning. Years later, during a retreat, Doug outlined longer-term goals for his business and determined that he didn't want to just fix problems, but proactively deliver solutions before they arose. Doug now has a solid reputation for advising and speaking to businesses on leadership, communications, and planning. Doug admits that, though he had a specific goal, the path to get there was less clear, direct, and planned than he originally thought.

Do not write your plans in stone; you can, and likely will, change your focus and direction at some point. You won't know what to adjust if you don't get started!

Get It Done

- Research businesses that deliver similar products and services using online tools and search engines.
- Think about your customers' needs and decide how you'll deliver your products and services.

- Test price points and track leads to help determine pricing.
- Complete the competitive analysis for each business comparable to yours.
- What businesses also touch your customers and could refer business?
- Identify people to serve on your board of advisors.
- Remember, some options include people with a background or experience in operations/process management, customer service, sales, accounting, or marketing. Inviting people from different industries to your board provides new perspectives. You could select someone with solid knowledge of your desired business practice, strong financial knowledge, or start-up experience. You could also invite someone who is already a potential customer or can see the big picture, or someone you just greatly respect for any other reason. What compelling reason or benefit will you provide to help entice your invitees to serve on your advisory board?
- Reach out to SCORE, SBA, and SBDC to learn what resources are available to you.

7

How to Market Your Brand or Your "VIV-id" via Social Media

Unless you're in the enviable (but unlikely) position of being the only business selling or offering your product or service, you need to convince your clients or customers that you are the best person for the job. In Chapter 6, we talked about how to size up the competition to see where you stack up. In this chapter, we provide advice to help you evaluate what you offer and how to use social media to demonstrate your expertise.

Personal Branding, or Your VIV-id

Social media is an interactive way to market your business. You'll be creating a business for yourself as a brand of one. Your reputation (what people know about you) and expertise (what you know how to do) will be the foundations of your business. If you have not already recognized this, now is a good time to embrace the idea that you must sell yourself as an expert if you want to convince people to pay you for your products and services.

Personal branding is a common catchphrase you may read or hear about, which captures this concept of marketing yourself. The exact definition of personal branding is a sensitive and contentious topic, even among personal branding aficionados. Therefore, we decided we needed a new, modern, and specific term to describe a business owner's unique attributes. We hope you agree, **VIV-id** is the perfect new term:

> **V**irtual
> **I**ndividualized
> **V**erified
> **id**—psyche or self

If you look up the word *vivid*, on Dictionary.com, it means, "*Clear, colorful, conspicuous, definite, evident, eye-catching, flashy, forceful, lively, loud, manifest, plain, prominent, pronounced, showy, spirited, and strong.*" In other words, exactly the attributes you need to embrace as a business owner.

How do you define your VIV-id? Jorgen Sundberg, Founder and Director of Link Humans (LinkHumans.com), suggests you answer these three questions:

- What value do you provide (what problem do you solve)?
- How do you do it uniquely?
- Who is your target audience?

What Do You Offer?

What makes you different from many other people who probably offer the exact same product or service as you?

You can ask your network of contacts and colleagues to help you describe your best marketable qualities. Reach, an organization focused on helping people with personal branding, offers a tool to help you do just that. Visit http://www.reachcc.com/360reach and try out their free trial for their 360-degree assessment, which encourages you to send a survey from Reach to people who know you so you'll be able to learn how they perceive you.

WHAT DO YOU KNOW? WHAT DO YOU WANT TO BE KNOWN FOR?

Maggie Mistal, Career Consultant and Radio Host, suggests entrepreneurs ask themselves and others who know them, "What are my best skills, abilities, talents, and qualities?" The other question she suggests exploring is, "Have I and how have I been of service to others with these talents and skills?"

Maggie explains, "*I find it's always easiest to articulate your value when you have the people whom you've helped describe what you did, said, or provided, that was valuable to them. A budding entrepreneur can also reflect on the types of conversations they prefer to have. Those are clues to where your passions lie! One more question I like to ask my clients is, 'If you were known as a wise man or woman, what special wisdom or expertise would you most enjoy sharing with others?'*"

Why is VIV-id Important to Entrepreneurs?

Would you ask yourself, "Why do I need to get the word out about my business?" Of course not! If you are planning to earn money, you know you need to solicit customers. Think of VIV-id as a way to create your own success.

In *Personal Branding Magazine* (August 2011), Nikolas Allen, who runs BAM! Small Biz Consulting (bamsmallbizconsulting. com), reminds readers, "One of the best results of creating a strong, coherent and positive personal brand is that, in time, opportunities start seeking you." This statement is so true. We all need to remember how much control we have over our career paths.

Biz Stone, co-founder of Twitter, said, "Opportunity can be manufactured. Yes, you can wait around for the right set of circumstances to fall into place and then leap into action, but you can also create those sets of circumstances on your own. In doing so, you manufacture your opportunities."

This is a great way to think about your VIV-id—an opportunity to manufacture your own opportunities. Once you outline your unique value proposition, it's time to consider how you are going to let the world (or, more specifically, your target market) know about what you offer.

Your goal is to attract business to you. In this book, we are going to teach you how to use social media tools to do just that. Would you love to hear people say that you are exactly what they have been looking for? The more people who know about you and your message, the more opportunities you will have to attract business.

Where To Use Your VIV-id

Take your VIV-id everywhere with you!

Networking
When you introduce yourself, you need to be able to provide a snippet of your VIV-id, sprinkled with several keywords to connect with your target audience. The trick to a branded introduction is not to overdo it. We know, you've heard about the "two-minute elevator speech," and pitches of this length do have their place (for example, at formal networking events when you're asked to introduce yourself or in interview settings). In most cases, sound bytes sell. Put yourself in the other person's shoes; when you're meeting someone for the first time, are you really going to listen to his or her entire two-minute introduction? Most likely, after about 20 or 30 seconds, your mind will wander to that night's dinner plans.

In *100 Conversations for Career Success*, Miriam and co-author Laura Labovich suggest you include the following topics when composing your perfect pitch:

- What is your goal/objective?
- What do you want to do? (Consider your audience's needs.)
- What impact do you have?
- What results do you create?
- What problem(s) do you solve?
- How do you create positive results?

> **⇨ TIP**
>
> If you are speaking to an audience unfamiliar with your industry, be sure your pitch is free of industry-specific jargon, terms, and abbreviations. Try to speak in sound bytes, as if members of the media will be quoting you.

Do your research to help identify what skills, experiences, and accomplishments your target clients will appreciate. Keep an eye on what thought leaders in your field are sharing via social media outlets (including blogs, LinkedIn, Twitter, and Google+).

Talk to people about industry trends. Here is a template to keep in mind when you write your pitch. You can adjust the order once you decide what to include:

> *I work with* [**target audience**] *to* [**what problem you solve**]. *This is how I* [**your impact/results**].

For example:

> *As a graphic designer, I use my extensive arsenal of design and software skills to collaborate closely with dental professionals to make sure their online and printed materials showcase their unique skills.*

You'll want to have a VIV-id value proposition. Jorgen Sundberg of Link Humans (http://linkhumans.com) collected a number of value proposition statements, for example:

"I help people to clear their head trash and find their mojo. And, once they've found their mojo I help them to set it on fire!"

—ALEXIA LEACHMAN

"Help thought leaders write great books in just 90 days. 300 satisfied clients so far . . ."

—MINDY GIBBINS-KLEIN

"With a passion for wine and a natural, open approach I inspire others to appreciate the pleasure of good wines in a fun way."

—WINE TASTING HOST

"I use my enthusiasm, forward thinking, and passion for self-direction to help clients identify their uniqueness and use it to take control of their careers and lives."

—WALTER AKANA, Career/Life Strategist

"Through my intuition and genuine concern for—and interest in—others, I build long-lasting, fruitful relationships with my team, my business partners and clients to drive consistent, recurring revenue for my company."

—BUSINESS OWNER

In the next chapter, we'll outline some tools you may want to use to help get the word out about what you offer and suggest how you may want to decide which tool (or network) is best for you.

Social Profiles and Bios

In Chapter 9, we'll suggest ways to incorporate your VIV-id message into your story via your social media profiles and bios. Keep this concept in mind whenever you do or say anything related to your business.

Business Cards

Make them unique, distinct, and memorable.

Email Signature

Include details about you and your business in your email signature. Consider using WiseStamp.com to include links to your website and social media sites.

Why It's Important

Whether you call it a personal brand, VIV-id, or something else, you need to know what is special about you, your skills, and your accomplishments if you want anyone else to choose you, your service, or your product from all of the choices available. Think about famous personal brands: Oprah, Madonna, Tiger Woods, Donald Trump. When you think of them, you have an opinion. What opinion do you want people to have about you?

If you are the go-to graphic designer for dental offices, then that's your VIV-id. Maybe you are the blogger who always posts the best, most inexpensive, and easiest ways to prepare meals. Perhaps you're the consultant who knows how to explain exactly how to make a boring presentation exciting and enlightening. Whatever your expertise, it's your job to market you and your business as if you were a company like Nike, Coca-Cola, or McDonald's. If you don't take on this challenge, you'll be just another small fish in a very big ocean of similar experts.

Get It Done

You need to prepare to market yourself to win business. Answer these three questions:

- What value do you provide (what problem do you solve)?
- How do you do it uniquely?
- For whom do you do it (who is your target audience)?

Know what you offer: What makes you different from many other people who probably do the exact same kind of work that you do?

What do you know, and what do you want to be known for?

Answer these three questions, suggested by Maggie Mistal:

- What are my best skills, abilities, talents, and qualities?
- Have I, and how have I, been of service to others with these talents and skills?
- If I were known as a wise man or woman, what special wisdom or expertise would I most enjoy sharing with others?

Consider using Reach's 360-degree assessment tool (www.reachcc.com/360reach) to solicit information from other people about what they think about you.

To help you identify your pitch, consider the following questions:

- What is your goal/objective?
- What do you want to do? (Consider your audience's needs.)
- What impact do you have?
- What results do you create?
- What problem(s) do you solve?
- How do you create positive results?

Use this template for your short pitch:

> *I work with* [target audience] *to* [what problem you solve].
> *This is how I* [your impact/results].

Once you identify your VIV-id, you can use it everywhere you go: at networking events, online, in social profiles and bios, in your email signature, and on your business cards.

8 Naming Your Company

One of the most fun, yet challenging, aspects of getting your business up and running is naming your company. Your business name is the launching pad for all of your social media and online monikers. Naming your business helps make your entrepreneurial ventures more concrete.

IS IT TIME TO UPDATE YOUR BUSINESS NAME?

Maybe you've been running your business informally for a while, but have not officially chosen a name. Alternatively, perhaps you have an official name, but you're just now thinking about how to incorporate social media into your business. When you start to think about keywords and how they influence whether or not people can easily find you online, you may want to consider changing or updating your business name. (See Chapter 6 for more details about keywords.)

You have many choices. Maybe you'll want to choose a meaningful name. For example, Miriam's business is named Keppie Careers because "keppie" is the Yiddish word for "head." Keppie Careers' original tagline was, "a head above the rest," which made the alliterative name significant.

Another approach is to personalize your business name, for example, "John Smith Consulting" or "Mary Jones Eateries." It's a natural choice for many business owners, but consider the advantages to keeping some distance between your own name and your business's name. For example, if you spend several years running your business full time and decide to return to a more traditional work arrangement, listing your business as Your Name, Inc. makes it immediately obvious that you've been working for yourself. Unfortunately, not everyone jumps at the chance to hire someone who is accustomed to being the boss. Another consideration: should you ever sell your business, it will be awkward if it is closely associated and branded with your name. These may be remote concerns now, but you should keep them in mind in case your needs change in the future. Of course, these examples don't include keywords, either, which may be a liability. Let's face it—no one is searching online for "consulting" and hoping to find a good match. "Consulting" is an overly broad term and would not likely yield specific results.

Tips from the Small Business Administration

The U.S. Small Business Administration (SBA) is a government agency that provides support to entrepreneurs and small businesses. These are their suggestions for small business owners (or soon-to-be owners) to consider when it comes to business naming:

Find Out if Someone Already Legally Claimed the Name

Check with your state (see Chapter 10 to learn how to investigate). Depending on your type of business, it is possible you can still use the name if the other business is in a different geographical region and it would not confuse potential customers. However, even if the business is in Timbuktu, if it owns the URL and uses the social media handles you want to use, it is not a good idea to overlap names—you will be out of luck owning your online properties. Consider using tools such as Thesaurus.com to find new ways to name your company if your go-to choices are already taken.

Check for Trademarks

The SBA notes, "*Trademark infringement can carry a high cost for your business. Before you pick a name, use the U.S. Patent and Trademark Office's trademark search tool to see if a similar name, or variations of it, are trademarked.*"

Is Anyone Else Using It?

Even if they don't have a legal claim, this is an important box to check on your to do list. Type the URL into your browser and make sure someone else doesn't already have your business name reserved online. You can also check the WHOIS database of domain names (http://www.networksolutions.com/whois/index.jsp). If it is available, be sure to claim the URL right away and move forward with reserving social media names. (Facebook allows you to claim your business page name once you have 25 "likes.")

Pick a Keyword Focused Name

Not only do you want to claim a website address or URL that is unique and available, but you should also choose one that is rich in keywords that reflect what your business does. If you've had your business name for a while and never thought about keywords before, consider whether it makes sense to reinvent and rename your business to take advantage of online tools. For example, operating a golf business with the name "Swing on By," is clever, but it does not do anything for you in the keyword department.

You probably don't want to totally give up your fun name, so consider adding it as a tagline with a more keyword focused name for the Web. For example, "Golf Strategies: Swing on By to Win." Your website may be called GolfStrategies.com.

What Connotations Does it Evoke?

Do you want a very corporate sounding name? Will a witty or funny name appeal to your audience? What will people think about when they see your business name? The SBA.gov site asks, *"Does it reflect your business philosophy and culture? Does it appeal to your market?"*

Other Considerations

Keep these suggestions in mind when naming your business so you won't be sorry later.

It should be easy to remember and spell. Ken Revenaugh is the owner of Fast Track Tools (www.fasttracktools.com), a consulting firm that helps sales professionals persuade, influence, and win business. He notes, *"The trend in recent years is to make up new words when naming your company. It might be original, but is it easy to remember and say? Creating new words can be great—especially when reserving a website name or trademarking your name—but if your name is so unusual no one can remember how it's pronounced or how it's spelled, it's a flop. Try out your new business name on a few friends. If they have to ask you to repeat it a few times, or if they're having trouble remembering the name you just told them, or how to spell it, that's a problem."*

Focus on your audience. Think back to when you envisioned your target audience. When naming your company, make sure you consider them. What would appeal to them? Are there any cultural references that would be appropriate to use or to avoid?

Does your business name have an expiration date? Ken reminds soon-to-be business owners, "*Your company name should never be based on trends or include a date. Do you remember a company named 20th Century? Hmm. Not much foresight there.*"

THINGS TO CONSIDER WHEN YOU RESERVE YOUR URL

Once you decide what to call your business, you need to reserve your URL—your business' website name. Here are some factors to consider:

- You may want to reserve many domains. For example, if you have the .com, you may wish to own the .net and .org as well. If your name has a common misspelling, you may wish to own both. If there are plural versions of the name, you may wish to reserve those as well. You do not need to host all of them on a site, but owning them will prevent anyone from using them, as long as you renew the domains.
- How does it look when it is on the screen? Think about if letters blending make it difficult to read, or if it includes a word that many people may misspell and not find your domain. Another consideration: if the business name is very long, how might you shorten it as a Twitter handle, which can only be 15 characters? Most importantly, make sure it doesn't spell anything with an embarrassing result.

IndependentSources.com made this list of unfortunate domain names:

1. A site called "Who Represents," where you can find the name of the agent that represents a celebrity, made their domain name . . . wait for it . . . www.whorepresents.com.
2. Experts Exchange, a knowledge base where programmers can exchange advice and views, resides at www.expertsexchange.com.
3. Looking for a pen? Look no further than Pen Island at www.penisland.net.
4. Need a therapist? Try Therapist Finder at www.therapistfinder.com.
5. The Italian Power Generator Company can be contacted, day or night, at www.powergenitalia.com.

continued from page 105

6. The Mole Station Native Nursery, based in New South Wales, purchased the URL www.molestationnursery.com.
7. If you are looking for computer software, there is always www.ipanywhere.com.
8. Finally, there are these brainless art designers and their wacky website: www.speedofart.com.

All joking aside, your domain name is important. While it is not expensive or difficult to reserve, it is crucial. Ask your trusted friends for their opinions, carefully review the choices, and pick one (or more than one) that makes the most sense for you.

To secure your URL, visit a domain registrar, such as:

Godaddy (http://www.godaddy.com) or Bluehost (http://www.bluehost.com).

When you do reserve your domain, find out if the company will remind you before it expires. Some of the larger companies will email you a reminder, but we have heard of bloggers who find their blogs inactive because they failed to renew their domains after never receiving any notifications. Regardless, it is up to you to keep track of your domains, so be sure to note the renewal dates.

It is important to own the URL for your company name, as well as to secure the name on social media sites, including Facebook, Google+, and Twitter. (Depending on the nature of your business, Pinterest, Instagram, or another visually focused site may be on your list of "must haves.") If you're very ambitious, be sure to visit namechk.com and knowem.com. These sites help you identify what names are available on the various social networks.

Get It Done

Naming your business is a bit like naming a child or a pet—you do not want to pick something you will regret later! Answer the questions in this chapter and check twice to find out what is available online before you choose your business name. Read ahead to Chapter 10 so you'll understand key legal concerns that could affect your business name before you make a final choice. This should be fun! How often do you have a chance to name something? Enjoy it, but do so with an informed and researched approach.

Consider factors such as:

- Is someone else using your name legally? (Don't forget to check for trademarks.)
- Is your name easy to remember and spell?
- Does the name include keywords that will help you with SEO?
- Will it resonate with your audience?
- How will it look online?
- What type of logo are you able to create?

Once you choose and fully vet your name, decide if you want to reserve multiple URLs; for example, you may hold the .com, .net, and .org for your business name and visit a domain registrar, such as: Godaddy (http://www.godaddy.com) or Bluehost (http://www.bluehost.com).

Congratulations: you're the owner of a brand new domain!

9

How to Choose the Best Social Networks for Your Business

You're marketing yourself, so it is all about you, right? Wrong! If you've read any of the previous chapters, you should already know that everything you do when you market your business has to do with the intersection of what you offer and what your audience wants from you.

Since you already identified your customer (see Chapter 4) and nailed down your unique value (or selling) proposition (in Chapter 7), your next job is to identify what social networks are most useful based on what you know about yourself, your business, and your audience.

When you choose the best networks to use, consider two major factors:

1. Where can you find your target clients or customers?
2. Where are you most comfortable posting content online?

For example, if you can't say anything in less than three paragraphs, Twitter (with 140 characters per tweet) will be tough for you. We advise every MOXIE and business owner to explore all of the networks before choosing the best-fitting tools as their go-to online marketing platforms.

Where Are Your Targets?

There are no fixed data about exactly which social networks attract which type of customers or clients, but the following statistics may surprise you:

A Pew Research study (August 2011) found, "Fully 65 percent of adult Internet users now say they use a social networking site . . . up from 61 percent one year ago." They further note, "The frequency of social networking site usage among young adult Internet users under age 30 was stable over the last year—61 percent of online Americans in that age cohort now use social networking sites on a typical day, compared with 60 percent one year ago. However, among the Boomer-aged segment of Internet users ages 50-64, social networking site usage on a typical day grew a significant 60% (from 20 percent to 32 percent)."

In August 2012, Pingdom (a company that provides website monitoring tools) did a demographic study that showed social media is not just a younger generation's phenomenon:

- 55 percent of Twitter users are 35 or older.
- 63 percent of Pinterest users are 35 or older.
- 65 percent of Facebook users are 35 or older.
- 79 percent of LinkedIn users are 35 or older.

Their research found that LinkedIn has the oldest user base at 44.2 years old. In comparison, the average Facebook user is 40.5 years old, and the average Twitter user is 37.3 years old. Facebook and Twitter have the same gender distribution: 40 percent male and 60 percent female.

Even if your target audience is baby boomers, you will not want to discount social networks as great tools to reach them. An April 2012 Pew study concluded, "One third (34%) of Internet users age 65 and older use social networking sites such as Facebook, and 18% do so on a typical day."

Content Marketing and Blogs

Content marketing is a phrase you should know. It's the umbrella term for your efforts to create and share content online (in the form of posts, updates, visual information, videos, etc.) that you hope will prompt your target audience to hire you or purchase something from you.

We believe your most important online property is your website/ blog (see Chapter 11 for more details about how to get your site up and running). Why? Because it is the hub, or centerpiece, of your other content marketing efforts. Think of your website as your business's virtual home. Before you create outlying posts for sharing information (via social networks), you need to build and maintain a strong, useful content platform on your own site.

We recommend you create a site built on a WordPress platform. Even if you are not technically inclined and need to hire someone to create it for you, with a little effort, you'll be able to update your site on your own.

Who Reads Blogs?

Anyone who searches for any type of information online reads blogs. How do we know? Most of the time, when you search for information on Google, it delivers links to blogs as the top results. That's no accident—Google loves regularly updated content, and blogs tend to be updated frequently. You can assume that you will be able to reach just about any online demographic via a blog, but there is one caveat to being successful: you must write well or hire someone to help you to successfully demonstrate your expertise via a blog.

Should You Blog?

If are not a strong writer, it's probably not wise to author your own blog as a way of demonstrating your expertise, as it may have the opposite effect. You don't want someone to land on your site and see numerous grammatical or other errors, then quickly click away. Does your blog need to be perfect? Probably not. As regular bloggers ourselves, we know errors can sneak in, especially during a particularly busy week or when we are bleary-eyed from other work.

However, we recognize that our blogs represent a large percentage of our professional faces online. If we couldn't keep up with a quality standard, we would each consider taking a break from blogging rather than posting content that would not represent us well. You should think about this, too.

Depending on your writing skills, you may be able to generate publishable content by hiring an editor to brush up your work. An editor can help ensure you demonstrate a solid thought process, produce interesting and grammatically correct content, and have a clear flow to your blog. Some people can eventually learn to self-edit their work from regularly working with an editor. (Although, we

DON'T BELIEVE THE HYPE

Please do not believe the hype that you are going to be the next Internet millionaire by selling ads on your blog. In our opinion, blogging for business is about showcasing your expertise, not about creating an avenue to advertise for other people.

both admit, you cannot catch all of your own mistakes. Having an editor, if you can afford one, is invaluable.)

If the last time you put two sentences together was in a high school or college writing course (and it was a business writing class, at that), you may want to consider hiring a writer to collaborate with you on your blog. Ideally, you will generate the content on your business site. However, if the expertise you market is unrelated to communicating well through writing, there is nothing wrong with contracting competent writers to help you share information about your business, news related to your field, and other content your customers may find useful.

Here are some resources to find writers and editors (freelancers) who may be able to help you:

- oDesk.com
- Freelancer.com
- Guru.com
- Mechanical Turk (https://www.mturk.com/)
- Elance.com

How a Blog Can Help You

What can a blog do for you? The list could go on and on. A blog can:

- Help connect you to a community of colleagues, experts, and potential mentors.
- Provide opportunities to expand your network, instigate two-way communication, and meet new people from around the world.
- Help you further define your message and potentially become known as a subject matter expert.
- Provide a 3-D portfolio of your work.
- Influence how Google and other search engines index your name, and what people find when they search for you.

What Should You Write About on Your Blog?

You want to try this blogging thing, but what should you write?

- Comment on the news of the day as it relates to your field.
- Post a Q&A or top tips for something related to your business or industry.
- Interview someone of interest to your target audience.
- Comment on another thought leader's recent blog post or other social media share, and be sure to link to that person.
- Post a video on YouTube and share it on your blog (this is known as a video blog, or vlog).
- Share an intriguing photo along with some brief comments or a thought-provoking question.
- Use a conversation on another network (Twitter or Facebook, for example) as a launching point for a blog. Showcase a conversation from those platforms and respond on your blog. (Be careful about sharing content posted in a closed forum; do not repost it online without permission.)
- Interview clients or customers, either in writing or on video (use Skype if it is long distance, or Google+ Hangouts) and post it on your blog.

If you're stuck for ideas, Google {blog, ideas} and you'll likely come across some inspiring suggestions or lists of ideas.

BLOGGING TO ATTRACT BUSINESS

As Todd Schnick explained in Chapter 3, when you blog about a client or company you want to notice you, it is a great way to get their attention. For example, if a company related to your expertise gets acquired by another firm, and you write about how the news is an opportunity for other organizations to win business, it's possible those organizations will notice your post. Then, they may get in touch with you to learn more about your ideas to influence their growth in the new market.

Connecting With Your Audience via Facebook

Facebook is known for having the largest social graph (number of people using it), with over one billion people of all ages and demographics using it every day. You would be wise to incorporate a Facebook strategy as part of your social media plans. Facebook gives you an opportunity to spark discussions, share visuals, and create a community of people who care about you, your business, and your products or services. People who are successful with Facebook provide frequent, useful, and engaging updates to build credibility and collegiality. Consider creating a Facebook business page full of useful information for your community of potential clients.

When you think about Facebook for your business, the opportunity to advertise or promote your business may come to mind. While this option is available, it's not the only way to get the word out about your products or services. In a true social media business strategy, Facebook's platform offers much more than just ads. We do not recommend relying on Facebook alone for an online presence (your website or blog should be your home base); however, a business page highlights what you have to offer, engages with your community, and connects you with potential new customers.

Learn from Your Own "Likes"

Think about the businesses you like on Facebook. Maybe you signed up because of an incentive or a contest (read more about contests in Chapter 17). Perhaps you were inspired to connect because the organization provided coupons, special deals, or promises to notify you of sales. How did you learn of the business' page to begin with? Was it because you were a current customer? Was it through an ad? Maybe it was an ad incorporating a QR code (see Chapter 13 for more on QR codes). All of these are likely approaches to encourage potential and current customers to like your page. Especially if you fit the description of your target customer, think about what motivates you and incorporate those incentives to motivate others to join your business' Facebook community.

Remember when you envisioned your target customer or client? What information or resources would that person want from you? Shape your Facebook and social media strategy to answer this question: how can you provide exactly what that person needs? What information is so valuable that your prospective or current client will welcome your business' Facebook feed into his or her daily routine?

Assess Your Facebook Audience

What can you post via Facebook (and other networks) to help keep people informed about the things they need and want to know?

Do not assume; rather, continue to research your audience. Facebook business pages have analytics to help you understand your readers. How can you find out what they will want to see on your Facebook feed? Ask them! Take note of shares, and pay attention when people respond (or do not respond). Do they respond more actively when you post stories or when you ask questions prompting for their opinions? Do they seem to like to view videos? Before long, you will have a good idea of what interests your audience and what type of information you can provide to keep your business relevant and top-of-mind.

Types of Things to Share on Facebook

Cater to your audience; what do they want and need to know? Below are some examples of Facebook updates catered to specific audiences.

A relevant news story from a food blogger:

> *Corn and soybean prices are up, which is likely to raise a myriad of food prices, since these items are key to our food chain. Here's how to find the best food at the lowest prices where you live* [link].

An update from a leadership consultant who companies hire to train new managers:

> *Common mistakes new managers make? The Wall Street Journal shares 5 myths that may surprise you. Have you fallen victim to any of these?* [link]

What type of update is appropriate for a freelance graphic designer specializing in working for dentists? Posting all about graphic design won't interest this business owner's target market. Instead, think about what content will appeal to his target customers. For example:

> *The number of people with dental insurance climbs for the first time in years* [link]

> *How to stop chewing up your brand and start spitting out profits—branding works for this dental office* [link]

A golf equipment salesperson may ask:

> *Who has the best chance to win this week's Open? Read what the experts say; it may surprise you. What do you think?* [link]

Look at the American Express Open page on Facebook. They do a great job involving their audience in conversations about small business topics.

THE BEST TIMES TO POST ON FACEBOOK

When are the best times of day to post to your Facebook business page? It's not entirely clear, and it depends on your target audience, but a study by Socialbakers.com says you shouldn't just stick to posting during business hours. As Facebook expert Mari Smith shared on her page (https://www.facebook.com/marismith), posts shared on Sundays get the highest engagement at 11 percent. Fridays come in at the

continued from page 117

second highest with nine percent, followed by eight percent on Saturdays. Mari recommends, *"Be sure to keep an eye on your fan demographics and 'people talking about this' demographics (fans and non-fans) so you know in which time zones the bulk of your community reside—then you can better target your timing."*

A different study by bitly, a URL shortening and bookmarking service, found that Facebook links sent between 1:00 p.m. and 4:00 p.m. ET generate the most clicks. They also found that Wednesday at 3:00 p.m. ET (noon Pacific) is the best time to post on Facebook. Links posted after 8:00 p.m. and before 8:00 a.m. get less engagement on Facebook.

On Facebook business pages, you can schedule your posts, so be sure to take advantage of the best timing to win engagement.

Keep Mobile in Mind

With so many people using smartphones to review their Facebook updates, you should consider how your posts will appear on mobile devices. It is a good idea to view your own status updates via your smartphone so you will know what people are seeing.

Here are some tips for catering to mobile devices:

Post photos. You know what they say about a picture being worth a thousand words. A photo will usually translate well on mobile. Unlike a text update, it will not be cut short. Photos will likely get you noticed. Use them wisely to tell a story. For example, show a happy customer, or highlight a new product that you offer.

Be brief. In general, this is useful for all target audiences, but people are viewing mobile devices while in line at the post office or watching their kids play soccer. Make sure your posts are short and to the point.

Incorporate Facebook Groups in Your Strategy

Like all online groups, Facebook groups allow you to meet people who have common interests. You may even want to consider starting a group as a meeting place for your target audience.

First, search for groups to join. Just type "Groups" in the top search toolbar. On the right side of the resulting screen, a series of search filters will appear to help you refine your search. You can even search groups where people you know are members.

Don't jump in a group and start advertising your wares or services; that will turn people off. Instead, contribute to the conversation by sharing relevant articles or information, engage with the people there, and wait for the right time to specifically invite them to your Facebook page and to highlight what you offer.

Facebook's Benefits

When you adopt this social media approach and create a resourceful and informative stream of information, you will begin to create a community of people who support you. Your community will not just buy your product or hire you to perform services; it will include people who pass along the information you post about local events and news related to your industry. Those same people are more likely to refer you to their friends and let their communities know about your products and services.

In the old days, a business might have been able to garner this kind of goodwill by sponsoring a local sports team or club, by or volunteering at various community events. Those can still be great, face-to-face ways to meet people, but if your business is national or global, you will not want to ignore Facebook as a means to connect with influential people and potential customers.

The Benefits of the Social Media Approach on Twitter

Twitter is a great network for people who enjoy skimming and posting headlines, quick tips, and resources. You'll excel at using Twitter if you can say something important in 140 characters or less. People generally read tweets in "real time," which means you should tap into Twitter if your business relies on the news cycle or if you want to respond immediately (and publically) to customers online.

Your goal in using Twitter is multi-fold: you want to meet new people and expand your network, learn new things, and demonstrate what you know. When you incorporate an engaging Twitter strategy, you can accomplish all of these goals.

We are both unabashed fans of Twitter. Miriam even asserts that most every important business contact she's made resulted initially from a connection via Twitter. In fact, the two of us first met via Twitter, which led to us becoming members of an online community, and ultimately meeting in person and collaborating on projects.

WHO IS USING TWITTER?

Is your target audience on Twitter? As with any network, it can be difficult to tell from statistics. While Twitter is not the largest network, you may find a very active group there of people interested in what you offer, depending on your field.

The numbers of people on Twitter are not as large as on Facebook. Pew Research finds, "as of February 2012, some 15% of online adults use Twitter, and 8% do so on a typical day." However, they also note, "The proportion of online adults who use Twitter on a typical day has doubled since May 2011 and has quadrupled since late 2010—at that point just 2% of online adults used Twitter on a typical day." Pew acknowledges that the rise in the number of smartphones probably accounts for this increase, as "smartphone users are particularly likely to be using Twitter."

Since smartphone usage continues to skyrocket, expect your target audience on Twitter to grow.

Unlike Facebook, where it's not generally good etiquette to search for and introduce yourself to random people, Twitter allows you to access people who interest you, and, if you finesse your interactions, invite them into your community without any intermediary.

Use the tools in Chapter 9 to begin to locate the best people on Twitter for you to follow. For example, if you want to meet alumni of the University of Georgia (UGA), you can use followerwonk.com to find the term "UGA" in Twitter bios. You can also think creatively by searching, "Go Dawgs!"

However, don't focus your search on individuals. While we are being creative here, think of other easy ways to find people you want to meet. Continuing with the fan theme, if you want to meet people interested in a particular sport or sports team, search Twitter during major televised sporting events for words related to the event. One way to search Twitter is through hashtags (a # sign plus a key term, as discussed in Chapter 3). Searching #superbowl would be one way to find people tweeting about the Superbowl during the big game.

If your target audience includes likely movie fans, search #Oscars during the awards season, or other variations of that term (for example, #AcademyAwards) during that televised event. Do your potential clients tend to fit the demographic of people who watch a particular television show? If so, you should identify and follow the hashtag for the show (many networks are actually posting hashtags on screen; it doesn't get much easier than that!).

Finally, if your target clients are news junkies, you can easily find them by tweeting about whatever topic is making the news. It may take a little trial and error to find the most-used hashtag, but it will be worth it if you can identify people who may be good contacts for you.

WHEN SHOULD YOU POST ON TWITTER?

A study by Bitly suggests, "For Twitter, posting in the afternoon earlier in the week is your best chance at achieving a high click count (1 p.m. to 3 p.m. Eastern time, Monday through Thursday)." They suggest that

continued from page 121

people are less likely to click through to read a post after 8:00 pm ET, and that few people click through to links after 3:00 pm ET on Fridays.

Statistics are great guidelines, but every community is different. Keep an eye on your Twitter feed and notice when people tend to retweet (pass along something someone else tweeted, giving that person credit) your posts.

Alternatively, if you'd like to automate your Twitter feed (which you may want to try from time to time, although we do not recommend it as a rule), investigate Crowdbooster.com, Buffer.com, and SocialBro.com, sites which can help you time and automate your posts, and provide updates about engagement after your tweets go out. You can also choose an application (we like TweetDeck or HootSuite) to schedule your tweets in advance.

What to Do Once You Find People on Twitter

First, make sure you establish a Twitter feed (the collection of things you say and have said on Twitter) that demonstrates your expertise or interest in the information your target audience will want to know more about. Your Twitter bio should be specific and describe exactly what you do and what you know. (Remember those keywords? Use them!)

Once you establish your feed and identify new people to follow, begin following and seeing what they tweet. Jump right in and participate in the conversations people are having via the hashtags. For example, if you're a fashion expert, comment during any red carpet televised event. Include the hashtag in your tweets and feel free to include the Twitter names of people involved in the discussions. For example:

> @fashionista I agree! Angelina looks terrible in that color, and what's with that headband? #oscars

What if you're a caterer? Are you tweeting during important cooking and foodie shows? Even though most of the people you will meet will probably not be local enough to purchase your food, you never know how raising your profile and making smart comments may affect your business:

I can't believe they are using cinnamon for that dish. I would try cumin for a really unique flavor! #CelebrityChef

What about when there are not any relevant events happening? What should you tweet about then? When it comes to your updates, the same advice applies to Twitter as Facebook. Include commentary about what is going on in the news relating to your niche, share useful information people need or want to know, and provide resources to help possible clients learn more about you and your expertise.

Don't hesitate to mention the Twitter names of people you want to know, ask them questions via your tweets and retweet (RT), or pass along their information. Don't forget to add your comment at the beginning. For example:

A must read! RT @BizCoach: Don't miss @careersherpa and @keppie_careers' new book, Social Networking for Biz Success.

In that tweet, the Twitter user added her comment ("A must read!") and attracted everyone in the message's attention. You can keep up with people who mention you through columns in Twitter applications (different online tools to view your Twitter stream), such as TweetDeck or HootSuite. You can also click on the button that says @connect on your top toolbar when you use Twitter.com itself. Twitter will show you tweets including your Twitter handle, so you can keep up with anyone talking to or about you!

GETTING RETWEETED

One affirmation that you are doing something right on Twitter is when many of your followers retweet (RT)—your content. On the Hubspot blog (http://blog.hubspot.com/), Dan Zarrella reported the following factors as being important in winning RTs:

continued from page 121

Include a link in your post. *Dan says, "Users who tweet more links (as opposed to more replies and conversations) were the winners."*

Use an unusual or novel word in your tweet. *Dan suggests that uncommon words may be better than typical words to get people's attention. It goes to show that, even in 140 characters or less, people appreciate creativity and originality.*

Ask for a RT. *Dan reminds us that we should be incorporating calls-to-action in our tweets. He notes, of tens of thousands of tweets, he found that, "tweets that contained the phrase 'please retweet' were retweeted 4 times more often than tweets that did not contain a call-to-action." He also found RT activity peaks on Fridays, when other Twitter activity goes down.*

Don't talk about yourself. According to Dan, fewer people RT posts that are too self-referential. In general, talking about yourself too often doesn't win friends and influence people on social media. Always think about how to create and join communities, and be a good listener on social media.

Benefits of the Social Media Approach on Google+

Google+ is useful for people who like to start and see a series of responses to discussions or questions about a topic. It can be useful if you're looking to share late-breaking news and want to solicit customer feedback through discussions. One main differentiator between Google+ and the other networks is its "Hangout" feature, which is a live video conference or get-together, which you can post to YouTube to amplify your message. Using Hangouts is just another way to differentiate your business. For example, if you are a chiropractor, you could invite a massage therapist, a back surgeon, and a patient to talk about different methods to treat back pain. Use the resulting video (if you record your Hangout) as content for a YouTube channel. Since YouTube is the second largest search engine (after Google), and because people go to YouTube when they are looking for information, having this content can help you get the word out about your business.

The other benefit of using Google+ is that Google gives you a boost in search results. People signed into Google+ who are connected to you are more likely to see your content as results for their searches. That's not a coincidence; Google's goal is to provide the most relevant results for customers. Google hopes that providing content from people in your network makes their service more useful.

While the actual numbers on Google+ are not as large as the other networks, the benefit to using this tool is Google's "Search, plus Your World" feature, which we explain in Chapter 8. Google indexes and delivers search results based on who is connected to you. When you connect and engage via Google+, you increase the chance that people will find you in searches when they need someone in your field of expertise.

How to Connect with People on Google+

Like Twitter, Google+ is a completely open network. Users are welcome and encouraged to find and follow Google+ streams belonging to people they do not know (in Google+, following is called "adding to your circles").

You can create circles of people in Google+ to represent any group of people you want to track and follow. For example, you may have a circle called "Potential Customers." You can then see what these people discuss and what interests them by viewing their streams. People do not know what categories of circles you have them in. Depending on their settings, Google+ may send a notification when you add them to your circles, though.

When you find people, follow the same guidelines as we suggest for Twitter. See what people say, add them to your "circles," and engage in online conversations.

Find New Contacts via Hangouts and Communities

In addition to posting useful content on Google+—including updates containing your keywords—Google+ also has a "live" component. You can find public video Hangouts where people are meeting to talk about mutual interest topics. Just click "More" on the left Google+ toolbar and follow the link to Hangouts. Search for Hangouts by keywords or topics that relate to your business, or start a Hangout to see if you can meet new people.

Find "Communities" of people on Google+ (similar to groups on LinkedIn, as described in the next section) through the Communities link on the left side of the Google+ screen. This can be a great place to connect with like-minded people.

The Benefits of the Social Media Approach on LinkedIn

LinkedIn is the premier professional network. It is a great site for business-to-business networking as well as direct customer contacts. People go there to search when they are looking for an expert, and the more people you know, and the more contributions you make, the better the chances that customers will find you.

If you are not demonstrating your expertise via LinkedIn, you are missing many great potential connections and possible business opportunities. In fact, Miriam's first online client initially noticed her because of information she posted on LinkedIn.

Useful LinkedIn Tools

Ask Questions in Groups. Join some groups and ask and respond to questions relevant for the members there. Try not to directly solicit business; it is better to simply state your expertise and, if possible, provide a link to something wrote (on your own site) that elaborates on your comment.

For example, if the question is about how to fix a problem on a website, do not say:

> *I am actually an expert developer and have a lot of experience handling these kinds of problems. Please visit my website and learn more about how I can help [Link].*

WHO IS USING LINKEDIN?

LinkedIn's website reports that its network includes over 200 million members, including executives from all 2011 Fortune 500 companies. There are more than one million LinkedIn Groups, and 23 percent of unique members visit LinkedIn through mobile applications.

That response is nothing more than an ad, and it is unlikely to win you clients.

Instead, consider posting something along these lines:

> *The problem you are describing is complicated; I can imagine why trying to add that code to your site frustrates you. Try this: go to the backend of your site and open the "Appearance" tab. Then, click on "Widgets." Go to "Custom Menu" and drag it to your sidebar. Then, copy the code and save. Hopefully, that will work. If not, try checking out my post about how to add widgets to your WordPress blog—I'm adding the link here. Don't hesitate to connect with me or be in touch if I can help.*

Consider asking a question if you're looking for new contacts or partners. Don't be surprised when complete strangers ask to connect with you after you interacted with them in Groups. If you are open to learning about new contacts—some of whom may be able to hire or refer you business—it probably can't hurt to connect with them. Review their profiles first to make sure you think the person is a legitimate contact.

Learn Information Via Groups. LinkedIn's Groups section provides many opportunities to find people who are interested in the same topics as you. Frequenting Groups allows you to see what problems (and solutions) people discuss, and gives you a great opportunity to connect with possible clients and customers. If you are motivated, consider starting your own group, especially if there is not another active group in your niche. You'll need to work hard to build the group's membership, but if you are successful, you can become a natural leader in your sphere of influence, which will help you grow your business.

In Miriam's first book, *Social Networking for Career Success*, she interviewed several people who created groups on LinkedIn to help them with their business plans.

Chris Perry, a Gen-Y brand and marketing generator, entrepreneur, career search, and personal branding expert, and the founder of CareerRocketeer.com said:

> "*Starting and managing a LinkedIn group is a great way to boost your brand, build a network and identify opportunities. Your members come in contact with you at multiple touch points, including your announcements, discussions, and external resources/sites/networks, and can't help but view you as a leader in the area or industry associated with your group. As the owner/manager, career stakeholders, including both member and non-member recruiters, employers, hiring managers and potential partners will view you as an industry leader.*"

Chris suggested the following advice to leverage your role and enhance your personal brand as a LinkedIn Group leader:

- Share unique and insightful news and resources on a consistent, but not overly frequent basis.
- Limit self-serving updates or promotions to 20 percent or less of your outgoing outreach and interaction.

Chris cautioned,

> "*Unless you already have a large network prepared to join your newly created group, these groups take time, effort, and planning to build and manage, and must be launched and nurtured strategically. As a result, growing a group to any substantial size is an impressive accomplishment to share in your interview or with potential networking contacts.*"

Chris started two LinkedIn groups: Career Rocketeer and MBA Highway. He noted that growing a targeted group is easier than building a general membership. He said,

> *"I started MBA Highway as a targeted networking group for MBAs and MBA employers and recruiters to fill an unfilled group niche. As a result, this group grew quickly, especially as I invited MBA programs to share the group with their students at the same time as those programs were discovering the value of online networking to enhance their students' job search. This group has grown to almost 20,000 members thus far, and is still going strong."*

If you don't have the time or desire to start your own group, Chris suggested getting active in someone else's group and asking how you can become involved and potentially help them as a manager. He explained,

> *"This will inevitably help you build your brand within the community without the trials and errors of launching your own group. When doing this though, be cognizant of the group owner's guidelines, needs, and comfort zone."*

Benefits of the Social Media Approach Using Video

Many people predict using video is one of the most important things you can do for your business. Even if you don't enjoy watching videos online yourself, consider adding video content to your arsenal of online information to make it easier to find you online.

Videos are particularly useful for people who like to talk more than they like to write!

Depending on how old you are, the song, "Video Killed the Radio Star" may echo in your head when you think of online videos (or,

HOW MANY PEOPLE ARE WATCHING VIDEOS ONLINE?

In July 2012, comScore reported that 85.5 percent of Internet users watched videos that month. Where are they watching them? The report says YouTube had 157 million unique viewers, followed by Facebook with just over 53 million, and finally, Yahoo! with around 49 million. Yahoo! users watched 625 million videos compared to Facebook's 327 million.

Don't forget that YouTube is the second largest search engine in the world! If you don't create videos, no one will find you there.

maybe that's just Miriam!) Whether or not it killed the radio star in 1979, video (and YouTube in particular) is important for your business.

Before you get your iPhone ready to shoot some footage, spend some time researching what is online. What are your competitors posting? How can you differentiate yourself?

What can your videos include? Only your creativity limits the content! Smallbizsurvival.com suggested these topics for possible video content:

- Feature client interviews
- Show your product in action
- Give a tutorial
- Promote others
- Go behind the scenes of an event or program
- Interview an expert
- Highlight new promotions or specials
- Share your success stories
- Answer frequently asked questions
- Say "thank you" to your customers
- Share cultural things of interest
- Film events and conferences
- Share others' videos

Here are some more ideas for potential video posts:

- **Post how-to videos relevant to your customers.** If you sell makeup, demonstrate how to use the newest product. If you inspect cars, film a video of you doing your job and show how to fix the problems on an example model.
- **Give tips and tricks.** If you have a service business, record a short clip of you answering a question that one of your customers might ask. If you can use props or visuals, your video will be even more interesting.
- **Show a "day in the life."** Insert some humor! Film a clip that is a day in your life, or the lives of one of your clients.
- **Post video testimonials.** It's great to have written recommendations, but how much more interesting and valuable might an actual client video testimonial be?
- **Interview someone your audience recognizes.** You can also interview someone who has great ideas that supplement the content you typically provide.

Follow the instructions in Chapter 4 to "tag" your posts with keywords to make it easier for people to find your posts online.

CREATE A VIDEO WITHOUT STYLING YOUR HAIR!

Maybe you don't want to feature yourself as the star of your video, but you'd prefer to showcase some online resources your audience would like to know about. In this case, you can use CamStudio, Camtasia, Screenr, or Jing to conduct a "live" tour of some tool, or to highlight tips from the Web. This type of video, called a *screencast*, is a digital recording of computer screen output, also known as a video screen capture (see Chapter 15 for more about these resources).

When you create your videos, they do not need to be professionally produced, but be sure to use appropriate lighting. Take all the necessary steps to ensure quality control. If you cannot post videos that you would be proud to show on your business website, do not use this medium. It is better to have nothing on a network than to have sub-standard content.

Places to Post Your Videos Outside of YouTube

- Vimeo.com
- Metacafe.com
- Revver.com
- Blip.Tv
- Yahoo! Video
- TubeMogul.com
- Brightcove.tv (http://www.brightcove.com/en/)
- Dailymotion.com

The Benefits of Using Pinterest

If your business has products that you can display through pictures, Pinterest will be a great tool for you. For example, if you are an artist, a jewelry designer, or another type of artisan who sells products or goods you can photograph and share, we recommend you try out Pinterest. For service businesses and people who don't have obvious visuals to share, Pinterest can be more challenging to implement. However, if you are creative, you can figure out how to leverage this popular tool (we have even seen accounting firms on Pinterest).

WHO IS USING PINTEREST?

- TechCrunch, a website that reports on Internet and social networking trends, noted that Pinterest receives around 28 million

continued from page 133

visitors a month. Pew research says 15 percent of adult U.S. Internet users visit Pinterest, and the visitors tend to be white, female, and affluent. In fact, women are five times more likely to use Pinterest than men (25 percent compared to 5 percent).

- According to comScore, the average Pinterest user spends 98 minutes per month on the site, compared to 2.5 hours on Tumblr, and 7 hours on Facebook.
- comScore reported Pinterest was the fastest independent site to hit 10 million unique monthly visitors in the U.S.
- Users stay on Pinterest for long periods. Pinterest ties with Facebook as the top time zappers at 405 minutes per month per user. Research also shows that people spend more money when they visit a site via Pinterest compared to Facebook.

It is difficult to predict what the future holds for Pinterest; however, it appears that the network is growing, thriving, and making efforts to monetize. There is a minimal learning curve and it may be worth testing the waters while it is still popular.

How to Use Pinterest

You may want to think of Pinterest primarily as a sharing platform more than a networking tool. While you can follow, "like," and add discussions to pins, you may realize business opportunities through Pinterest by drawing attention to the actual items you share, or "pin." Similar to Twitter and Google+, Pinterest is an open network, which means you don't have to follow someone to see what they share—you can just visit their public boards. It is simple to use: just click and re-pin, like, or tweet a link to a pin! Pinterest is best for giving your visual content the exposure it may not otherwise garner. The site is also a useful branding tool. Your unique business identity should come through in the boards you create and the pins you post and share.

Use the search bar at the top to look for keywords related to your industry to find other people in your niche.

TIP

> Create your business Pinterest account at http://business.pinterest .com for access to resources and tools specifically for businesses!

Types of Pins to Create and Share

As we mentioned, visual content gains the most attention on social networks like Facebook and Google+. When creating images or pictures to help your clients or potential customers, think about what they would like to see. What can you show them that will make their lives easier or more entertaining? Be sure to use the correct keywords in the description and to link back to your site.

You can share links to videos, books, infographics, quotes or sayings, photographs, and even blog posts or articles. You will need to name your Pinterest boards; be sure you give some thought to how you name them so they align with your business and contain appropriate keywords whenever possible. It helps to use your imagination and creativity as you build your visual content, but don't be afraid to lift ideas from other active pinners.

For example, you could name a board, "Top Up-and-Coming Photographers," or share your "Favorite Images of All Time," or even, "Websites that Rock." For the less visual business, you could name one of your boards, "Tools That Get Me Through" or "Go-To Technical Resources."

If you are selling items from Etsy or your e-commerce site (more about these in Chapter 11), add your product images to Pinterest to gain greater exposure. When you include the price of your product in the description, it will display on the pin.

How to Make Pinterest Social

When you see a pin you like, you have many different choices of what you can do with it: You can add it to your own pinboard, like it on Facebook, or re-tweet on Twitter. You can share it on Google+, too.

Use Pinterest to strategically select and comment on pins of people you respect and to target people you want to notice or partner with. Create a memorable impression by leaving a comment on the pin, especially if the pinner owns it. You should also check out your competition to see if they are on Pinterest, and observe how they are using it.

Pinterest allows you to create community boards and invite multiple pinners to contribute to it. This is another way to build partnerships and community.

Get It Done

When it's time to choose networks, you need to think about a variety of things. It is as much an art as it is a science.

1. Consider your own skills and expertise as they relate to successfully engaging in the various networks. If you're a writer, you will probably start with a blog. If you can't say anything in less than a book chapter, Twitter will be

tough. If you're a talker, an audio or video channel may be best. Remember, your website will be your hub, and creating a blog on there will provide a platform for anything else you do online. Ultimately, your blog/website is your most important online property; don't underestimate how important it is to share information there.

2. Once you consider your skills, try to identify where your target audience may exist online. Review the research and data in this chapter, and use it as a guideline. When you decide where to start, remember, your social media goal should be to:

   - Demonstrate your expertise.
   - Build your network.
   - Be found.

   You can accomplish all of these by identifying what your audience wants to see and hear from you, and providing it to them consistently and regularly. In all of your networks, cater to your audience: What do they want and need to know?

3. Keep in mind how people are consuming your content. Are they accessing Facebook via mobile devices? What percent of your audience visits your blog and website from their smartphones? (You can find this out via Google Analytics.) Once you know how your audience consumes your content and notice how often they share, retweet, or comment on your content, you'll be able to tweak and customize what you post to get the most return on your time investment.

   Things to consider:

   - Visual shares are very engaging. Consider posting pictures and videos.
   - Be brief—people online have short attention spans. You don't need to write a book (or a chapter) for each blog; 500-750 words are probably plenty.

- Find groups to join on your favorite networks.
- Use open networks such as Twitter and Google+ to grow your network and meet thought leaders in your field. Use their network names (@name or +Name) when you communicate online so people you want to meet will notice you.
- Take advantage of opportunities to get online during televised entertainment or sporting events—you never know who you may meet while cheering for your favorite sports team or commenting on your favorite television shows.
- Try the great tools LinkedIn provides to connect with new people and potential clients, including Answers, Groups, and the various news resources (LinkedIn Today and LinkedIn Signal).
- If you have a business suitable for sharing visuals, try Pinterest. You can connect with new communities and get the word out about your products or services there.
- Don't forget about video; people love watching videos, as long as they are short and sweet!

CHAPTER 10

Sharing, Disclosure, and Transparency in Today's Online Economy

When you share information online, you should know something about sharing etiquette. What is okay to share, and how can you protect your own online content? Protecting your information is important, but don't be too stingy with what you will and won't share. Unless your process, procedure, or system is truly a trade secret, what do you have to lose by writing about it? It's unlikely someone would be able to steal or implement your ideas on his or her own. By sharing your information, potential clients may become interested in your services. A good rule of thumb is to see what others are sharing. A trend in online business (especially service-oriented business) is "freemium," which means giving away quality content, information, videos, or instruction for free. Entrepreneurs have an ongoing debate about freemium information.

Just as your grocery store may give samples of a new soda or granola bar to entice you to buy it, providing freemium content (sometimes in the form of a free teleseminar or webinar) may convince a prospect you know exactly what you are talking about, and that he or she cannot move forward without hiring you!

In essence, providing a stream of information and advice via social media is the ultimate freemium offer. When you provide useful tidbits of information via Twitter or give away useful, practical advice on your blog, you're teaching your audience that you are an expert and you know what you are talking about.

Attributing and Referencing Others' Work

Protecting your rights is important, but you want to consider other content creators' rights, too. This section addresses the different rights on the Internet and what they mean. You can use this information to label your own work and decide how you can use others' work. Referencing authoritative sources is a good SEO strategy (as we talked about in Chapter 5), as long you do it ethically and legally. You don't want to make a careless mistake and inadvertently "lift" content from someone else.

Others' Copyrights

If you use or copy someone's writing or use their images, you must cite your source. Depending on how much content you want to use, you may also need to receive permission, which should keep you out of trouble and help you to avoid plagiarism charges.

These are some formats for crediting a photo from another source:

> *Image courtesy of Stock.XCHNG user Jan Willem Geertsma*
> *Photo by RambergMediaImages*

In a blog post where you reference a direct quote from someone, be sure to name the source and include a link to the post on the site you are quoting from. For example, "This would be the quote you would use in your post," by Waldo Weird, *Thinking Outside the Lines*.

Creative Commons Licensing

If content is labeled Creative Commons (CC), the owner grants permission to use the copyrighted material. When you create written or graphic content unique to you and your business, you should learn about different versions of Creative Commons licensing and include the appropriate CC term on your website, blog, software, or music. You can use the license builder at creativecommons.org—complete the information, submit the link, and it will generate the code for you to put on your site so the license image appears on your page. It is also helpful for you to understand what the usage terms mean when it comes to you re-using or sharing other people's work. It is your responsibility to credit the creator as they specify in his or her CC license.

Though the terms of the license may be clear, many people who apply CC licenses to their work do not specify how they want to be credited. In these cases, use your best judgment and always provide attribution.

Attribution (by)

Licensees may copy, distribute, display, and perform the work, and make derivative works based on it only if they give the author or licensor the credits in the manner specified by these.

Noncommercial (nc)

Licensees may copy, distribute, display, and perform the work, and make derivative works based on it only for noncommercial purposes.

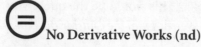
No Derivative Works (nd)

Licensees may copy, distribute, display, and perform only verbatim copies of the work, not derivative works based on it.

Share-alike (sa)

Licensees may distribute derivative works only under a license identical to the license that governs the original work. This is also referred to as copyleft.

Fair Use

Fair use means using an excerpt or portion of someone's copyrighted work for the purpose of reviewing, reporting, critiquing, or educating. This means you should be able to use a portion of the copyrighted material for these purposes without asking permission. Unfortunately, fair use is debatable, so if you're republishing more than a few lines of someone else's work on your site, the best practice is to ask for permission first, and to cite the source on your website or in your work. Be sure to clearly highlight content you get from others, and make sure you're not copying more than the necessary sections to illustrate your point.

The Importance of Linking

Many authors who write blogs mention another blogger's content with an appropriate citation and a link back to the source post, known as a *trackback*. In these cases, it is usually enough to provide attribution and a link back to the source. Don't "borrow" the full post on your site, and never use any part of someone else's work unless you credit the author.

The Scoop on Trackbacks

If your blog is hosted on WordPress (we will talk more about this in Chapter 11) and the blog you want to link to is also using WordPress, all you need to do is include a link to your target post in your post. WordPress sends a message automatically to the referenced blog. This message notifies the author that you referenced their post and serves as a little self-promotion. Some people will look at the site referenced in the notification, which means they will visit your blog and have a chance to learn more about you! This could be a useful way to help build relationships with other bloggers.

If the blog post you want to reference has a link at the bottom saying "trackback," obtain the trackback URL and copy it into your blog post's trackbacks section. Note: not all blogs allow trackbacks, so it's possible you may not be able to find a trackback link on some blog posts.

Using Images on Your Site

Whether you are setting up your website or blog or hiring someone to do it, you will want to select images, artwork, and icons for visually appealing content. Using the best quality and appropriately branded images is important in a quality site. We don't recommend skimping on these. If you are lucky enough to have a friend who is a graphic designer or photographer, you may be able to buy or barter his or her services.

Free Images

For blog posts, articles, or presentations, you can use photos that provide the Creative Commons licensing with attribution (meaning you give credit—and a link—to the artist). Many of the resources listed below allow you to specifically search images you are allowed to use. Please be careful to read the fine print in each site you visit and intend to use.

- CC Search (http://search.creativecommons.org/)
- Commons.wikimedia.org
- Everystockphoto.com
- Flickr.com

- Freedigitalphotos.net
- FreeFoto.com
- Morguefile.com
- Stock.XCHNG (http://www.sxc.hu/)
- Zemanta.com

Purchase Stock Photos

Sometimes, you can't find the photo you are looking for on the free sites or you want to modify a photo for your website or book cover. The following sites grant rights to edit their photos after you purchase them. Most of these sites are royalty-free, which means you pay a one-time fee to use the image multiple times for multiple purposes. Some of these sites give you the option to subscribe for access to a larger number of downloads or you can pay per download.

- Alamy.com
- Bigstockphoto.com

A NOTE REGARDING PINTEREST

When you re-pin (or share) from Pinterest, we advise you click through to the original source to ensure you don't link to content disguised as something else. Always pay attention to the pinner and consider their reputation and authority. There has been a buzz about copyright infringement issues on Pinterest. For example, is it okay for someone to pin something that they did not create or develop? Pinterest claims they are protected in the same way YouTube is protected when people share video content. The bottom line is that you should always credit the original source of material you do not create. Pinterest is taking steps to monitor pins and ensure there is linking to the original source, and there is a clear definition of their copyright policy on their site.

- Corbisimages.com
- CanStockPhoto.com
- Depositphotos.com
- Dreamstime.com
- Fotolia.com
- FotoSearch.com
- Gettyimages.com
- iStockphoto.com
- Photopin.com
- Photos.com
- Shutterstock.com
- ThinkStockphotos.com
- 123RF.com

Social Sharing Icons

Whether you call them icons or buttons, these visual elements help give your site personality. Their purpose is to draw the reader's eye and direct them to your social outlets. There are thousands of different buttons and icons available to you and website developers. The collection of social sharing icons includes all the important choices, such as Twitter, LinkedIn, Facebook, Google+, and much more. Icons come in different colors and designs—some are flag-shaped, others are square, and some are even shaped like bottle caps. This is all part of adding personality and flair to your site. As we move more towards mobile computing, having icons makes navigating your site easier for the user, plus, they are more visually appealing than text. Here are two sites to help you find icons or buttons you like. We chose these because they did not require attribution or link backs to the developers' sites for credit.

- Icons Etc. (http://icons.mysitemyway.com/)
- Iconfinder.com

Get It Done

Consider the following:

- Will you use Creative Commons Licensing?
- Understand what fair use means to you and the content you want to share.
- Know how to appropriately link to cited content and understand what trackbacks do.
- Know where to go to get images to use on your site, both free and for fee. Also, know how to give the appropriate attribution.
- Social sharing icons give your site character and direct visitors to your social networks.

11

Create Your Website and Choose the Right Way to Sell Your Products Online

Creating a constantly evolving web presence that doesn't break the bank will help you get your business off to the right start. You want a site that will grow as your business does! In this chapter, we will recommend options to help you create (or redesign) the right type of website, and explain different e-commerce solutions for your business.

Here are some factors to keep in mind as you create your ideal site:

Function

What is the primary role of your site? Is it an online store to sell products? Is it mainly a virtual brochure to inform consumers about your company or services? Will it create an online community where people come to exchange ideas and information? Perhaps you need a hybrid of many of these formats.

Nail down exactly what you want your site to do before you get started. Your goals will influence what features your site needs, how it functions, and its design.

Aesthetics

You have many aesthetic decisions to make about your site: color, font, design elements, images, logos, and the overall layout. Your site should reflect your personality and style (remember your "VIV-id") and represent how you do business. Research and review sites you like; collect ideas from websites within and outside of your niche. When you have some ideas, you or your website designer will have a definitive goal with ideas in place. Collect these ideas in an electronic or paper scrapbook so it will be easy to reference later. Evernote (www.evernote.com) is a popular choice for clipping and saving ideas you find online.

Usability

Make sure your site is uncluttered and easy to navigate so people can find information easily and quickly. Consider that people may land on your homepage by Googling a question or term related to your product or service. Remember, most people don't go online intending to buy anything. Typically, they search for information or have a problem they want to solve. Your site should convince them that you have the answers.

What primary action or actions do you want your visitors to take? Do you want them to:

- Read your blog?
- Buy your products?
- Hire you to speak or buy your services?
- View your "how-to" videos?
- Sign up for your newsletter?

Feature the most important action on your home page, and create clear directions for your visitors to follow. We will talk more about how to write effective calls to action in Chapter 16.

Designing Your Site: Use WordPress

We've said it before and we'll say it again: use the self-hosted Word-Press site (WordPress.org) as your website platform. It will do virtually everything you need it to do with ease. If you scope out the competition, you may notice their sites use WordPress. Perhaps one of the greatest benefits of using WordPress is you can update the content yourself, once you get the main design features set up. There's no need to hire a developer to tweak HTML (website code) every time you want to add a new special offer! You can add landing pages, and even an online store if you're adventurous. Your Word-Press site can expand to meet your needs; there are thousands of plug-ins (tools to add additional functionality) for you to use when you want to make updates.

Option 1: Use a Theme

If you already have website development skills, or are willing to learn new ones, you can set up your own WordPress site. One reason we like WordPress is because you can customize the way your website looks by using pre-programmed frameworks and themes. Themes, otherwise known as "skins" in the web development world, are ready-made designs you can use on your site. If you know about web design and programming, you can customize the themes, or you can hire someone to customize your site. Depending on what themes you choose, your website can look like an online newspaper or feature a photo gallery, for example. Themes act like templates and give your website the look you want without requiring coding and advanced technical skills to achieve your visual goals.

When new trends in website design emerge, or when new styles become popular, you can choose from thousands of themes to give your site an updated look. Whether you choose WordPress or another website building tool, be sure you can easily change, add pages to, and update its appearance and functionality. While there are free themes, expect to pay between $40 and $100 to use a theme that provides the functionality you'll need.

If you use a WordPress site, a web designer can modify the theme you select to give your website the feel and functionality you want. The small amount you invest upfront to purchase a theme will save on development hours, which makes this a cost-effective option.

POPULAR WORDPRESS FRAMEWORKS/THEMES

Visit these sites to view galleries of different themes. Thesis and Genesis are popular choices for many bloggers with well-trafficked sites.

- **Catalyst Theme:** http://catalysttheme.com/
- **Elegant Themes:** www.elegantthemes.com/
- **Elemental Framework:** http://prothemedesign.com/themes/elemental/
- **Genesis Framework:** http://my.studiopress.com/themes/genesis/
- **Headway Themes:** http://headwaythemes.com/
- **Thesis 2.0:** http://diythemes.com/
- **WooThemes:** www.woothemes.com

Option 2: Hire a Web Designer to Build it from Scratch

If you have a clear vision for your site but feel overwhelmed by all of the choices, decisions, and technology, forgo the template approach and hire a designer. Hiring an expert gives you more time to focus on your marketing strategies and your products or services. Ideally, you want to select a website designer or developer who understands your goals, has built similarly functioning sites for online businesses like yours, and is skilled in SEO, social sharing tools, and cutting edge website development. You don't want to pay to be the first e-commerce site in a designer's portfolio, or to educate him or her on which social sharing tools you should use on your site.

What Assistance Will You Require?

Are you planning to do the setup, theme selection, and customization yourself, or will you contract someone else to do this work? Here are some of the things you may need a designer's help with:

- Structural set up (setting up the shell of your site, then you include the content).
- Site design concepts (logos, graphic design elements).
- Programming for online transactions such as a shopping cart/e-commerce solution, contact forms, sales pages, or linking your newsletter signup with your email provider.

Ask for Recommendations and Testimonials

You get what you pay for, so it pays to do your research up front. Ask other business owners who they used to design their sites and if they were satisfied. If you've developed an online network, you can even ask your communities for recommendations. Find sites you like and ask the owners who designed them! Don't just limit yourself to your competitors; review a broad range of sites that have the same goals as you. Once you get close to settling on a designer, ask for references.

Call the designer on the phone to gauge if his or her approach and attitude are a good match for you. Also, don't forget to ask about timing issues to be sure your schedules align. If you want a site in a month and the designer has a waitlist, you need to find a new designer.

What is Your Budget?

What can you expect to pay? It depends on the scope of work and the designer's experience. If you need someone to modify or customize a template you purchase, expect to pay an additional $300 to $800. If you want someone to build a site from scratch, you could expect to pay $3,000 on the low end, and up to $10,000 or more for more complex sites.

Once your site is built, the designer's work is done, unless you want to keep paying him or her for minor updates and changes. You will need to learn how to maintain the site yourself or hire someone else to do it. You may ask your designer/developer for some training on how to do this, but be willing to compensate them for their time.

Get It in Writing

Make sure you know what you are paying for and get it in writing. During the discussion with your designer, you probably talked about many things. Ask for an estimate in writing and be sure it explains exactly what the designer will provide. Set deadlines and, if necessary, roll out the site in phases. These are some questions you should have your designer address:

- Do they provide webhosting?
- Will they purchase themes or will they use their own developer's version?
- Will they provide graphics, images, or stock photos?
- Are periodic updates included?
- Will they register your site with search engines?
- What search engines will they include?
- Will they optimize your site for SEO?

DO YOU WANT TO SAVE SOME MONEY?

Here are some ideas:

1. Do as much as you can by yourself. If you have printed material or content you want to include, type it into a Word document, email, or onto the site itself, if possible. You don't want the designer to bill you at their rates for data entry.
2. If you already have images and graphics you like, give them to your designer. It will save time. These are some sites to get ideas and inspiration for the visuals. You (or your designer) can purchase images and photographs from these sites:
   - http://www.istockphoto.com/
   - http://www.veer.com/
   - http://www.gettyimages.com/
   - http://www.shutterstock.com
3. Know when and where to make compromises. The easiest way to run over budget is to continuously send the designer back to the drawing board to rework an idea, or continue to make small modifications that may not be very important in the end. Know which issues are non-negotiable, which are must-haves, and which are not worth extending your budget.
4. If you don't mind, you may let your designer add their logo at the bottom of your site in exchange for a lower fee.

Don't forget, your completed site should include these elements:

- **Home Page:** This is where you showcase what you know and what you offer. Why are you the expert?
- **About:** Be sure to read Chapter 12 about writing online bios to populate this section.
- **Products/Services**
- **Contact Us**
- **Blog**
- **Free Newsletter Subscription E-mail Capture:** See Chapter 16 for details about how to choose a provider for your e-list.

Setting Up Shop on Third-Party Sites

Eventually, you might want to sell products and/or services from your site. Depending on your available finances and time, setting up a fully functional e-commerce website may take longer than you want. The fastest and easiest way to begin selling online is to leverage the power of existing site resources. These sites are pre-formatted with templates, which makes it faster to get your products up online. You also become part of an online marketplace that is searchable by potential buyers, making it more likely buyers will find your products because they are already looking for similar goods. Once you list your products on third-party sites, you can link to them from your own site, but all purchases must occur on the third-party site. Sites such as Etsy (www.etsy.com), Zazzle (www.zazzle.com), Redbubble (www.redbubble.com), and CafePress (www.cafepress.com) are known as third-party online store solutions that allow you to start selling your products quickly and begin testing the market. These online stores are communities where people go to find unique, artistic items. These sites are fairly easy to populate with your product information, which gets you online faster and less expensively than building an e-commerce site from scratch within your own website.

GETTING FOUND BY A GLOBAL MARKETPLACE

How do your customers hear about you? Elaine Barge, owner of Relevant Vintage, sells her mid-century wares and vintage jewelry on Etsy. She said she was shocked by the amount of overseas sales she's had. Last year, her collection of 1950's structured wicker handbags sold immediately, and most of them went to Australia! She says she sells quite a bit of jewelry and bags to Europe as well. Elaine regularly ships jewelry and handbags to cities such as New York, Los Angeles, San Francisco, Atlanta, Chicago, and Portland, where vintage products are in vogue. The market for vintage is much larger than Elaine had expected, and her presence on Etsy placed her in a global marketplace. This enabled people who want to buy what she sells to find her more

continued from page 154

easily than if she did not use the marketplace. Trends and fads vary greatly by geography, and Etsy's reputation for being a go-to source for vintage items helped increase her sales.

One drawback to the third-party system is that you don't own the site. If the third-party site goes out of business, or increases its fees, you have limited recourse. The advantage is that the community already draws consumers looking for specialty products. You're opting into the virtual equivalent of renting a store in the part of town where everyone goes to shop for the thing you sell. For example, many cities have a furniture district, or stores clustered around mall areas. Similarly, when you join an existing platform, you'll compete with a lot of other sellers, but everyone benefits because consumers know to visit these sites when they want unique or handcrafted items. This increases the odds that someone looking for items such as yours will find you, although there are no guarantees.

TRICKS FOR STANDING OUT ON THIRD-PARTY SITES

To stand out from the thousands of other online shop owners, develop relationships with your potential and existing customers so they will continue to revisit your e-commerce pages. To communicate and market to them, you need their email addresses. Maybe you'll want to provide a discount on a future purchase in exchange for joining your list. You can also offer a discount or free sample if they "Like" your Facebook page, since being connected there can help you keep in touch with customers. If you have not already, you could include discount coupons off the next purchase when people buy your products.

Make sure you're not an anonymous Etsy store when you ship packages. Your packaging should make it clear where the product came from—make it easy for people to reconnect with you the next time. VIV-id (branded) packaging and materials can help make memorable impressions. All

continued from page 155

these ideas can make it easier for past customers to remember you the next time they need a product you offer or have a chance to recommend you to a friend.

Build Your Own Online Store

If your business was profitable using Etsy or another third-party store, you may want to take the next step and build your own store online. Doing so eliminates the "middle man" and gives you control over your own business. You may also decide to build your own online store from the start. You can set up your website and store using templates especially designed for selling products online using a virtual store option. There are many e-commerce storefront solutions, offering these features:

- Website
- Domain name (or create/use your own customized domain for a small fee)
- Secure shopping cart
- Product catalog
- Payment gateway
- CRM (Customer Relationship Management) database
- Email accounts
- Marketing tools
- Reporting
- Mobile-optimized store

SOLUTIONS TO HELP BUILD YOUR VIRTUAL STORE

Bigcommerce: www.bigcommerce.com
Shopify: www.shopify.com
Volusion: www.volusion.com

These solutions either include their own blog option or allow you to import or start your own. The prices range from free to $70 per month for up to 1,000 products. When you create your own store using one of these all-inclusive solutions, it serves as your primary site and you benefit from the direct traffic to your new store.

Shopping Carts for Digital Downloads

A shopping cart lets your customers order from a link on your website and easily pay for products and services online without you needing a full-fledged e-commerce website. Shopping carts are especially good for selling digital downloads such as eBooks, mp3 music or audio files, or other digital files. It's easy to get started. Create an account at a provider's site—examples are below—and upload the files you want to sell. Next, include a link to the product listing on your own website. When someone clicks to buy your product, the link takes them to the shopping cart where they pay. Then the file is sent directly to the email address they provide. This simplicity and ease comes with a price tag, but we are talking pennies on the dollar. Using a shopping cart automates the delivery system, so you will not be chained to your computer sending files and processing orders all day. When a customer buys your product, the system sends the file and the buyer automatically receives a thank you message.

E-junkie and ClickBank

E-junkie (http://www.e-junkie.com) and ClickBank (http://www.clickbank.com) are two shopping cart options that

RELY ON YOUR SOCIAL NETWORKS FOR ADVICE

Consider joining a group of other small business owners on LinkedIn to gather information about different online store platforms. You may find you can easily access a brain trust of advice from other entrepreneurs who have "been there, done that." Then it's up to you to decide what direction to go.

provide similar services. E-junkie does not have a payment option built in, which means you will have to integrate it with PayPal or another solution. The bonus to using either of these is their built-in affiliate option. Offering your products to affiliate re-sellers can help boost sales and awareness. We talk more about affiliate programs in Chapter 15.

⇨ TIP

Don't forget to evaluate how the site appears and functions for mobile device users. According to Forrester Research, customers are slightly more likely to convert to a sale (4 to 5 percent) on a tablet than PC users who convert into a sale 3 percent of the time. Tablet users are also more likely to place larger orders, usually adding 10 to 20 percent more to their cart than other mobile and desktops users.

Classified Sites

Many people use online classified sites to get rid of unwanted household items, but they are becoming much more popular with small business owners. Listings are free; however, you will need to invest time experimenting and incorporating lots of keywords to ensure your ads stay at the top of the classified search rankings.

Here are some online classifieds to try:

- **Backpage:** www.backpage.com
- **eBay Classifieds:** www.ebayclassifieds.com
- **List Here:** www.listhere.com
- **Oodle:** www.oodle.com
- **PennySaverUSA online classifieds:** www.pennysaverusa.com
- **Sell.com:** www.sell.com
- **WebClassifieds.us:** www.webclassifieds.us
- **Craigslist:** www.craigslist.org

Additional Distribution Channels: eBay and Amazon

There are entire books written about how to sell on eBay and Amazon. These distribution channels help you break into the market and let people know about your products and services. Like the third-party solutions, eBay and Amazon take a cut of your sales and charge listing fees. These fees start from $.20 per listing, plus an additional 7.5 percent of total sale (up to $50). Because they are so well-known and have large amounts of traffic, you may be able to convert some buyers to visit your own site!

Selling On Your Business Facebook Page

Consider using your business Facebook page to sell certain items to your target audience. *F-commerce* is the term used to describe making purchases directly on Facebook's platform; in other words, you do not direct purchasers to your site to make the actual transaction. This is a relatively new function, and the results have been mixed among large retailers.

While some businesses sell on their Facebook pages, the majority of consumers are not quite comfortable making purchases this way, yet. They may be concerned about a secured server and other online purchasing best practices.

However, just because the big stores aren't seeing strong results does not mean F-commerce won't work for your business due to the uniqueness of the products you sell.

One strategy is to try selling lower-cost items through your Facebook page. The lower cost may encourage some people to buy. For example, established businesses may be able to tap into loyal fans and sell unique, branded promotional items such as pens, flash drives, t-shirts, stickers, or calendars. Another strategy might be to offer "early release" or discounted items to your loyal fans on Facebook.

We think it would be unwise to put your entire "store" on Facebook and abandon your own site, given the mixed results and

MARKETPLACE ON FACEBOOK
(POWERED BY OODLE)

Marketplace offers classified advertising on Facebook. Use Marketplace to buy and sell products and services within your group of friends, networks, or other networks.

You can list anything used, new, or intangible on Marketplace including things like books, DVDs, furniture, or real estate. What makes the classified ads on Marketplace different from other classified ad sites, such as Craigslist, is that you control who sees your ads. If someone is interested in learning more about an item you sell, they can simply reach out to you through Facebook.

TIPS FOR EFFECTIVELY USING MARKETPLACE:

1. Learn what other sellers are charging for comparable items.
2. Use high-quality images.
3. Use keywords and unique descriptions.

---

consumer hesitancy. Instead, make your Facebook store a place you reward fans and followers.

The following applications enable your business Facebook page to operate as an e-commerce site. The best way to find these applications is to log into your Facebook account and search for the application in the main search bar:

- Payvment
- Bigcommerce Social Shop
- Storefront Social
- Ecwid
- Wishpond Social Store

Pinterest

Pinterest is gaining momentum as a go-to site for sellers. It currently ranks as the third top social networking site and fourth source of referral traffic (after Google, directly visiting the site, and Face-book). According to a BizRate survey, more than 70 percent of Pinterest users say they turn to the network for inspiration when they want to make a purchase and keep up with trends. This represents a golden opportunity to build a loyal following by creating inspiring ideas. For example, if you sell recipes or a cookbook, pin your pictures of beautiful main dishes or crafty appetizers to entice people to purchase your recipes. If you sell golf accessories, create coordinating golf clothing and golf accessory packages to inspire purchases for fashion conscious golfers.

When people click pinned images, they link back to your website or store, which provides another opportunity for you to engage with potential customers, encourage them to sign up for your newsletter, or to sell products.

> **TIP**
>
> 57 percent of Pinterest users interact with food-related content, the number one category on Pinterest.

Think carefully about the images you use. The more unique or artistic the image, the greater the likelihood people will share it with their Pinterest communities. It may seem counterintuitive, but add a price to your pin. According to Shopify, Pinterest pins with prices receive 36 percent more likes than those that do not.

You might want to look outside your industry to see how other businesses are using Pinterest and what pins seem to generate the most shares. You can use PinReach (www.pinreach.com) to search for popular and influential pins. PinReach lets you search for a keyword or category and view the most shared or liked pins.

Using tools like Pinterest can give you a jump-start on the competition, netting you additional traffic and more business. Consider this stat provided in comScore's 2012 webinar, "State of the Internet in the U.S.": Pinterest buyers spend more money, more often, and on more items than any of the other top five social media sites.

Selling and Collecting Money

You have a few choices when it comes to collecting money. You can open your own merchant account, which allows you to process online payments via your own website, or you can use a third-party merchant such as PayPal. It will cost more money initially, and may seem more complex to have your own merchant account. There will be monthly and other fees. On the other hand, using PayPal or a similar solution will cost you more per transaction; you'll pay more each time someone buys something from you.

A merchant account may require you to hire someone to install it on your website, thereby incurring a website developer's programming and setup costs. You could also potentially open your business to credit card risks since you'll be processing the credit card payments yourself. The cost may outweigh the benefit if your business does not generate enough sales and income.

Third-Party Merchant Options

You want to make it easy for your customers to pay you, and you want a reliable and effective system to collect money online, or in person, for example at a book signing. Checks are passé. Not to mention, they take time to clear, and who wants to deal with a bounced check ordeal? Keep it simple for you and your customer, and find a system that allows you to easily collect money.

PayPal

A significant benefit to using a reputable third-party merchant is that your visitors may be more willing to buy from you online since they trust PayPal to keep their credit card numbers safe. Well-recognized and easy to use, PayPal is a solution both of us use. PayPal allows you to collect money, make payments, and even send invoices.

Opening a PayPal Merchant account is free, and it allows you to do all the basics of collecting money from a website with their "Pay Now" button, which takes the buyer to the PayPal website to complete their transactions. There are upgrades available for advanced features, such as keeping the transaction confined to your own website. Your customers do not need to have a PayPal account to pay you, just a debit or credit card. Note that PayPal charges the business 2.9 percent on the total sale amount, plus a $0.30 fee per transaction.

We suggest you start by using PayPal, since it is so easy to use and install. Once you start earning money, you can decide what solution is most cost-effective and convenient for you.

Google Wallet

Google Wallet is another payment option gaining popularity. Google boasts several differentiating factors. First, customers who come to your site to purchase digital products can do so in just one click. Second, Google Wallet sends payment directly to your bank account, unlike PayPal, where money collects in your designated PayPal account. If monthly sales are less than $3,000, Google Wallet charges the business 2.9 percent on the total sale amount, plus $0.30 per transaction.

In-Person Payments via Mobile Phone or Tablet

PayPal allows businesses to collect money in person by swiping a credit or debit card into your phone. You will need a special gizmo to process the swiped card, but PayPal provides it at no extra cost. Your mobile phone provider will also be happy to sell you a reader to go along with your smartphone.

Square.com is another tool that allows you to accept credit cards in person via a device that plugs into your mobile phone or tablet. It also provides the functionality to manually enter credit card information without having the card. For example, you could accept an order over the phone using this tool.

These tools charge business owners fees, however, so be sure you are aware of the costs and how you will receive the money from your sales.

Get It Done

Before you build your site, take into consideration three key elements:

1. **Function:** Your site may serve as an online store, billboard, or community hub. It may be a combination of all three. Think about what you need immediately, and about your vision for the near future.
2. **Aesthetics:** Align your site with your VIV-id and give careful consideration to font, images, and other visual elements on your website.
3. **Usability:** Your visitors' needs should come first. Be sure your site is easy to navigate and makes sense to the user.

Will You Build it Yourself or Hire a Designer?

Decide which option makes the most sense for you. Each option has advantages and disadvantages.

Option 1: Do it Yourself With WordPress

Will you take on the challenge of building and managing your website? It isn't as difficult as it might seem, given the numerous templates available. This option provides you with more design power without needing programming or coding skills.

Option 2: Work With a Designer

Working with a designer can save time, so you can focus on building your business. If you choose this option, keep these things in mind:

- Ask for recommendations and testimonials to make sure the designer has the right skills, is someone you feel comfortable collaborating with, and can complete the project within your time frame.
- Expect to pay anywhere from $300 for simple customization to $10,000 for a complex site.

- Be sure to get an agreement in writing from your designer so you fully understand what is being delivered.

Setting Up Shop on Third-Party Sites

Getting your online store up and running quickly is one of the benefits of using a third-party site. Test the waters to see what demand there is for the products you offer among a community of sellers and buyers.

Build Your Own Online Store Easily

Setting up your own e-commerce site with templates is an option to consider if you already have many items to sell online. Choose a solution that fits your style, budget, and technical aptitude.

Shopping Carts for Digital Downloads and Affiliates

You may not need a full-blown e-commerce site. If you are selling digital downloads (eBooks, podcasts, mp3s, etc.) you can use e-Junkie or ClickBank to easily process orders.

Classified Sites

Classified sites are often free and provide another outlet to explore and test the viability and earning potential for your products. eBay and Amazon are the largest online shopping communities, and you may acquire new customers from these sites.

Selling On Your Business Facebook Page

F-commerce, or selling directly on Facebook, is relatively new. With over a billion users (and counting) there may be potential here. Facebook has its own classified ads, known as Marketplace. This unique classified ad option gives buyers the ability to ask you or a friend about the product or service you are selling.

Pinterest

Promoting your products on Pinterest, one of the hottest new social networks, is another way to build awareness and attract new customers. According to comScore, Pinterest buyers spend more money, more often, and on more items than any of the other top five social media sites.

Selling and Collecting Money

If you plan to sell products and services, you'll need a way to collect money online. PayPal and Google Wallet are two popular options and both charge you the same transaction fees, 2.9 percent of the cost of the purchase, plus $0.30 per transaction.

If you plan to collect payments in person, Paypal, Square, and Google Wallet offer solutions to collect money from your mobile phone or tablet.

CHAPTER **12**

Creating a Branded Bio: How to Tell Your Business's Story

You got this far in our book because you want to be a successful business owner. Now, you're about to find out you also need to be a storyteller! Consider this: when you actively create, own, and tell your story online, you form a virtual online imprint, or digital footprint. By including information you want people to know about you, your expertise, and your business, you make it easier for people to find, understand, and hire you.

Small business owners, or *solopreneurs*, walk a fine line between including personal information and business information in their bio or story. When you're a small business owner, your personal biography may actually *be* the organization's story. The "About Us," page on your website and the information you need in your social media profiles may overlap quite a bit or be the same.

No matter what type of business you have, you need to explain who you are and how you can help your clients solve problems. Your goal is to convince people that you have the best qualities and credentials to get the job done. In order to do this, you need to stand out from the crowd and be interesting. Keep in mind, your "VIV-id,"

If you are a MOXIE, you may choose to say something about your day job in your online bios, or you may prefer to focus only on your business goals. If your side business is a secret, you may decide to omit it from your personal LinkedIn profile. However, be aware that it's hard to hide anything online. When people Google your name and find your LinkedIn profile, they will expect to see information pertaining to your business ventures.

One example of how to incorporate your day job into your persona profiles is to say: "By day, I'm a dedicated, overachieving customer service provider. Every other minute of the week, I'm a writer and recipe-tester."

or your Virtual Individual Verified id (psyche or self), will be an important part of your business bio on your website and on social networks. Make sure you remember the lessons about how to define yourself, what you offer, and what you want to be known for as we described in Chapter 7. Ask yourself, "What do I want people to know about me that will help them decide I am the best qualified person to serve their needs?"

Questions to Answer Before You Write Your Online Bios

Start out by answering a few questions about yourself and your business:

What's your back story?

Don't make this section your autobiography ("I was born in. . . ."). Instead, explain how you wound up doing what you are doing now. Did something or someone influence you? Tell your potential customers why you love what you do. Of course, clients want to work with someone who is successful, but displaying enthusiasm for your work will help your audience connect with you.

What Are Your Qualifications?

Do you have a degree or a recognized certification in your field? Include specific accomplishments and results people should know about.

What is Your Approach?

How do you solve problems better than your competitors? Give examples of your style and personality, and demonstrate how you handle obstacles.

What Do Other People Say About You?

Your bio isn't only about what you think of yourself. Incorporate information about what others think of you and your work. Quotes from clients or colleagues can be very powerful ways to let people know how you are unique and what you offer.

Do You Have any Third-Party Organizational Endorsements?

Do you have well-respected media outlets quoted or have they used you as a source? If so, refer to them in your business bio.

Do You Have Any Relevant Awards?

It can't hurt to mention them!

Demonstrate Your Personality, Keeping in Mind your Target Audience

Are you interesting? Let your audience know. If you have a wacky, offbeat personality, and your audience is a buttoned-up, conservative group, you'll need to think twice before inserting humor and wit into your professional and business bios! What you include in your bio depends on the nature of your business and your target audience. For example, if you consult to very conservative industries or professionals, your bio should mirror their sensibilities. On the other hand, if you run a pet sitting business, you have more leeway with what you share, and it should definitely include something about why you love furry friends. Envision your target customers and consider what will resonate with them.

> Consider telling your story (writing your bio) in the first person—using I, me, and my—to describe yourself and your attributes.

Include Some "About Me"

Robert Cialdini, author of *Influence: The Psychology of Persuasion* (HarperBusiness, 2006), suggests you list something personal about you in your "About Us," even if it does not relate specifically to your work. As Roger Dooley explains in *Forbes*, one of Robert's suggestions is, "List your three favorite 'driveway songs'—those songs that keep you in your parked car until they are over . . . (it's) irrelevant to business, but humanizing. And, if a prospect says, 'Hey, I'd sit in my car for that song, too,' you'll have established a bit of commonality."

A BIG BRAND'S BIO

Chipotle Mexican Grill is a fast food chain with a VIV-id story that separates it from other eateries. Its website explains how the company is committed to providing food with integrity. It notes how they choose the best ingredients while respecting animals, the environment, and farmers. They market sustainability, taste, nutrition, and value. On its website (www.chipotle.com), the company includes a link to its story, which includes information about founder Steve Ells:

> *Steve Ells may be the founder of Chipotle, but he's not your typical CEO. Steve is a chef first, you will almost never see him in a suit, and he can still mash a mean batch of guac when he wants to.*

The site includes several videos and photos, as well as a letter from Steve that explains his company's goals. The result? Customers understand the company's origins and what it believes in. This can inspire people to become loyal, return buyers.

continued from page 170

Visit their site to see a great example of how a story can help sell a brand. You don't need to be big or accomplished to have a great story to tell. Focus on the basics: why should people take a second look at you and your company?

Using Your Bios Online

You'll use your story and your bios differently depending on where you post them. The social networks dictate how long your bios or profiles can be. It will be up to you to select key points from your longer online story to share in your "quick and dirty" profiles via Twitter and Pinterest, for example. Keep in mind, even in short bios, you'll want to demonstrate your expertise and incorporate keywords so it is as easy as possible for potential clients and customers to find you.

Here are a few additional things to consider when you're writing your social media bios:

1. **Identify your target audience.** To whom do you provide value? (Is it universities? Fortune 500 accounting departments? Individual consumers?) If you are unsure, ask yourself, "Whom do I want to attract with my message?"

2. **Consider the value you provide.** Be specific and narrow your focus whenever possible. This is known as your Unique Selling Proposition, or USP. Ask people you trust about your best business skills. For example, are you the organizational maven? The go-to HR process expert? Are you a marketer to small medical practices? Be sure to include your unique value as part of your online profiles.

3. **Make it memorable.** Be creative, so your bio will leave an indelible mark on readers. Add humor, if it fits your personality, and avoid making it cheesy or overly self-promotional.

Your LinkedIn Profiles

Assuming you are not hiding your business while in a day job, create overlapping personal and company bios on LinkedIn. We recommend starting with your personal LinkedIn profile and then extracting the best parts of it for your company bio.

Your Headline

The headline field is capped at 120 characters. You do not have to include your job title. In this chapter, we revist the sample LinkedIn information we used in Chapter 4, inspired by Maria Hancock, senior graphic designer at The BOSS Group in Atlanta. Note: we sacrifice keywords in this example for a strong and unique pitch.

> *Create on-deadline, dynamic visuals. Bring your needs to life from paper napkin drawing to final print production.*

Your Summary

The summary is your opportunity to convince someone to want to know more about you. People generally read your summary once your headline enticed them to click through to learn more, so it is your opportunity to seal the deal and inspire someone visiting your LinkedIn profile to get in touch with you.

You'll probably see many LinkedIn summaries written in the third person. For example, "John Smith is a very strong manager and spellbinding author." While there is no rule saying third-person summaries are bad, we prefer the more engaging first-person structure, where you speak directly to readers about yourself, your accomplishments, and what you can do for them.

YOUR BUSINESS SUMMARY

Depending on your business, and unless you run a big company, it's likely your business page's summary will be similar to your personal profile's summary. Don't work too hard to make them different if they logically mirror each other.

Here's a great start for a LinkedIn summary, either for a personal or a business profile, inspired by Maria's materials:

Known for my ability to execute on-deadline, dynamic visuals with minimal client direction; if you need a strong conceptual thinker who can develop designs from idea to market—you've found one! With a portfolio of customized visual solutions that effectively interpret clients' corporate branding, experience, and expertise, I'm the artistic partner you need to help accomplish your strategic business goals.

Develop dynamic, creative visuals:
Print marketing collateral, web media, multimedia designs.

Effective communication skills:
Exceptional listener, facilitate verbal and written co-worker interaction, engage with customers.
Social media development & maintenance expert.
Mentor team members on new tools.
Oversee cross-departmental project management.
Adapt schedule to effectively prioritize concurrent projects, fluctuate project goals to achieve deadlines.
Identify and execute innovative solutions to complex marketing problems.

Proficient in Adobe Applications:
[Photoshop, Illustrator, InDesign, Bridge, Acrobat, Framemaker, Flash] and Quark. MS Office Suite [Word, Excel, PowerPoint, SharePoint, CRM, and Outlook].

Specialties (Note: LinkedIn no longer includes a designated Specialties section, but you can write one into your Summary, as long as you have room. It can be a great way to include keywords.):
Website Design, Logo Design for Dentists/Dental Offices, Website Designer, InDesign, DreamWeaver, Sign Designer, Graphics Design, Create Facebook Fan Pages, Concept Art,

Illustrations, Animation, Graphic Design. Proficient in Adobe Photoshop, Illustrator, InDesign, 3DS Max, Premiere After Effects, Final Cut Pro. Experienced using Cinema 4D, Avid, and CSS.

Twitter

Consider whether you want to tweet as yourself (using your own name) or as your business name. Both of us tweet as our business names (@careersherpa and @Keppie_Careers). You should own both your actual name and your business name on Twitter (so no one else can capture them), but it's not necessary to tweet from both accounts.

Your Twitter bio should make it easy for people to know what you do and how you can help them. Remember, the easiest way to create an appealing bio is to identify the skills, experiences, and accomplishments your target audience will value, and demonstrate you are a strong match for their needs.

Twitter allows you to use 160 characters (letters and spaces) for your bio, so select every letter wisely. While it's fun to incorporate aspects of your personality, limit non-keyword content until you incorporate the most important details. For example, if you are a "fun dad," "soccer mom," "love Mickey Mouse," or "can't live without chocolate," consider opting to leave those details out until you are certain you have enough room for your content-rich information. Focus on what is special about you and how you solve problems, and avoid any vague or nonspecific language or information.

In *100 Conversations for Career Success*, Jorgen Sundberg, social-recruiting and online-branding consultant at Link Humans in London, suggests getting directly to the point and incorporating the following structure in your Twitter bio:

1. **Be specific.** Start with: *I provide banks with insurance solutions or I help people achieve fitness through Pilates.* Make sure you include your relevant keywords so you will appear

in search results. List any product or service names you expect potential customers to enter in search boxes.

2. **List a few specialties that set your personal brand apart.** For example: *First certified scuba instructor in Greenland* or *Passionate about your customer experience*. You can also include any notable achievements or people you are associated with, such as: *Author of the best-selling book* Twitterati; *Previous owner of the Springfield Isotopes;* or *Special advisor to Henry Kissinger*.

3. **End it with a call to action, a statement, or a question.** For example: *Contact me for details*.

When you write your Twitter bio, take a close look at your LinkedIn headline. If you wrote a strong headline, you can replicate parts of it into your Twitter profile. This sample, an extension of the graphic designer's bio, clearly illustrates how easy it is to turn a LinkedIn headline pitch into a consistent Twitter bio:

> *Create on-deadline, dynamic visuals. Bring your needs to life from paper napkin drawing to final print production, and you hardly have to do a thing!*

Be sure to incorporate your actual name and a location in your Twitter profile, include a photo (which should be a picture of you, as people relate better to people than they do to icons or logs), and include a link to your website so people know where to learn more about your business. If you choose, you may create a specific landing page to direct people from Twitter to learn more about you and your business. It's not necessary, but if you want to track your Twitter traffic, it may be helpful to have a designated page on your site where people from Twitter land.

Facebook

You need to sign up for a personal Facebook page before you can create a business page. Once you sign up for your personal account (follow directions from Facebook.com—it's simple; over one billion people have accounts!), just Google "how to create a business Facebook page" when you're signed into your personal account, and you will be on your way.

About

This is a good place for your tagline; it will appear on your Facebook page's cover. We bet it looks familiar:

> *Bringing visuals to life from paper napkin drawing to final print production.*

Company Overview/Mission/Description/ General Information

Facebook provides a variety of categories for business owners, and you may not see all of the categories listed here. Don't worry; just fill in the sections that make sense for you; we think there would be a lot of overlap if you complete every section.

Here's a sample Overview. Notice how it is the same as the LinkedIn personal bio:

> *Known for my ability to execute on-deadline, dynamic visuals with minimal client direction; if you need a strong conceptual thinker who can develop designs from idea to market—you've found one! With a portfolio of customized visual solutions that effectively interpret clients' corporate branding, experience, and expertise, I'm the artistic partner you need to help accomplish your strategic business goals.*

General Information

> *Develop dynamic, creative visuals: print marketing collateral, web media, multimedia designs.*

> *Effective communication skills: exceptional listener, facilitate verbal and written co-worker interaction, engage with customers.*

Social media development & maintenance expert.

Mentor team members on new tools.

Oversee cross-departmental project management.

Adapt schedule to effectively prioritize concurrent projects, fluctuate project goals to achieve deadlines.

Identify and execute innovative solutions to complex marketing problems.

Proficient in Adobe Applications [Photoshop, Illustrator, InDesign, Bridge, Acrobat, Framemaker, Flash] and Quark. MS Office Suite [Word, Excel, PowerPoint, SharePoint, CRM, and Outlook].

Specialties include:

Website Design, Logo Design for Dentists/Dental Offices, Website Designer, InDesign, DreamWeaver, Sign Designer, Graphics Design, Create Facebook Fan Pages, Concept Art, Illustrations, Animation, Graphic Design. Proficient in Adobe Photoshop, Illustrator, InDesign, 3DS Max, Premiere After Effects, Final Cut Pro. Experienced using Cinema 4D, Avid, and CSS

Your Google+ Personal Profile

First impressions count, and within Google+, that means your profile is king. Review and revise it until you clearly articulate your value.

Introduction

As promised, you can continue to repurpose your LinkedIn bio on this social network, too! Target your audience, and incorporate keywords you want people to use when they are searching for you, which will "teach" Google search about your areas of expertise.

Within your personal profile, you have the following categories to complete:

Bragging Rights

Keep it professional here. It's tempting to add something funny or sarcastic, such as "survived raising teenage children" or "learned to avoid traffic in L.A." Instead, incorporate awards or professional accolades to help raise your reputation or credibility. For example:

> *Won Award for design and definition, 2014.*
> *Earned "Competitive Manuscript Award" from the American Accounting Association, 2013.*
>
> *Recognized as Business of the Year, Tempe, Arizona, 2014.*

Occupation

You could simply include your job title here or add some flair or humor. For example:

- *Making your design dreams come true.*
- *Resourceful artist and designer . . . passionate about sharing ideas!*
- *Designer by day. Designer by night.*

Employment

Google+ uses your recent employment as your tagline—this information appears under your name and is the first thing people will see when they find you on Google+. Instead of just listing your company, expand your business' description to include accolades or useful information:

> *Graphic Design Central: Bringing visuals to life from paper napkin drawing to final print production.*

Peachtree Petcare, Dog sitter caring for your pampered pup.
Gold Business Foundation triple award winner.
HR Consulting International. Creating HR processes from scratch.
Special Occasions 4U. Creating unique, themed special occa-
sions to meet all budgets.

Be sure to fill out this section completely, including all of your past experience, as it can help potential clients who are searching for contractors to decide if you are qualified.

Your Tagline

Choose something short and sweet that describes you.

Bringing visuals to life from paper napkin drawing to final print production.

> Your current employment shows up when someone scrolls over your profile on Google+ (along with your tagline), so it's important to make sure you list more than just your title! Listing "owner," or "president" won't help someone learn more about you!

Your Google+ Business Profile

Once you have your personal Google+ page set, develop your business page. Visit http://www.google.com/⁺/business/ to get started with your business page. Google provides many resources to help you learn to make the most of your page.

It is very easy to fill out the details you'll need in Google+, as your business bio includes a tagline, introduction, contact information, website, and links. Feel free to repurpose information from your previous descriptions.

Pinterest

Like on Twitter, Pinterest provides you with a short bio, known as "About." Luckily, this is a slam dunk, since you've already written so many other profiles. It's easy to use your Twitter bio or your LinkedIn headline on Pinterest; for example:

> *Bringing visuals to life from paper napkin drawing to final print production.*

Share Bios Beyond Online Social Networks

Once you create and share your online business bios, don't forget to look for places to share beyond social media and your own website. For example, you may find professional directories you can join, and then ask to include your bio on their websites. Chamber of Commerce sites may include bios on your profile when you join (there is usually a fee).

Get It Done

Consider your target audience. What information will appeal to them? If they might not appreciate your humor, keep it to yourself, but if they'll think you're hilarious, bring out the funny bio stories! Think about how much of your personal story will be in your business bios. For most solopreneurs, personal and business bios are very similar.

Start out by answering a few questions about yourself and your business:

- What is your backstory?
- What qualifications do you have?

- What is your approach?
- How do you solve problems better than your competitors?
- What do other people say about you?
- Do you have any third party organizational endorsements?
- Do you have any relevant awards?

We like bios to be in the first person and to describe yourself, your business, and your attributes.

Do some research and find business bios you like. Think about how you can use the best attributes of the bios you appreciate for your own business pages and profiles.

Use your story and your bios differently depending on where you post them. The networks themselves dictate how long your bios or profiles can be, and it will be up to you to select the key points from your longer online story to share in your "quick and dirty" bios via Twitter and Pinterest, for example. Demonstrate your expertise and incorporate keywords so it is as easy as possible for potential clients and customers to find you.

Keep the following points in mind:

1. Identify your target audience.
2. Consider the value you provide.
3. Make it memorable.

As the examples in this chapter illustrate, a strong LinkedIn profile and bio can be the foundation for all of your online business profiles. Do it right once and then duplicate as necessary, and you'll be golden!

13 How to Market Your Business

Your marketing plan doesn't have to be complicated or complex, but it does help to have a simple road map to keep you focused. As a MOXIE or business owner with so many roles to fill, it is tempting to focus on doing the work you enjoy while ignoring the details that will help your business grow. Ironically, one of the most important projects you handle as a MOXIE or a business owner probably has nothing to do with your core expertise. Just as you may need to stretch outside of your comfort zone to morph into a storyteller to create compelling business and personal bios, you also need to make sure you focus on marketing if you want a successful business. A solid marketing strategy involves more than putting an announcement in the newspaper and hoping to win some news coverage. You need to reach your audience consistently and constantly for best results.

Developing strong marketing materials will help you attract more business, and sell clients your services. You don't want to be scrambling at the last minute to pull together documentation for a proposal, client request, or opportunity for press coverage. We created a list of marketing tools you should have ready to streamline your processes and help keep your head on straight while you drive activities that will result in measurable—and hopefully profitable—outcomes.

Why Do You Need a Marketing Plan?

A marketing plan outlines a strategy to introduce a product or service to the marketplace. It will help you drive an organized "plan of attack," especially in the complicated and sometimes confusing social media landscape. With a little planning up front, you'll be more likely to stay on track and develop a consistent online presence and message for your business.

One-Page Marketing Plan for Using Social Media

Building your one-page marketing plan requires you to identify who exactly your target audience is, what content you plan to deliver throughout the year, what marketing methods you will use to reach your target audience, and how often you will implement them.

> **⤳ TIP**
>
> When you keep your marketing plan in front of you, you can use it to help you stay on course and prioritize your activities, and you won't be as easily distracted by the myriad tasks and requests you encounter.

Social Marketing Plan Template

Market: *What specific niche do you serve? Where will you find them? (geography). Who are your target customers? (If business to business, list industries. If business to consumer, list precise demographics.)*

Positioning: *State your unique value proposition. (What value do you provide or what problem do you solve?) How do you do it uniquely? For whom do you do it (your target audience)?*

Key Target Customers (Business to Business)

INDUSTRY YOU WILL TARGET PRIMARILY	SECONDARY INDUSTRY YOU WILL TARGET (IF APPLICABLE)
1. Company name	1. Company name
2. Company name	2. Company name

High Level Goal: *[Increase revenue X%, Generate X% of income from speaking, Increase site traffic by X].*

Campaign Theme: *(List the topic or theme of the content, product and/or service you will promote. These will be based on "hot issues" or reoccurring problems you can solve for others and tie into the product or service you want to promote that quarter.)*

Q1: *Topic/Theme*	**Q2:** *Topic/Theme*	**Q3:** *Topic/Theme*	**Q4:** *Topic/Theme*

Campaign Schedule *(Specify what goal you want to achieve each quarter.)*

Q1: *Goal*	**Q2:** *Goal*	**Q3:** *Goal*	**Q4:** Goal

Campaign Details
Quarter 1: *(Q2-4 To be determined based on Q1 results)*

Content: *What will you create? Blog posts, case studies, eBooks, images, or other content?*		
Communication Vehicles: *What methods will you use to reach target customers?*	PR: Ads: Content:	Events: Email: Social Networks:
Distributing Content: *Which social networks will you use?*	Facebook Twitter LinkedIn Google+	YouTube Pinterest Other

Tactical Actions

Goal: *How many website visitors/followers or other measurable outcomes?*	
How: *How many posts, tweets, Facebook shares, etc. per week or per day?*	

Business to Business (B2B) Sample Social Marketing Plan

Market: *Small to medium businesses within a 100 mile radius of Chicago. These companies fall within high-growth rate industry clusters and struggle to train new employees on internal procedures and work etiquette.*

Positioning: *Partner with rapidly growing small businesses to acclimate new employees to new work settings for improved engagement, performance, and retention.*

Key Targets

IT & SERVICES	IT PROFESSIONAL ASSOCIATIONS	ADVERTISING/ MARKETING
TradingPartners	Association of Information Technology Professionals (AITP)	Wirestone
Arrow Strategies	Association for Women in Computing (AWC)	Imagination Publishing
Align	Software Development Forum (SDF)	Turn
Lucidity Consulting	Network Professional Association (NPA)	Manifest Digital
CS Technology		Marketing Werks

High Level Goal: *Generate $50,000/yr through consulting, and training (in-person and online).*

Campaign Schedule

Q1:	Q2:	Q3:	Q4:
Creating Company Culture	*Employee Engagement*	*Dispersed Leadership*	*Multiple Generations in the Workplace*

Campaign Goals

Q1:	Q2:	Q3:	Q4:
Acquire one new client with ongoing training needs	*Launch one free and three for-fee webinars*	*Acquire two leadership consulting jobs*	*Deliver six for-fee webinars and sell 50 eBooks*

Campaign Details

Q1:

Content: *What will you create? Blog posts, case studies, eBooks, images, or other content?*	• Create four case studies on small company culture • Draft a blog post on winning on-boarding programs • Create a checklist of onboarding best-practices • Reference resources for calculating cost of turnover
Communication Vehicles: *What methods will you use to reach target customers?*	**Ads:** LinkedIn ad campaign targeting IT small business owners **Email:** Outreach to PTA, libraries, YMCA, and gyms
Distributing Content: *Which social networks will you use?*	LinkedIn, Twitter, Google+

Social Actions

Goal: *How many website visitors/ followers or measurable outcomes?*	• 150 downloads of checklist • 50 new email subscribers
How: *How many posts, tweets, Facebook shares, etc. per week or per day?*	• One blog post per week (share on LinkedIn and Google+) • Participate in LinkedIn HR groups in Chicago area two times a week

Sample Business-to-Consumer (B2C) Social Marketing Plan

Market: *U.S. or English speaking consumers, initially within local area. People who value healthy and easy-to-prepare recipes for their families.*

Positioning: *Helping families eat healthier foods everyone will enjoy. Providing menus that fit within tight budgets and can be prepared in under an hour for busy lifestyles.*

Key Targets

DEMOGRAPHICS	GROUPS/ACTIVITIES	LIFESTYLE
Women 25-40 years old	PTA/school volunteer	Subscribe to magazines such as *Real Living, Healthy Living*
Family income between $60-200K annually	School athletics/ community sports for kids	Visit farmers markets
Suburban lifestyle	Gym or YMCA members	Drive fuel efficient vehicles
Part-time work or stay-at-home		Will visit hairdresser, dentist, and physician offices regularly
		Use local libraries

High Level Goal: *Build income to $10,000/yr and generate 10% of income from speaking; increase email subscriptions to 350.*

Campaign Theme:

Q1:	Q2:	Q3:	Q4:
Healthy Menus	*Local Products*	*Busy Schedule Menus*	*Holiday Menus*

Campaign Goals

Q1:	Q2:	Q3:	Q4:
Sell 100 eBooks during launch quarter	*Develop five new partnerships with local vendors & suppliers*	*Establish distribution of eBook through school & community sports groups*	*Build affiliate program to benefit new partners and groups*

Campaign Details

Q1:

Content: *What will you create? Blog posts, case studies, eBooks, images, or other content?*	Create weekly blog posts highlighting a healthy menu from eBook Take pictures of finished menu items
Communication Vehicles: *What method will you use to reach target customers?*	**PR:** PR Web and one local press release **Ads:** Facebook ad campaign targeting women 25-40 with families **Content:** Submit guest blog post to *Healthy Living* **Events:** One presentation at library or PTA meeting **Email:** Outreach to PTA, libraries, YMCA, and gyms
Distributing Content: *Which social networks will you use?*	Facebook, Pinterest, YouTube-maybe

Social Actions

Goal: *How many website visitors/followers or other measurable outcomes?*	• 3,000 unique sales page visitors • 500 new email subscribers • 200 new Facebook page likes
How: *How many posts, tweets, Facebook shares, etc. per week or per day?*	• One blog post per week (share on FB and Pinterest) • Two Facebook updates per day • One new pin to Pinterest per day

Marketing Materials You Want to Have Ready (Online and Hard Copy)

Business Cards

Your business card is a valuable source for referral marketing, even in the digital age! Visit sites like Vistaprint.com or Moo.com to see examples of business card designs. (Do not select free business cards with ads on the back—it doesn't look professional.) At a minimum, your business card should include your company name, your name, contact information, and website. If you want people to take your business seriously, you'll need some type of logo and a branding statement that makes it clear what you do and whom you help. If you are active on LinkedIn, Facebook, Twitter, or Google+, adding the logo for those particular networks or listing the URL will help new contacts find you online.

INNOVATIVELY LINK TO CONTENT

Often you see Quick Response (QR) codes on business cards and marketing materials, which anyone can scan using a smartphone equipped with a QR code reader (the readers are applications you can download to the phone). These QR codes direct the person scanning them to upload your contact information, navigate to your website, open a specific video, or go anywhere on the web to learn more about you, your company, or your products and services. Get creative and have fun testing QR codes on your business card and maybe on your printed collateral. There are free QR code generators and readers available as apps for mobile devices. To download a QR code reader, visit your Android Market or Apple App Store from your smartphone or mobile device:

QR Code Generators
- **Azon Media:** http://azonmedia.com/qrcode-generator
- **BeQRious:** http://beqrious.com/qr-code-generator/
- **Delivr:** http://delivr.com/qr-code-generator

QR Code Readers for Your Smartphone
- Barcode Generator/Reader (Android)
- ScanLife Barcode Reader (Android)
- QuickMark QR Code Reader (Android)
- QR Droid (Android)
- Scan (iPhone)
- Qrafter (iPhone)

Build Your VIV-id Media Kit or Press Kit

Create a media or press kit to include on your website, submit with proposals, and include when you apply for partnership opportunities. Have these materials ready to send potential clients, for outreach to partners, presentations, and media requests, or just for people wanting to learn more about you. Ideally, you will want most (if not all) of this information visible on your website. You will also want to have a PDF version you can easily email upon request, and some copies if you need to send one via snail mail.

Your kit should contain a professional looking, well-written collection of materials that clearly communicate and market your business and services. You should include the following information:

Company Overview

Your company overview should clearly explain what you do, your background, and perhaps your future goals. If you are comfortable doing so, list your rates (or a range) to eliminate confusion and dissuade window shoppers or tire kickers from taking up your time if they cannot afford to hire you.

FAQ Page

You can probably anticipate certain questions people will ask when they want to find out about a business in your field. When you put your company's features and benefits in a question and answer format, it helps your potential customers find what they are looking for, especially when you link part of your answer to other content on your site. Visiting other sites may generate some ideas for creating your FAQ page in a way that incorporates your VIV-id. A carefully thought out FAQ page lets people know what differentiates you from the competition.

Bio

A bio, as discussed in Chapter 12, helps people get to know you so you're not just a faceless company. Your bio should contain a professional headshot you use across your social media platforms for consistency and recognition. Don't forget to include your contact information—your email, phone number, and website are important. Equally important are links to your LinkedIn profile, Facebook page, YouTube channel, Twitter handle, and any other social profiles where you are active.

Media Coverage

Include links to news or any coverage that mentions your business, as well as press releases either written by you or other media outlets about your company. In Chapter 17, we talk about how to generate buzz, and offer advice and recommendations about press releases. In addition to links, have hard copies of the articles to give to prospective clients during in-person meetings. You should also link to radio or TV interviews, speeches, performances, and any other events with media coverage.

Additional Pages to Have Ready

If you create the following content, it will be a lot easier for you to respond quickly when people inquire about your business:

- Pricing page
- Website traffic, number of Twitter followers, number of Facebook likes, Google+ circles, YouTube hits or subscribers, Klout score, and any details about your online successes
- Samples of your work
- Testimonials
- References
- Nonprofit and community-service involvement
- Recent awards
- Photos (if appropriate)
- White papers or other factual background material
- Upcoming promotions and event schedules and details

- Statistics specific to your industry, demographics, and target audiences
- Feature articles, such as articles that have appeared on major media outlets
- Missions, goals, and objectives
- Camera-ready logo art
- Order form (if applicable)

Your press or media kit should be unique and convey your VIV-id. It should also make it as easy as possible for those interested to learn about your company, whether their intent is to become a customer or to write a story about your business.

SPEAKER'S REQUIREMENTS

If you plan to enter the speaking circuit, you should know about the unique requirements of speakers' bureaus. Many companies turn to these bureaus to find speakers for their company meetings or events. These are just some of the items the All-American Speakers Bureau asks you to provide to be included on their listings:

- **Biography**
- **Your Introduction:** (The one you use when delivering a speech.)
- **Brief program(s) description outlines** (preferably one page)
- **Detailed (topics) program descriptions** (one page)
- **Investment Schedule:** Define your fees, services, travel requirements, and terms
- **Product Descriptions:** Include products for review.
- **References and Testimonials:** From clients and other speakers' bureaus
- **Photos:** Black and white 5 x 7 and/or 8 x 10 head shots, color head shots, and action photos
- **Published Work:** Copies of books you authored, or co-authored, published, or sold the rights to publish
- **Publicity and Press Clippings:** Copies of articles you have authored and had published as well as interviews

continued from page 194

- **Live Demo Samples:** Professionally produced DVD (Recent within 12 months) video of speech before a live audience.
- **List of Instructions:** Clearly define the best group(s) for which we should attempt to book you, and the list of group(s) you prefer we do not
- **Current Speaking Schedule**

If speaking is part of your plan, add your information to directories or registries to help people find you and your business. Companies looking for a speaker often turn to these registries to find suitable people to address their audiences. Be sure to read Chapter 12 about creating bios to ensure you include keywords and terms most likely to be searched. Below are some registries where you may want to add your name and information to increase the likelihood of being invited to speak:

- **BigSpeak:** www.bigspeak.com
- **International Speakers Bureau:** www.internationalspeakers.com
- **Keynote Speakers, Inc.:** http://keynotespeakers.com
- **National Speakers Association:** www.nsaspeaker.org
- **Professional Speaker Directory:** www.professionalspeaker directory.com
- **Speakers' Spotlight:** www.speakers.ca
- **Washington Speakers Bureau:** www.washingtonspeakers.com

Elements of a Great Sales Page

A sales page is any page on your site that you send to someone who is interested in your product or who requests more information. For example, if someone wants to buy your cookbook, instead of sending him directly to the order form and asking for payment, send him to a sales page that includes the link to order your new book, alongside other elements. Your sales page might convince the customer to purchase your new cookbook, because it contains numerous easy and healthy recipes, all in one place. On this page, the customer might also see endorsements from others who were delighted by your cookbook and its recent review by *Bon Appétit*. If, for some reason, customers had second thoughts about purchasing your cookbook, a strong sales page will convince them they can't live without it.

Include these elements on your sales page:

- The product or service's unique selling proposition.
- A photo or video to show off your product in action (if applicable).
- Three to five bulleted benefits as they relate to the customers needs.
- A link to a shopping cart or product page on an e-commerce site.
- A form to capture leads. You should collect names and email addresses from people who want to be contacted (either by newsletter updates or for a specific event or product). We describe tools to help accomplish this in Chapter 15.
- Testimonials and other sources of outside credibility (quotes in newspapers or magazines, for example).
- A single call to action. This is what you want page visitors to do. For example, order a product or provide an email to subscribe to your newsletter so you can keep in touch with potential clients and customers.

SAMPLE CALL TO ACTION

Join over 170,000 people who get fresh content from Copyblogger! You can see more examples of calls to action in Chapter 16.

Get It Done

One-Page Marketing Plan for Social Media
Building your one-page marketing plan requires you to give some thought about what your goals are, and specifically what you need

to do to achieve them. Outline the strategy you will use to build and share content, and to create awareness of your business in the marketplace.

Marketing Materials You Want to Have Ready (Online and Hard Copy)

Business Cards

Make sure you have business cards to hand out at events and meetings. Your card should include: your company name, your name, contact information, website, logo, and branding statement. It may also include social network references. Visit Vistaprint.com or Moo.com to see business card designs.

Build Your VIV-id Media Kit or Press Kit

Create a media or press kit to include on your website, to submit with proposals, and to use when you apply for partnership opportunities.

- Company Overview
- FAQ Page
- Bio
- Media Coverage

Additional Pages to Have Ready

- Pricing page
- Website traffic, number of Twitter followers, number of Facebook likes, Google+ circles, YouTube hits or subscribers, Klout score, etc.
- Samples of your work
- Testimonials
- References
- Nonprofit and community-service involvement
- Recent awards
- Photos (if appropriate)

- White papers or other factual background material
- Upcoming promotions and events schedules and details
- Statistics specific to your industry, demographics, and target audiences
- Feature articles
- Missions, goals, and objectives
- Camera-ready logo art
- Order form (if applicable)

Speaker's Requirements

If speaking is in your future, learn about the requirements for getting yourself listed with the different speakers' bureaus.

Elements of a Great Sales Page

Any time you have a new product or service to offer, it needs its own page! Be sure you incorporate these key elements to convert visitors to customers:

- The product or service's unique selling proposition.
- A photo or video to show off your product in action (if applicable).
- Three to five bulleted benefits as they relate to the customers needs.
- A lead capture form or link to shopping cart.
- Testimonials and other sources of outside credibility (quotes in newspapers or magazines, for example).
- A single call to action (perhaps your only request is to order your book or sign up for something).

14 Paid Advertising

E ven though you can accomplish a lot by marketing your business online for free, you can also attract business and generate income via advertising. We think it is important for MOXIEs and all business owners to promote themselves strategically and thoughtfully, and to take advantage of ways to earn a little extra money on the side.

> ⮑ **TIP**
>
> If you're thinking about investing in pay-per-click (PPC) advertising, we provide a high-level overview here. Setting up your advertising campaign can be complex, not to mention time-consuming to monitor daily results. Consider hiring someone with experience in PPC advertising to set up a campaign for you if you'd like to try that advertising route. This chapter also suggests some simpler, paid advertising options that may be useful for you.

You will need to be both strategic and frugal when you decide how to invest your money. Before you rush into spending your hard-earned cash to advertise your business, think about what you want to accomplish, and evaluate the best platform and strategy to achieve those goals. For example, if you want more subscribers to your newsletter, focus your advertising campaign on the social network most used by your target audience. Pew Research Center (http://pewresearch.org), Nielsen (www.nielsen.com), and comScore (www.comscore.com) regularly update statistics to show the latest social network demographics and trends in the consumer and business worlds.

Pay-Per-Click (PPC) Advertising

Pay-per-click (PPC) advertising is a way to help attract traffic to your site. In theory, it sounds pretty simple—you place ads that direct traffic back to your website, but you only pay when people click through. However, it's a little more complicated than it seems! In order for you to buy the ads, you bid (via Google's AdWords or Bing Ads) on keyword phrases relevant to your audience or potential customers. Then the ad, with a link to your site, appears in the top of search results. This allows your ad to reach all of the websites that host PPC advertisements as part of Google's Ad Network and the Yahoo! Bing Network.

You may need to experiment and rely on trial and error to find the right combination of keywords to generate a significant number of click-throughs to your site. Shaan Haider, owner and founder of the site Geeky Stuffs, where he writes about technology and social media, says:

> "A good PPC advertising campaign is by no means easy to pull off, and learning to successfully manage a PPC advertising campaign takes time and experience, so be prepared to put the hours in."

It may be best to subcontract this work to someone who has expertise and knowledge with PPC so you can spend your time on other business-generating activities.

SPONSOR PPC ADS

Your site can sponsor PPC advertisements. If you allow ads, you will receive a small percentage of the payout when the ads are clicked. In the beginning, when your site has very little traffic, you're likely to earn pennies, if anything at all.

If you are considering buying PPC ads, start with Google AdWords (adwords.google.com) or Bing Ads (bingads.com); they are the two largest search engines. While it is difficult to say how much you should budget for a PPC campaign, you can expect to pay anywhere from 50¢ to over $100 per click depending on the popularity of the keywords you use. Pay-per-click continues to get more expensive for competitive keywords, making it increasingly difficult for small business budgets to afford. A less expensive option is 7Search.com, which leverages smaller advertising networks and therefore has lower pay-per-click costs.

CHECK SETTINGS WHEN YOU ARRANGE PAID ADS

When you set up paid ads on any network, make sure you are very careful to check all of the settings, including your target audience and geographic preferences, and double check your daily maximum spend. Monitor your ads closely during the first 24 hours to be sure everything is going the way you expect. If you fail to do this, you may discover your entire monthly budget is gone in hours!

LinkedIn Ads

If your target audience is on LinkedIn (and it most likely is if you provide a product or service to businesses), this is a good spot for you to test your marketing. Start looking at the ads that appear on your LinkedIn profile. Gather ideas. Remember: though your ultimate goal is to generate new business, it doesn't necessarily mean that your ad has to be a hard sell. For example, your ad's purpose may be to help grow a bigger email list. In this case, your ad would include a link to your email sign up page instead of a link to one of your sales pages.

Where Do LinkedIn Ads Appear?

LinkedIn ads consist of a headline of up to 25 characters, a description of up to 75 characters, a company name, an image, and a URL. Your ads could appear on numerous pages on the LinkedIn website. LinkedIn determines which pages these are. To get a better idea of what the ads look like on the page, here are the pages to scope out:

- **Profile Page:** The page users see when they view someone else's profile.
- **Home Page:** The first page users arrive at after they have logged in.
- **Inbox:** The page where users see messages and invitations to connect.
- **Search Results Page:** The page that results when you search for a member by name.
- **Groups:** Any of the pages in LinkedIn Groups.

Getting Started

It is possible to write, target, pay for, and post your ad in minutes. Ultimately, you have control over how much you spend on a daily basis.

When you set up your campaign, LinkedIn will show you a suggested bid range based on what other advertisers targeting the same audience have bid. Usually, the higher bid will receive the most impressions and clicks. You determine you daily budget and only pay when people actually click on the ad.

> **⤳ TIP**
>
> LinkedIn sets a minimum $10 daily budget requirement. The cost-per-click for an ad is between $2.00 to $5.00, plus a one-time set up fee of $5.00 (this fee becomes a credit once you begin your campaign).

LinkedIn allows you to select your ad's audience. You can target viewers by:

- Geography
- Company name
- Industry
- Company size
- Specific job title
- Job function
- Seniority
- Group
- Gender
- Age

Be sure you are using the demographic information you compiled in Chapter 13 to select the most appropriate potential customers.

How to Create LinkedIn Ads

LinkedIn's site provides recommendations and examples to help you design and create an ad campaign. They suggest you include these elements in your ad:

- **Headline.** Make it short and catchy. This is what will inspire the reader to take action.
- **Ad copy.** Your ad copy explains the benefits of what you are asking them to do.
- **Destination URL.** Set up a special landing page tailored for referrals from LinkedIn. When people click through to your site, they have to immediately see the relevance to the ad on your site. Don't just take visitors to your homepage.
- **Photo.** A photo with a person works best, but any eye-catching image could work.

TIP

LinkedIn will occasionally email coupons or promo codes for $50 off LinkedIn Ads to users who "qualify." If you are a business, be sure you have a business page on LinkedIn to increase the odds you might qualify. Be on the lookout for this deal, or contact the LinkedIn team for one.

Suggestions/Examples of LinkedIn Ads

In your ad, ask viewers to "follow" your LinkedIn business page, subscribe to your website or newsletter, and connect with you on LinkedIn. Or, offer a discount code in the ad for people who come to your page through LinkedIn. Convince them to take action by providing something they'd want for free such as a checklist, case study, or eBook. LinkedIn provides tips to create effective ads and campaigns on their site (http://partner.linkedin.com/ads/bestpractices).

LinkedIn suggests a good ad would look something like this:

Need a Corporate Caterer?
Gourmet catering for private parties.
Affordable prices. Get a free quote.
www.tastyCorpCatering.com

TRACK YOUR AD CAMPAIGNS

Track how well your ads perform using LinkedIn's Ads dashboard. You can see and download detailed reporting of impressions, clicks, and click-through rates for your advertisements. Monitor which ad campaigns and keywords are most effective. As a benchmark, LinkedIn says click-through rates above 0.025 percent are acceptable, so don't wait to tweak or change your ads if they aren't performing at that level.

Facebook Ads

Facebook ads are relatively inexpensive and allow you to specifically target your audience by demographics (age, gender, interest, and location). Keep in mind, even though these ads are inexpensive, people log into Facebook to see their friends' interesting personal gossip and updates. Tearing them away from this with your ads can be a tall order.

A Facebook ad or sponsored story consists of a headline and text. The headline is limited to 25 characters and the body text limited to 90 characters. Facebook encourages a suitable, G-rated image.

How to Use Facebook Ads

You can promote four things with Facebook ads:

1. Ask viewers to "Like" your page.
2. Promote a specific post.
3. Link to an external website, perhaps your site.
4. Promote an event you created on Facebook.

Like LinkedIn, your Facebook ad should contain an appealing image or picture to help attract attention. Try to use your image to target an emotional connection.

> **⇨ TIP**
>
> Your Facebook followers expect special benefits for following your page. Offer them a pre-release special on your new eBook or a sneak peak of your photos, recipes, or project where your ad takes them to a special landing page on your site.

Be aware, your ad's life is one short week, and your target audience will see it on their pages multiple times during that period. You'll want to use words and an image that really grabs their attention quickly.

What Do You Want Your Facebook Ad to Do?

If your primary goal is making people aware of your business, then getting people to your site is your ad's mission. Hubspot recommends you draw them in by creating an ad featuring your most popular post or content via a "promoted" post. When you promote your post, it appears higher up in newsfeeds of people who have liked your page, which makes it more likely they will see what you shared. The more people see and engage with your posts, the better you will fare with Facebook's EdgeRank algorithm, which gives more visibility to content with high engagement.

> **⇨ TIP**
>
> The minimum daily budget for any campaign is $1.00 USD. Your budget must be at least two times your cost-per-click (CPC) bid. For example, if you have a $1.00 CPC, your daily budget must be at least $2.00.

You can also use Facebook ads to sell extra inventory or push a brand new product. Target your ad to meet the specific demographics of your desired purchasers. You may even want to include a special coupon to help boost traffic to your site.

You may also want to use an ad to promote an event you've scheduled on Facebook. Target the geographic area if it is an in-person event or target the appropriate demographics for a virtual or online event.

Facebook's Business page has ideas and help to set up your ad on their site: https://www.facebook.com/business/connect.

Samples/Examples

Hubspot recognized this ad for these winning qualities: attention-getting question in the headline, key words, special pricing, and sense of urgency:

> Struggling with SEO?
> All SEO, SEM & Other Online Marketing Services
> in 1 Place & For Just $5.
> Check it Out Now!

Don't Forget about Mobile!

According to the site Inside Facebook, almost 60 percent of Facebook users access it from their mobile devices. This trend continues to grow. Facebook's mobile ads are integrated in the users news feed because there is not space on mobile devices for sidebar ads. There are four types of mobile ads:

Sponsored Stories

These ads don't really look like ads at first glance. They fall in the user's news feed near the top of the status updates in a section called "Pages You May Like." If you look closely, you see the ads say "sponsored." These ads recommend pages to users based on their friends' activities. It even says which friends like that page when it appears in the status update field.

Page Post Ads

These ads are slightly larger than the "sponsored stories" and include some sort of a call to action at the bottom of the ad, for example a "like this page" action. Your ad can feature photos, offers, questions, videos, events, or links. As an added bonus, you can set these ads to appear in the news feeds of users beyond fans and friends of fans.

Promoted Posts

When you select the option to promote your post, it shows up in the news feeds of people who like your page. You cannot target specific demographics on promoted posts. Facebook users will see a promoted post appear in their news feed from a brand they have not liked if one of their friends likes it.

Mobile App-Install Ad

If you are selling an app, this ad makes it easy for people to instantly download it. When a user clicks on a mobile app-install ad, Facebook prompts them to install the apps on their mobile devices via iTunes or the Google Play store.

Making Your Ad Right for Mobile Users

If you want your ads to be mobile-friendly, either on your site or on other sites such as Facebook, here are some basic guidelines you need to be aware of:

1. Do not use an advertisement that contains Flash (programming that animates what is on the screen). The iPad, iPhone, and iPod Touch do not support Flash programming.
2. The size of the banner ads on your site may not fit on a mobile device screen. Create a square banner ad, which will most likely show up well on any mobile device.
3. Keep the file size as small as possible. Mobile devices cannot upload as quickly as a computer, so be sure you have compressed your ads.

MOBILE ADVERTISING DATA

Seventy percent of mobile users said they have clicked through on mobile banner ads according to Hipcricket's 2012 Mobile Advertising survey of 650 respondents. Hipcricket is a one-stop mobile marketing and advertising company.

According to this same study, 31 percent of mobile users have clicked on a mobile coupon redemption offer, 29 percent clicked on a sponsored text link, 28 percent downloaded an application, and 24 percent clicked through to a website based on an advertisement.

However, not everyone is so eager. Almost one-third of smart phone users (31 percent) thought the ad was spam, and 21 percent were unsure of the source. The key takeaway here is to focus your ad on the right target audience.

Twitter Ads—Promoted Accounts and Tweets

Before you start paying for ads on Twitter, invest some time to see if it's a good fit for your target customer demographic. Try following some of our recommendations in Chapter 9 for growing your presence on Twitter. If you find it easy to engage with people on Twitter and your followers have been steadily growing, then investing in Twitter ads may not be necessary. If you want to grow a big following quickly or promote a special product or event, you should acquaint yourself with Twitter's two ad types.

Promoted Accounts

The first ad is called Promoted Accounts. Twitter studies your current followers and looks for other Twitter users with similar interests. Twitter adds your profile to the "Who to Follow" section of similar people. This will show up on Twitter's mobile "Who to Follow" too. When you are ready to buy your promoted account ad, Twitter requires you to set a daily budget and bid on the cost you are willing to pay for converted followers. You only pay when new followers actually begin following you. If your goal is to build a larger following on Twitter, check the helpful details on how to set this up on Twitter's advertising page: www.business.twitter.com/en/advertise/promoted-accounts.

Promoted Tweets

The second ad type is Promoted Tweets. Twitter monitors your account and promotes your best performing tweets. The tweets that perform best (based on how often they are retweeted, generate retweets, or replies) will show up in your followers' Twitter stream, as well as the streams of those with interests similar to your followers. Twitter labels these tweets as "promoted." You will only pay when someone follows your account, retweets, replies to, clicks, or favorites your promoted tweet. The advertising process is the same as promoted accounts where you set a daily budget and cost per engagement, or click.

Twitter ads can help amplify your messages. Buying promoted tweets also reconfirms your presence among current followers and potential advocates. The following are examples of promoted tweets.

Promoted Tweets in Search

Your promoted tweets will appear near the top of the search results for search terms you choose. These ads are best for helping people who do not know about your business learn about it.

Promoted Tweets in Timeline

This puts your tweet at or near the top of your followers' timelines when they log in or refresh. You can target followers (those who already know about you) to increase their awareness of an event, special product, or service incentive you are offering. This type of ad will also target users similar to your followers, exposing your content to a new audience of potential followers and customers. Give them a reason to follow you, sign up for your newsletter, or at the very least, access your most relevant and compelling content.

Targeting Across Mobile and Desktop

Twitter lets you set promoted tweets to reach a specific platform (mobile to desktop). Promoted tweets on mobile appear at or near the top of the user's timeline.

Location Targeting

You can target your promoted tweets to a specific geography, such as a state or metro area.

Suggestions/Examples

Have you written a blog post about a new product you are releasing? A promoted tweet referencing the link to that post would be a great way to get the word out. Do you have a local workshop, presentation, or event, or a message for a specific U.S. region? Well, you are in luck! With Twitter ads, you can specify a specific U.S. region to promote your tweets. In your tweet, create a convincing call to action and share a link to the event information and registration page.

For the best results on Twitter, first become active there and attract followers. Twitter needs to find tweets and followers to analyze and make recommendations. Be sure you will have relevant and quality tweets. Also, be sure your Twitter profile will catch the eye of your potential new followers. See Chapter 12 for recommendations for writing a strong Twitter profile.

MOBILE BANNER ADS ON YOUR SITE

If your website is set up so that mobile users can see it clearly from their devices, and you have ads on your site, then your ads need to be adjusted to show up on mobile devices, too. If you are using Google's AdSense, they have a solution for mobile ads, AdMob, which puts mobile banner ads on your website.

Banner Ads on Websites

If there are websites where you'd like to advertise, you can approach the sites directly to learn about their advertising policies. Generally, you expect to pay a cost-per-click, but some sites prefer to collect a set monthly fee to recognize you as a sponsor. Target your demographics and learn about the site's traffic before you invest money. You can do this by checking to see if it has a Google Rank above four, or an Alexa rank better than your own. To learn more about sites' ranks, type the URL of the website you are interested in researching into these two sites to evaluate their ranking: www.prchecker.info and www.alexa.com.

These service providers make it easier to find sites to advertise on:

- **DoubleClick:** www.google.com/doubleclick/
- **Burst Media:** www.burstmedia.com/
- **247Media:** www.247media.com/
- **Commission Junction:** www.cj.com/

Ads on YouTube

If you are using video (and we hope you have considered it), you can advertise on YouTube via YouTube's Video Targeting. As we have mentioned before, YouTube is the number two search engine (after Google), and even if you aren't a video pro, it can help you reach a large number of people. You can chose between video or text ads on YouTube.

InVideo Ads on YouTube

If you've been on YouTube, you've seen InVideo ads. They appear during the beginning of the video and show up at the bottom of the screen. If you want to reach people who watch video (which is a lot of people, so you probably are), this may be one way to do it.

YouTube gives you two InVideo ad options: static image or Flash. To keep this simple, we'll just include basic technical requirements for the static image. The ad you submit to YouTube needs to be in a .jpg, .png, or .gif file format and have dimensions of 480 × 70. When you are uploading your image, be sure the file size does not exceed 50K.

YouTube also offers standard banner ads, which appear on the right side of the page. YouTube recommends you use Google's AdWords ad builder to create your standard banner to ensure it meets the ad requirements and specifications. Ad builder walks you step-by-step through building the ad. Start by logging into your AdWords account at www.adwords.google.com.

If you want to experiment with mobile, YouTube has Mobile Banner ads. Depending on your budget, there is a full range of sizes and placements. YouTube has thorough instructions about what to do and how to get started at www.youtube.com/yt/advertise/mobile.html.

TV Ads

Google recently unveiled a TV ads program specifically designed for smaller businesses to be able to purchase advertising on national TV. You can target up to 45 million households and purchase spots on such prestigious stations as ESPN, TNT, and CNN, plus over 100 other networks.

Inc.com ran a story about using TV ads and it says you can purchase ads for $2,500 to $3,500 a week. Now, having a national TV strategy may well be within your budget—and a great way to hit a massive amount of your target audience. We've discussed having a strong social media presence, but it's important to remember that this is only effective if you can drive eyes to your site. Having a targeted and relatively affordable television advertising campaign could be your door to big traffic. If you can combine a solid television advertising campaign with a strong online and social media presence, you've created a three-pronged strategy to set up your small business for success.

Get It Done

Keep Up-To-Date on Social Media Usage Demographics

Pew Research Center (http://pewresearch.org), Nielsen (www.nielsen.com), and comScore (www.comscore.com) regularly update statistics to show the latest social network demographics and trends in the consumer and business world.

Pay-Per-Click Advertising

If you are considering buying PPC ads via Google AdWords (adwords.google.com) or Bing Ads (bingads.com), expect to pay anywhere from 50¢ to over $100 per click depending on the popularity of the keywords you use.

LinkedIn Ad Details

http://partner.linkedin.com/ads/bestpractices

LinkedIn sets a minimum $10 daily budget requirement. The cost-per-click for an ad is between $2.00 to $5.00, plus a one-time set up fee of $5.00 (this fee becomes a credit once you begin your campaign).

LinkedIn ads consist of a headline of up to 25 characters, a description of up to 75 characters, a company name, an image, and a URL.

Facebook Ad Details
www.facebook.com/business/connect

A Facebook ad or sponsored story consists of a headline and text. The headline is limited to 25 characters, and the body text limited to 90 characters. Facebook encourages a suitable, G-rated image. The minimum daily budget for any campaign is $1.00 USD. Your budget must be at least two times your cost-per-click (CPC) bid. For example, if you have a $1.00 CPC, your daily budget must be at least $2.00.

Four Ways to Promote with Facebook Ads
- Ask viewers to "Like" your page.
- Promote a specific post to amplify great content you shared on Facebook.
- Link to an external website.
- Promote an event you created on Facebook.

Mobile Ads on Facebook
- Sponsored Stories
- Page Post Ads
- Promoted Posts
- Mobile App-Install Ads

Twitter Ads—Promoted Accounts and Tweets
www.business.twitter.com/en/advertise/promoted-accounts

Twitter offers two types of ads: Promoted Accounts, where Twitter will add your profile to the "who to follow" section of similar people, and Promoted Tweets, which will promote your best performing tweets.

Four Kinds of Promoted Tweets
- Promoted tweets in search
- Promoted tweets in Timeline
- Targeting across mobile and desktop
- Location targeting

Banner Ads on Websites

You can directly approach website owners to see if you can advertise on their sites. If you do, check to see if it has a Google Rank above four or an Alexa rank better than your own. Try using these two sites to evaluate their ranking: www.prchecker.info and www.alexa.com.

YouTube Ads

Want to reach people watching video? You don't need video skills to create an InVideo ad.

Submit a jpg, .png, or .gif file format that has 480×70 dimensions. When you upload your image, be sure the file size does not exceed 50K. Submission options include static image or Flash.

TV Ads

Google recently unveiled a TV ads program specifically designed for smaller businesses to be able to purchase advertising on national television.

15 Free and Low-Cost Ways to Get Visibility

Who doesn't love free stuff? While you may want to take advantage of the paid advertising opportunities described in the previous chapter, one great thing about learning how to leverage social media is that you can generate business without spending anything but your time and effort. We acknowledge that nothing is actually free—your sweat equity is worth a lot—but, in this chapter, we'll highlight ways to attract new customers without spending actual cash!

CHOOSE YOUR GIVEAWAYS CAREFULLY

This chapter suggests ways to help you gain some momentum, which sometimes involves giving something away for free. Make sure you maintain a high quality standard in everything you write, present, and share, via video, audio, or any other format. Your goal is to convince people who read or view your free offers to become paying customers. If you don't plan to offer your best, you might as well sit this chapter out.

Social Media Sites

We've already provided many suggestions to help use tools such as LinkedIn, Facebook, Twitter, and Google+ to get the word out about you, your expertise, and your business. Actively use these tools to connect with your audience and build a community of people who know, like, and trust you.

More Social Media Sites for Publishing Your Content

A variety of other online sites may be useful for publishing your content. While your own blog and website are always the best places to share content, sometimes it helps to find new places to reach an audience you can lure back to your own online properties! We thought you should know about these sites, in case you choose to share content beyond the standard venues:

Ning
http://www.ning.com/about/
Ning is a social network community. Some people will turn to this tool when they want to create an online group and invite contributors to their sites. It isn't free to create a presence there, but you can usually join these networks for free. Ning accommodates features such

TAKE ADVANTAGE OF Q&A OPPORTUNITIES ONLINE TO WIN BUSINESS

Pay special attention to sites that offer formal opportunities to answer questions. Why? Sometimes, people use online Q&A sites when they are looking for experts to hire. Everyone who hires you has a need (a question), so if you answer inquiries, it can be a great opportunity to connect with potential clients at exactly the right time. Quora.com is a useful site to find questions and answers, and to connect with new contacts.

as photos, videos, forums, events, etc., which you can customize. People may join via a customizable profile page.

HubPages
http://hubpages.com

HubPages bills itself as a website designed around "sharing advertising revenue for high-quality, user-generated content." Users write and publish any posts they want to share related to their expertise, and may be compensated via Google's AdSense, which manages a revenue split with writers. If you run some Google searches, you will find many HubPages come up as search results.

Squidoo
http://www.squidoo.com

Founded by Seth Godin, a bestselling author, entrepreneur, and marketer, Squidoo is a community website that allows users to create pages (called lenses) for subjects of interest.

Ezine
http://ezinearticles.com

Another place to share your expertise and potentially extend your brand, Ezine "serves millions of unique visitors monthly, has over 100,000+ RSS feeds, plus 600+ email alert lists designed to announce every new article posted to over 100,000 permission-based members/publishers." Visit their site to learn more about how to submit your unsolicited, expert articles to take advantage of their distribution system.

Be aware that you should not rely on article directories if you want to improve your Google ranking. Google may actually penalize you if low-quality sites pick up and share your content. Therefore, post your articles, but do not make an effort to have them widely distributed on sites you do not control. Use a Google rank checker, such as http://www.prchecker.info, to identify if the search engine considers the site to be of high quality. Anything ranked five or above is a suitable site.

Niche Sites

Don't forget to investigate whether sites exist that cater to your niche audience and allow you to become a member and contribute content. Find them by Googling {your niche topic, membership site}, and by keeping an eye on where industry experts post content. When you use these sites, be sure to follow their contribution guidelines and don't consider things you share there to be "throwaway posts" or shares. Your goal is to convince readers you are an expert and someone to follow closely to inspire them to visit your blog and site, and to follow you via social media.

SlideShare and Scribd

http://www.slideshare.net
http://www.scribd.com

SlideShare.com (60 million monthly visitors and 130 million page views) and Scribd.com (100 million registered users and 90 million monthly active users) are two tools where you can post content. If you are trying to gain market exposure, one strategy is to author an eBook, or the equivalent of a "white paper," about a topic in your area of expertise, and provide it for free. Scribd is a good place to

COMMENT ON BLOGS

You can get a little free advertising when you post comments on blogs related to your niche. This is especially useful when the sites have large and active communities. Be aware, it's inappropriate to try to use your comments to filter business away from a competitor with a successful website. However, if you can find a popular blog where the author does not offer or sell the services you sell, it's perfectly acceptable to visit, comment, and share your expertise. Do not overtly advertise your services, though.

share this content to extend its visibility. SlideShare, in comparison, is a popular place to share presentations.

Another option is to follow directions in Chapter 17 to find guest posting opportunities on highly-ranked blogs.

Social Bookmarking Sites

Social bookmarking allows you to see what articles other people like, which helps you find new content and useful information. When you use social bookmarking sites, you can flag your content via a "bookmark," which you add to your profile. This information is then listed and classified for other people to find. Some people use these sites as search engines, so you may find a new audience for your information. Using these tools also helps increase the likelihood that power social-bookmarking users will share your content with their communities. Try bookmarking some of your own content on some of these popular bookmarking sites:

- **Reddit:** http://www.reddit.com/
- **Digg:** http://www.digg.com/
- **StumbleUpon:** http://www.stumbleupon.com/
- **Delicious:** http://www.delicious.com/

Videos

Statistics show that people enjoy consuming video content. If you aren't comfortable creating and editing videos, you may decide to ramp up your other online and social marketing before trying your hand at video. However, remember YouTube is the second largest search engine after Google. People turn to video sites to learn how to do things and find out information they need to know. Be sure to have it on your list of possible ways to market your business for free, especially if your business lends itself to a "how to" video, or if you can envision how to demonstrate your expertise using this technology.

If you want to try your hand at video, but want to make it quick, try Twitter's six-second video tool, Vine. The application makes it easy to start and stop recording, and the micro length means you need to be creative and succinct.

Screen Casting

If you're camera shy, but would still like to have a YouTube or video presence or include video content on your blog, you can try one of these tools to create a *screen cast*. Screen casts allow you to video record your voice while you show something on your computer screen. These demonstrations are great for "how to" videos that you can illustrate from your computer screen. For example, you could illustrate shortcuts and tips to edit work in Microsoft Word by taking viewers step-by-step through the process. Viewers would be able to see anything you did on the screen. You could also feature software or an application you designed or like to use. Use the following websites for screen casting; not all are free to use, but most have free trials.

Camtasia Studio
http://www.camtasiasoftware.com
According to their website, Camtasia Studio allows you to, "Easily record your screen, PowerPoint, multiple audio tracks, and webcam video to create compelling training videos, screencasts, and presentations without ever leaving your desk."

ScreenFlow for Mac Users
http://www.telestream.net/screenflow/overview.htm
This website offers a variety of options for creating and presenting your information, and includes a free trial.

Jing
http://www.techsmith.com/jing.html
With Jing, you can "create images and videos of what you see on your computer screen, then share them instantly!"

Screenr.com
This is a free web-based video recorder used to produce screencasts for Twitter. Screenr is known to be easy to learn, and you do need to be registered with Twitter.

Webinars and Teleseminars

Webinars and teleseminars are popular mechanisms to entice people to hire you, especially if you provide a service. A webinar is typically an online presentation where people connect to a software program, then watch and listen to a virtual presentation on a topic. The only difference is that your viewers see your online slides instead of you. Usually, you create the slides in PowerPoint and talk through your points as you advance the slides, and your online audience watches from their computer screens. Make these presentations worthwhile by including a special paid offer for participants willing to hire you.

A teleseminar is similar to a webinar, except it is only an audio presentation. People listen to you talk, but you don't have supporting documentation for people to see while you speak. This can be a useful format for question and answer sessions, and for introducing you and your skills to a new audience.

We recommend that you identify other professionals who offer free, introductory webinars or teleseminars. Sign up to watch and listen to their presentations before creating your own. It's not hard to find some presentations. If you do not have a go-to list of people in your niche to observe, just Google {free teleseminar} and you'll find many options! Make a note about what you liked and didn't like about presentations you observe. This will help you to create a great online presentation for your potential clients.

Why Create Free Webinars and Teleseminars?

These free presentations help get the word out about what you do. When you give them away free, you can collect email addresses from potential customers in exchange for signing up. When you purposely build your e-lists, you will create a targeted market of people who may be interested in your services at some point (see Chapter 16 for suggestions of auto-responder tools to use to build your email lists).

During your presentation, make sure to include a special offer to entice those who are convinced that you are qualified and may want to hire you. Don't hit people over the head with the offer, but include information about you and your business. Successful free webinars share some details about their offer at the midway point of the presentation, before providing all the useful resources for listeners. That way, you won't be likely to see people hang up or sign off before you have finished your pitch.

You have two goals with your free webinars and teleseminars: to gain exposure and obtain email addresses. Develop a plan to follow up with people who attended. Be sure to send a follow-up note (you can set this up automatically in the program you selected to capture email addresses). Thank people for participating in your webinar or teleseminar, and let them know about your newsletter and blog. Invite them to join you via your various social networks. Consider asking them a compelling question and inviting them to one of your online properties to answer it. For example, if you're a graphic designer, post something on Facebook asking people to share their most pressing design questions. Invite new members of your list to visit your Facebook page to respond, and then follow up by providing insights and suggestions to help overcome those problems.

Prepare for a Great Presentation

Decide what you want to teach. For example, if you are marketing to people who want to save money on their food budget, you could create a presentation about the best coupon sites, best times of the year to buy certain items, and how to buy and store bulk food. Your goal may be to sell your eBook with complete details and checklists. Similarly, if you are a professional organizer, you could host a webinar to give tips about how to organize paperwork. Your goal could be to sell either a virtual consultation, or an organizing system containing labels and supplies to keep things in order. Always consider how your products or services can help solve people's problems. Demonstrate this during your webinars and inspire people to become customers.

Be sure to keep your presentations relatively short. People probably won't tolerate much more than a 20- or 30-minute presentation, unless your content is so compelling that they cannot turn away! That should be enough time to provide unique and informative content, while also being easier to record and share.

Next, create several slides on PowerPoint or another presentation creator to outline your content. Make them visually interesting by including pictures so people have something to focus on while you talk. Include important bullet points, but keep in mind that you do not need to include everything you say on the slide. Don't forget an introductory slide highlighting you and your business, and be sure to include contact information and details about your social media platforms. This way, people can stay in touch with you and redeem your special offer. Be sure your online seminars illustrate the vast array of information that you know, to entice participants to hire you and reap the benefits of your expertise.

TRICK TO SUCCESSFUL WEBINARS AND TELESEMINARS

The trick to successful webinars and teleseminars is to include enough information to demonstrate your expertise, but not so much that listeners will be prepared to go it alone. Your webinar is the virtual equivalent of the samples they pass out at mall food courts; you get a taste for what they sell and want to buy it. However, no one gives samples the size of dinner plates!

Finally, plan to use your notes. No one can see you, so it is okay if you don't memorize everything. However, even though you can read your notes, be sure you don't rely on your script word-for-word. If possible, keep your notes to bullet points so your presentation will have a natural flow and be pleasant and easy to follow.

Promote Your Event

You can have the most intriguing presentation in the world, but if you don't promote it, no one will ever experience it! Get the word out. Tap into all of your networks, market it via your newsletter, and generally promote the heck out of it. The more people who sign up, the more opportunities you will have to market your products and services this time and in the future (since you'll have their email addresses).

Choose a Platform for Your Presentation

You may not be surprised to learn that there are many applications to host your webinar or teleseminar. Review this list, which includes some of our favorites and the most popular choices, to see if any are good fits for you.

Webinars

FreeScreenSharing.com: The site notes it is useful for, "online presentations, sales presentations, product demos, webinars, and training." You can host webinars for up to 96 people for free.

JoinMe (https://join.me): This is a screen sharing application. You can't record, but you can invite 250 people to join you online for free.

GoToMeeting (http://www.gotomeeting.com/fec/webinar): With their GoToWebinar option, "you can conduct do-it-yourself webinars with up to 1,000 people—all for one flat rate." There is a free trial.

Conference Calls

www.freeconferencecall.com: The site notes that it is "a reliable, cost-effective, reservation-less, and easy to use audio conferencing service." You can have up to 96 callers, and there is an option to record the calls.

Video Interviews

Video interviews are also an easy way to create video content. Here are some tools you can use to conduct the interviews.

Skype (Skype.com): With Skype, you can "talk to more people on one call—for free if everyone's got Skype. Add people on phones using Skype Credit or at no extra cost with a subscription."

Google+ Hangouts: Use your Google+ account to host an online video chat. When you're signed into Google+, it is easy to start a hangout and to invite other people. You can also record and share the video on YouTube.

Audio and Podcasting:
Tips from Maggie Mistal

Podcasting and audio content are popular tools, and a good place to get started is BlogTalkRadio (http://www.blogtalkradio.com). All you need is a computer and a phone to create (un-editable) audio content to share online. It is much like hosting your own radio show reaching a global audience. If you like to talk and think this might be a good medium for you, review these tips from Maggie Mistal, career change consultant and professional radio host, which were also shared in *Social Networking for Career Success*:

What Skills Do You Need to "Do" Radio Well?

- **A true passion for radio.** "I have never met a successful host who didn't love radio. It's a great medium for great conversation. I myself listened to talk radio for years before becoming a host. Once you start hosting a show, you even look at life differently—everything becomes fodder for radio. If you have a conversation or read an article or react to a story, you start to think in terms of what would make for great radio conversation."

- **Creativity and an authentic passion for your show.** "To consistently come up with compelling topics, it takes a lot of creativity and passion for your show/what its all about. I have heard some people say that radio can be 'like a beast that needs constant feeding.' Unfortunately, if you get that attitude, I think it's going to be hard to come up with topics. Rather, I look at radio as a chance to share my message of 'soul search, research, and job search' in new and different ways so that people really get it. I share my own advice and stories, and I take listener calls to help them apply the soul search, research, and job search message in their own situations. I am constantly looking for new ways to get my message across via my show and I never get bored."

What Are the Key Mechanics of Radio Hosting?

- **Hosting skills.** "Opening/closing, resetting, managing the clock, managing guests, keeping the show moving at the right pace, eliciting callers, managing callers (respectful but not so polite you let them take over), and the ability to make listeners feel like you're "inviting them into your living room."

- **Content expertise.** "Sharing information, answering callers' questions in a quick, yet relevant and useful way."
- **Education and entertainment ability.** "Comedic abilities, able to share information in a fun and compelling way."
- **Presence.** "The ability to stay focused and engaged in a seemingly one-sided conversation, able to present without audience feedback."

What Should Someone Thinking About Creating an Online Show Consider?

For example, should they consider length of show, format, having guests, etc.? Maggie suggests:

- **Soul search.** What is the philosophy behind your show? What is your mission and purpose with it? What is at the core of your message, and why are you sending it? What audience do you want to attract? What are you trying to say, to whom, and what is the best way to convey that message?
- **Length.** How long do you need to give useful information, but leave them wanting more? Better less time than too much.
- **Format.** This depends on your topic/mission. Are you taking calls or is it you and your guests or some combination? Remember, it takes time to build a caller base because most people like to listen, and fewer actually call in. If you're going to have guests, you need to add that into your planning time. I find it takes about four hours of prep for every hour of airtime.
- **Sponsors.** Eventually, as you build popularity, you might want to approach organizations that would benefit from advertising on your show/gaining access to your listeners (a radio ad salesperson would be able to share ideas along these lines).

In terms of format, it depends on your mission. To elicit callers, however, you will want to:

1. Open with a compelling topic and share your own related anecdote.
2. Ask for calls from listeners.
3. Expound on the topic, tease the guest (tie the guest into the topic).
4. Reset the show (by saying who you are, what the show is about, today's topic, etc.).
5. Interview a guest.
6. Have a signature show close.

Maggie's Tips for Preparing and Do's and Don'ts?

- Prepare bullet points of what you are going to say in advance. Don't read verbatim; speak conversationally.
- Before going on air, take a few minutes to stretch out your chest, shoulders, neck, and face. It will also help you relax.
- Don't staple your papers together or rattle them while recording. Microphones pick up a lot of noise, and you don't want anything to distract the listener from your message.
- Focus on what the audience wants to hear, not just what you want to say.
- Remember that people often listen to radio while doing other activities, so keep your points simple and have examples that illustrate what you're trying to convey.
- Speak clearly and slowly.
- Remember to breathe.
- Drink only room temperature or warm water. Cold water will tighten your vocal chords and distort the normal sound of your voice.

- If you forget what you were going to say, it's ok. Rather than freeze, look to your bulleted list for guidance (this isn't TV, so no one will know).
- Don' talk over others. It's distracting to the listener.

What Are Good Techniques for Getting the Most out of Your Guests?

For example, how do you make them look and sound good?

- **Prepare for your guests.** Read or deeply skim their book, ask the guest to provide the top five bullet points on his/her topic.
- **Ask the right questions.** Ask yourself, "what will my audience benefit from hearing this person talk about?" How can I ask a pointed question to get a concrete answer? It helps to listen in to talk show hosts and take notes on how they interview guests. Incorporate what you like from their style.
- **Give topic and/or sample questions to your guest ahead of time.** Don't talk too much before the show, as it takes the spontaneity away from the actual interview.
- **Weave in your guest's bio.** Do this throughout the interview rather than presenting it all upfront.

Do You Have Advice for a Show Without Guests?

Is it possible to be engaging alone on radio? Maggie says yes, and offers these words of advice:

- Care deeply and speak passionately about your topic.
- Have real life examples.
- Ask for listeners' reactions.
- Use your radio voice. Love the sound of your voice on air (it may take some time getting used to hearing yourself, but you have to like the sound and have fun with it).

If you're a little more technically inclined, consider starting a *podcast* on a platform of your choice, and distribute it via iTunes (for free) and on your own site. A podcast is simply a voice recording you can share. You can choose the software program to create it. Check out http://podcast-software-review.toptenreviews.com/ for ideas about which tools to use. You can find Maggie's free podcast on iTunes.

Assume many people will be interested in what you say, so put time, effort, and energy into creating a professional podcast that will help people understand what you have to offer. Use the tips from Maggie about creating a great radio program. Consider collaborating with other podcasters and cross-promote your programs to help grow your audiences. Don't forget to include links on your website with information and details shared in the podcast so people can easily follow up when they want to learn more.

Press Releases

Don't forget to keep your local newspapers and other traditional media outlets in your area (including radio and television) up-to-date when you have news to share about your business. Are you selling a new product? Adding a service? Publishing a book? It's possible your in-town press will cover it. If you're looking for broader distribution, try writing a press release to send to a distribution site. Search Marketing Standard suggests investigating the following services to help you share your press releases:

- **Press Method (www.pressmethod.com):** Offers both free and paid press distribution.
- **Free Press Release Centre (http://www.free-press-release-center.info):** Provides press release distribution services for small and medium-sized businesses.
- **SB Wire (www.sbwire.com):** Provides free (with ads) or paid press release distribution

- **PR.com (www.pr.com):** offers options of paid and free press release distribution.
- **I-newswire (www.i-newswire.com):** Provides small business-oriented packages ($47 per month).
- **PR Web (www.prweb.com):** Probably the best-known option. This site offers one basic release for $89, with premium distribution running up to $369 per release.

Take advantage of the tips on the sites to be sure you create press releases that meet distribution standards.

Affiliate Marketing

Affiliate marketing is a way to extend your reach to potential new customers and clients. Effective affiliate marketers partner with other succesful businesses who may be interested in what they sell. In exchange for a financial reward, often 50 percent of the purchase price, your affiliate partner promotes your products or services (since the financial incentive is usually significant, this type of arrangement works best for products such as eBooks, where there is no actual cost to distribute them). Most businesses engage affiliate marketers as a strategy to extend their reach and earn more money.

There are two ways to participate in affiliate marketing. You can find affiliates to promote your products and services (this aspect fits the topic of this chapter—effectively, you are asking for free advertising, even though you pay a commission on sales). Alternatively, you can promote other products and services to sell on your site.

BECOMING AN AFFILIATE FOR OTHERS

One important point: if you plan to try to make passive income (commissions from selling other peoples' products) by signing up to be an affiliate, you're effectively endorsing whatever you advertise when you

continued from page 233

ask your customers to also be their customers. Make sure you are confident about the products' quality. If you choose to pursue this path, here are some resources to help find items to sell:

- Clickbank.com
- Amazon Asssociates—https://affiliate-program.amazon.com
- MarketLeverage.com
- Commission Junction—http://www.cj.com
- PepperJam Network—http://www.pepperjam.com
- Linkshare.com—Especially good if you have a fashion blog or music blog
- e-junkie.com

How can you market *your* content via affiliates? You'll need to identify affiliate partners willing to share your product or service with their customers. As we've mentioned before, your best partners attract an audience interested in your content, but do not compete with you or sell the same types of products or services. Before you begin to search for good partners, be sure you create information to help them market your materials.

Set up your program so it is ready to go. First, choose an affiliate tool—two of the most popular websites for managing your affiliate programs are clickbank.com and e-junkie.com, which allow you to easily track sales and fulfill your payment obligations. Contact people you think will be interested in marketing your product, and be sure to describe it convincingly so they will want to partner with you.

Then, provide a designated information page for potential affiliates. Include details about your eBook or other product, compelling ad copy, and relevant images for affiliates to use when they market your information. Don't forget to outline all the details about your affiliate program, such as how to sign up as an affiliate, what percentage they can earn of the sale, and how you plan to arrange payment.

Online Classifieds

You may want to consider placing ads in free, online classified sites. For example, you can use Craigslist (www.craigslist.org). Be sure to include keywords in your ad, and write it professionally to represent you and your business well. Keep an eye out for other free websites that allow you to place ads and track your success rate.

Online Forums

In addition to well-known social networking forums, there are many additional online "meeting" places for people in various professions. If you have time, Google, {forum, your profession} and see what you find. For example, {Forum, photographer} yields several results that may be useful for photographers. Similarly, consider skipping directly to forums where your customers might spend time. Do not spam and start peppering a parenting forum, for example, with ads about your products for new mothers. However, if you join respectfully and contribute useful advice, you may make some new customers.

In-Person Meetings

When you're working your social network, creating videos, and producing webinars, do not forget to incorporate some in-person networking. Attend conferences (speak at them, if possible), join local chapters of national groups, and look for business associations and chamber of commerce events to attend. Seek opportunities to expand your in-person audiences by speaking in libraries and at relevant interest group meetings. Be creative and think about where you will be able to meet your perfect clients. Once you decide, go there!

Get It Done

- Explore all of the major social media sites, and dabble in the less-known sites, including social bookmarking tools such as SlideShare and Scribd.
- People love video, so keep it in mind when considering how to get the word out about your business.
- Find a free or inexpensive program to help you run webinars and/or teleseminars. Remember: these opportunities may help convince someone that you are the expert they need to hire, so make the presentations great!
- If you enjoy talking, consider hosting your own podcast or online radio show.
- Write and distribute press releases when you have news to share—or make some news to share!
- Decide if affiliate marketing may be helpful for you. If you have a product to sell, maybe other people will help you sell it in exchange for a kickback!
- Don't forget online classifieds and forums; you never know—you could meet a great contact there.
- Never underestimate the power of in-person meetings and presentations.

16

Use Online Tools to Create Connections That Last

You have so many choices to help you get the word out about your business! Once you capture those coveted eyeballs, you want to be sure to convert potential customers into actual customers. One of the best ways to do that is to engage regularly with those clients through your online networks.

Sending out great content is step one of the lead generation process; it is kind of like getting customers to look into your store window. Step two is encouraging potential clients to give you their contact information so you can keep in touch. Step three is proactively reaching out to them with great information and deals based on their unique sets of needs and wants.

Keep these three things in mind as you build your marketing strategy. Your customers need to:

- **Know** about you, your company, and your products and services.
- **Like** what you are doing because it helps them in some way.
- **Trust** that you will be a smart investment in order to help customers part with their money.

LISTEN FIRST

Don't focus on *you* and what *you* want; listen to your customers. When you grow "big ears," you will learn how to improve your ability to respond to the problems your customers face. The content you create in response will help them see you as a trustworthy source they can rely on. Then ideally, the information you send out through Twitter, LinkedIn, Google+, YouTube, and other networks will keep them coming back to you and your website for more.

When you accomplish these goals, you'll have a much easier time generating leads and filling your sales funnel with potential clients.

Luckily, you can connect and keep in touch with people using all of the tools we've already discussed and more. Consider ways you can incorporate any of the following tools and suggestions into your campaign to be magnetically attractive to your audience.

Keep in Touch Via Email

One way to create "sticky," or returning, readers for your sites is to capture their email addresses. When you know how to contact people who express an interest in your business, you can let them know when you have special offers, new products or services, or an eBook to sell.

Email Services to Consider

You could use your existing email system; however, email marketing software provides more features and saves you time. For example, people interested in your business can subscribe to your email list, and you can create different versions of your newsletter to go to certain email subscribers. For example, first time subscribers should automatically get a welcome email shortly after they subscribe. Email marketing tools will do this for you, and ultimately save you time.

Most services have options to set up automatic responses to subscribers. For example, you may offer a free eBook to anyone who joins your list. The email marketing software you use should be able to deliver the free eBook automatically without you doing any work at all! These services offer different options for varying price points. Most will charge based on how many leads (email addresses) you collect. You've probably signed up for services like this yourself—you provide your email address to a business in exchange for something free, or to stay updated on content, information, or services they offer. The business owner sends an automated reply and perhaps a link to a free eBook or report. Once you confirm your intent to be on their list, you can sit back and wait for more content to appear in your email box.

Most of the email marketing software is easy enough that you do not need advanced programming skills to use it. Some popular choices include:

- **AWeber:** www.aweber.com
- **Constant Contact:** www.constantcontact.com
- **GetResponse:** www.getresponse.com
- **iContact:** www.icontact.com
- **Infusionsoft:** www.infustionsoft.com
- **MailChimp:** www.mailchimp.com
- **VerticalResponse:** www.verticalresponse.com

Visit these sites to learn what they offer, and be sure your choice can fulfill your business needs. For example, if you plan to market eBooks, make sure the program you pick has a robust solution to register a client's payment and then automatically deliver the link to download the eBook (AWeber is one such solution). Some sites have more active support than others, so if you prefer talking to someone when you have a question, make sure your choice offers phone support. Don't choose based on the cheapest plan. You may be sorry later when you learn you have your list captured into a program that doesn't suit your needs. (Be sure to learn how portable your list is—can you download it and transfer it to another service if you choose to do so later?)

Once you capture email addresses, you can begin to create marketing emails and newsletters. You may be surprised to learn that email marketing may be more effective than social media marketing, according to information collected by Monetate, an online marketing company. Almost everyone has an email address and most check it at least daily. Another speculation made by Jamie Turner, founder of 60 Second Marketer, an online video magazine, is:

> " ... *a visitor that lands on your site via social media is often a first-time visitor with no sense of trust or relationship with your brand. On the other hand, a visitor that lands on your site via email marketing has an established sense of trust and an ongoing relationship with your brand.*"

⇨ **TIP**

How frequently should you send emails or newsletters? It depends on the buying cycle and the amount of time you can afford. Weekly or monthly emails are fine, especially if you regularly write blog posts.

Keep in mind; your newsletters do not have to consist only of original content or your content. In his newsletters, John Jantsch, author of *Duct Tape Marketing* (Thomas Nelson, 2006) and *The Commitment Engine* (Penguin, 2012), includes excerpts written by other experts and authorities. You can also repurpose or summarize themed content you've already written. For example, your email could list the top five posts you've written on a specific topic. Just make sure you provide useful information via your emails. When you give readers practical tips and helpful advice, they're more likely to read the next emails you send.

How to Build Your e-Lists

Your goal is to build email lists of potential customers' contact information. This isn't always as easy as it sounds. Generally, people do not like to provide their email addresses because they don't want to receive spam or annoying sales pitches. You need to inspire your readers and visitors to trust you with their contact information. One way to help convince them is to give something in return for this information.

When you ask someone visiting your site to sign up for your newsletter or opt in to get updates, you need to provide something valuable as an incentive. Think about what information your potential customers want. You may want to entice them with some of these items:

- Audio recordings
- White papers or case studies: For example, "Best SEO Techniques for Businesses," if you provide SEO services for clients
- Cheat sheets: For example, "12 Ways to Improve Your Eating Habits"
- Check lists: For example, "Top 10 Ways to Save Money on Your Grocery Bill," "How To Eliminate Clutter in the New Year," or "10 Items You Must Have Before You Travel"
- Newsletters
- E-courses
- Mini eBooks
- Resource lists, templates, and forms: For example, "Top 15 Leadership Books to Read This Year," or "Labels To Make Your Potluck Dinner A Snap"
- One-time teleseminars
- Free consultations

Immediately after someone provides an email address, you can send the free product via an email autoresponder such as AWeber, MailChimp, or the others on the list provided. The other option is to use E-junkie, which you can configure to automatically store and send the digital content you upload and make available. We talk more about using E-junkie in Chapter 11.

Convert Your e-List Subscribers to Customers

Now that you have newsletter subscribers, be sure you make the most of the opportunity to turn these leads into customers. How? Ask them questions. For example, send a message a week after new subscribers join your list and ask them what information they would like to see from you. This won't take much time if you use the autoresponder function supplied by the email service you selected. Use information they provide to create new blog posts and articles for upcoming newsletters or emails.

It often takes multiple touches or encounters for a subscriber to convert from a reader/subscriber to a paying customer. Be proactive—interact purposefully and engage with your audience. When your readers believe you are talking directly to them and providing useful information, they are more likely to continue opening your newsletters. Every time someone opens and reads what you send, you have another opportunity to nurture relationships and convert them to paying customers. Once you've convinced them you have good products or services, you'll need a clear call to action.

Call to Action

Whether you want people to sign up for your e-list, buy your products or services, or register for your webinar, you need to tell them exactly what you want them to do. This is known as a *call to action*. There is some psychology behind using the correct wording and design. You should test different language, colors, and page placement with your readers to see which generates the best response. Look at other sites and find businesses that have an attractive call to action to help them collect email addresses before you decide how to create your own.

Creating Your Call to Action

Calls to action can appear as hyperlinks within blog content, as buttons, or as banners within newsletters, emails, or websites.

A call to action should be specific; in other words, it should tell readers what action to take, how they benefit, and ideally, imply a sense of urgency. Include a legitimate benefit to encourage people to take action. Think about it, which would entice you to take action: "Click Here" or "Get it Now"? Here are some examples:

OK: Submit

Better: Get free quote

OK: Download

Better: Download now! Get your free eBook

OK: Buy Now

Better: Add to cart—Save 25%

These calls to action are more popular:

Call for a Free Quote: Use this alongside other information about your services.

Buy Now and Save 20%: Combine a sense of urgency and entice your visitor with a discount.

Download Now, Free (Download Our Free eBook Now!): People like free downloads and respond to immediacy.

Join Now: Great for membership and social network sites.

Talk to an Expert: This is a great way to prove credibility, especially if you provide expert advice as a service.

Start Your 30-day Trial: Trial periods are a great way to lure prospects. It's not too committal, and people can form their own opinions by trying your product or service.

Stay Up-to-Date on Industry News: For a softer sell like a newsletter sign-up, this speaks to the value.

Where to Put Your Call to Action?

The basic rule of thumb is to place your call to action where the reader can easily see it. Your primary call to action button, image, or text link should appear at the top of the screen, or "above the fold," where visitors can see it without having to scroll. Do not overwhelm your readers with too many calls to action.

You can use social media to create the following calls to action, too.

Sample Tweet

Never get left behind again! Read this newsletter today "Leadership News for the Rest of Us" [URL to newsletter sign up form]

Sample Google+ Update

Have you ever missed a promotion? Keep in tip-top shape by reading this weekly newsletter filled with ideas to boost your career! "Leadership News for the Rest of Us" [URL to newsletter]

Sample Facebook Update

Hot off the press for our Facebook friends, "Leadership News for the Rest of Us!" These weekly tips will help get you a promotion! [URL to newsletter]

Your sales page should have few distractions (no side bars, ads, or links to other pages) and a clear call to action: "**Buy Now.**" Clearly state the benefits and what the buyer will get once he or she has shelled out money for your product or service.

Keep in mind, your calls to action on your website should be visually appealing with few words, ample white space, and just the right use of color to draw the reader's eye.

Use Calls to Action to Engage and Interact

"Buy Now" is not necessarily the first or most important call to action. For example, if your visitor comes to your site for the first time, they are unfamiliar with your VIV-id and perhaps not quite ready to buy. Remember, one reason someone may purchase something from you is because they trust you. You need to encourage and grow this trust.

While some of your calls to action will obviously direct people to buy something or sample your products, you can also successfully encourage and convince people to engage with you, especially online. Direct visitors to view other content on your site, ask them to post comments, and inspire them to share your posts with friends. When they engage, they begin to learn more about you and your expertise.

Derek Halpern of Social Triggers has tested these calls to action. In this example, Derek wants you to engage with him on Twitter:

> "*Before you scroll down to the action steps, if you've enjoyed the NEW Social Triggers TV episodes, let me know by saying "What's UP!" on Twitter [link to Derek's Twitter page."]*

Notice how he tells his readers what he wants them to do!

Another example of how Derek uses calls to action in his blog posts is by asking the reader a very specific question and requesting the answer in a comment such as:

"Now I have a question for you:
Are you focusing on your email list as your MAIN priority?
If yes, share with me how your email list has helped you and your
business in the comments below."

This request entices readers to show off their knowledge via the comments to provide other readers with a valuable assortment of ideas. Readers will then review the comments, stay longer, and possibly revisit later to see more comments and advice.

Part of Derek's VIV-id includes humor, which comes across well during the calls to action he makes during videos. He asks viewers to share his videos with someone who would benefit from the information, and to subscribe to his YouTube channel. Derek believes that if you don't tell someone what to do, they most likely won't do anything. The power of suggestion is, well, powerful!

⤳ TIP

If you make it easy for the user to understand what action to take, why to click through, and what to expect once they do, you'll be well on your way to successfully engaging them.

As we've said before, engagement happens when you provide information your readers and potential customers find valuable and interesting. Polls are a way to add variety to your content and interact with your target audience differently. You can use the data collected to fine tune products, promote products or services your customers say they want, uncover potential customer problems, or discover where they are in the buying cycle. Conducting a poll might also show that you care about your customers and value their input.

Create Effective Polls

What do you want to accomplish by running the poll and what information are you looking for? Do you want feedback on your products or services? Do you want to learn more about the problems or issues your target audience faces? Alternately, are you simply looking for another way to interact with your followers?

Ask Good Questions

Here are some ideas for types of questions to ask your audience:

- What are their greatest concerns or questions about a topic?
- What prompts them to buy or make a decision related to your industry, service, or product?
- What do they consider to be good customer service?
- Invite them to vote on topical issues that are in the news and relevant to your business.
- Ask a question to make people laugh (if it fits with your VIV-id).

You can create a poll and host it on your site using one of these free tools. Many of them have pre-designed questions to make it easier for you to collect unbiased answers:

- **99Polls:** www.99polls.com
- **Acepolls:** www.acepolls.com
- **Checkbox:** www.checkbox.com
- **Constant Contact:** www.constantcontact.com
- **eSurveysPro:** www.esurveyspro.com
- **FreeOnlineSurveys:** www.freeonlinesurveys.com
- **GetResponse:** www.getresponse.com
- **Inquisite:** www.inquisite.com
- **Mineful:** www.mineful.com
- **Pollcode:** www.pollcode.com
- **Polldaddy:** www.polldaddy.com
- **SurveyGizmo:** www.surveygizmo.com

- **SurveyMonkey:** www.surveymonkey.com
- **Vizu:** www.vizu.com
- **Wufoo:** www.wufoo.com
- **Zoomerang:** www.zoomerang.com

Run Your Poll

Once you've tested your questions with colleagues and made sure your poll generates the right type of response, launch it on your site and share a link to it on your social networks. Ask your social network connections to include a comment in your posts when they vote—more dialogue often results in more buzz and traffic. Comments may also make the poll results more meaningful and interesting.

For example, if the question you create is, "How many times per week does your family eat out?" ask them to include their favorite restaurant in a comment. If the question is on Facebook, encourage people to tag (include the @Name) the restaurant!

Promote Your Poll

Creating a poll won't guarantee responses. You have to invite people to respond. Run your poll for about a month to give enough time to collect responses. Here are some suggestions to get the word out about your poll.

- Write a blog post and embed or link to your poll (wherever it is).
- Share a link to the poll in your status updates across LinkedIn, Facebook, Twitter, and Google+.
- Ask your network to share the poll.
- Send reminders and ask colleagues to help you.

Tempting status updates and messages such as these (in any social network) should help encourage participation:

- *Only one week to go! Please cast your vote!*
- *We've gotten over 85 responses so far . . .*

- *26% of respondents said this . . .*
- *What is the most popular response to our poll? The result might surprise you!*
- *Thanks to all 112 respondents for sharing your opinions!*
- *Thank you [@name] for your recent response!*

Share the Poll's Results

It isn't often you see a formal summary report after a poll has run. You could summarize the findings in a blog post, a slideshow, or even an eBook. Be sure to share the results across all the same networks and with all the people who responded. Additionally, in your summary, be sure to thank respondents and people who helped you get the word out about the survey or poll. By sharing the summarized results, you create greater loyalty, respect, and trust.

LinkedIn Polls

LinkedIn makes it easy to create a poll. You can choose who you want to have access to the poll, such as all LinkedIn members, groups, or a subset of people you hand select. Once you have created your poll on LinkedIn, you may decide to send individual invitations to your LinkedIn connections asking them to contribute or share your poll. This direct appeal is generally more effective than a status or group update.

Facebook Polls

A poll adds variety to your Facebook page by giving your fans an easy and different way to interact with you. Additionally, if your fans like your poll or think it is interesting, funny, or useful, they can easily share it with their friends. As a result, even more people and potential customers may notice your page. If you want to invite specific friends to respond to your poll, tag them in your status update by adding the @ sign to their Facebook user name. (For example, if you wanted to get our attention, you could tag us on

Facebook by using our Facebook business names: @KeppieCareers and @CareerSherpa.)

An easy, non-high tech way to engage your Facebook audience is to post regular questions or statements intended to illicit replies on a regular basis. For example, Dan Schawbel, a personal branding expert and founder of Millenial Branding, consistently posts questions and statements that inevitably attract many replies and engage his Facebook audience. For example:

> Stat of the Day: "The average teenager sends 3,400 texts a month: more than 100 a day." [Nielsen]

> You can always make time for someone so stop making excuses.

> Companies who care about their employees' careers will retain them, while others will lose the battle for talent.

When his readers respond, it helps him maintain their attention and keeps his Facebook stream top-of-mind. In turn, this helps him when he wants to share information or details about his business.

Facebook Questions is Facebook's poll service. There are a couple of different options for setting up a poll. You can ask an open-ended question or create a custom multiple-choice poll. Unfortunately, with Facebook Questions, you can't limit your poll to a specific demographic subset of your fans—your poll can either be viewed by the entire Facebook community (public) or just on your page.

FACEBOOK POLLING APPS

Below is a list of polling tools available as Facebook applications. The best way to learn more about them and decide which you'll choose is to search for them while logged into Facebook. Just add the application name into the search bar at the top of your Facebook page.

- Poll
- Polls for Facebook
- Polldaddy for Facebook

Your Facebook page audience is already interested in what you have to say, and some members may even be current customers. Use this opportunity to poll your more dedicated viewers with product or service-related questions. Ask what they want to see more of, or which product or service they liked best.

Engage On All Social Networks by Asking Questions

Use your status update on any or all of your social networks to engage people with a question. You can also consider posing a question within a group discussion on LinkedIn, Facebook, in a Google+ community, or through social networks specifically focused on questions, such as Quora.com. (Quora is a Q&A social network that is very popular with a high-tech audience, so if you have a tech-y question, consider asking it there.)

It's always a good idea to reveal that you're interested in what people say and that you will listen. As you know, listening is one of the first rules of social networking and building relationships.

Here are some sample questions to get you going.

On LinkedIn

> *Small Business Owners: When it comes to content marketing, which would you choose: hiring a professional copywriter, or investing in training to learn to DIY?*

This question was submitted by a copywriter in a LinkedIn Group and resulted in five answers, which provided an understanding as to why someone may not hire a copywriter, and when someone would not.

> *"I will be selling audio CDs about fruit tree care. What's the best way to distribute them? I'm thinking about using CreateSpace and backing it up by promoting them on my website*

and through my work. I'm open to also having an option for people to download just the audio and listen on their computers. How could I charge for this, though?"

Six responses later, this consultant has options and ideas for a better strategy for distributing her CDs.

Short questions with quick asnwers will work well across social networks:

Conference planning: Do you prefer urban or exotic/isolated venues?

On Your Own Blog

Sharlyn Lauby is an HR Consultant and runs a website called HRBartender.com. She regularly runs polls to engage her readers. In a recent poll she asked:

Do job seekers need to color their gray hair to get hired?

Answers included:

Men should color their hair for a job interview. Women can do whatever they want.

No! Hair color doesn't matter during a job interview.

Women definitely need to color their hair. Men can get away with gray hair.

Yes! Both men and women need to consider coloring their gray to look better for a job interview.

Sharlyn's polls regularly address topics with varying opinions. They are educational and entertaining, and help draw readers to her site.

Are you wondering if answering questions will help your

business? Follow these basic guidelines to make the most of your answers:

- Zero in on sites where your ideal customers participate.
- Answer questions in line with your business and expertise.
- Provide good quality information that will benefit both the person asking and others reviewing.
- Clearly disclose who you are and what you do using your branding statement.

Ask Questions on Twitter

Twitter is a fast-moving open platform, and if you build a strong, collaborative network here, you can post questions to gain insights about your potential customers. Try these suggestions to connect with potential customers and learn new information via Twitter. Here are some examples of tweets to elicit answers:

What is the healthiest #snack your kids will eat?

If you could improve your #golf game, what is the one thing that would help?

What do you think is the most underappreciated #leadership quality?

What do happy, successful, balanced mom entrepreneurs have in common? Add your tips here: [shortened URL]

It's mid-afternoon here and we've already got dinner on the brain! Any suggestions for inspiration? #recipe #dinnertime

Search for tweets by asking questions about your company. From the Twitter search window, type in "# [yourcompany]?"

See who is asking questions that include one of your keywords or hashtags by using this type of search formula: "[keyword]?"

Use the advanced Twitter search function (https://twitter.com/search-advanced) if you want to omit certain tweets from your search results, or search only for tweets near a geographic location.

Promote Your Events

Never overlook the power of face-to-face networking events to engage and interact with your potential and existing customers. Luckily, it's easy to use social networks to promote your in-person events. For example, Facebook lets you create and share "events." When people are invited and respond, their attendance status becomes public. This is a great way to draw a crowd. If an invitee sees someone attending the event that he or she has always wanted to meet, there is a good chance that person may also attend. These events are easily shared, not only with friends on Facebook, but via broader audiences on Twitter and Google+. Ask other invitees and attendees to help promote the event among their extended social networks.

There are online events as well. You can host a Twitter chat, webinar, or Google+ Hangout (or join with an existing one) to talk about your industry's best practices, hot new technology, trends, common work-arounds, or time saving tips.

Being Social *After* the Sale

Saying "thank you" immediately after the sale is one way to help develop stronger connections to your customers. Create a thank you page or an automatic email that tells your new customer what to expect next, and don't miss the opportunity to let them know about the other services you provide and where they can go to learn more or get questions answered.

Continue to nurture relationships with your new customers, too. Think about how you can provide the best after-sale support. Will you delight and overdeliver? With social media, you have the opportunity to do both. Tell your customers how they can have immediate access to you. Ask them to opt-in for a special free gift after purchasing something from you. Follow up in regular increments after the sale to see how things are going, gather feedback, and continue to communicate with them to create a loyal, life-long fan.

Endorsements, Recommendations, and Testimonials

We've mentioned informal endorsements, so now is a good time to mention formal endorsements, recommendations, and testimonials. As part of your follow up strategy with customers, build a system to collect feedback—the good and the bad. You can use the feedback to modify your products and of course, share the praise publically. Remember, people need to be told what to do, and they trust the recommendations of their friends! (See Chapter 18 for more about how to inspire customers to recommend you.)

Get It Done

Social engagement strategies are about providing answers, inspiring or surprising, and educating your community. We hope you will implement some of these ideas to engage more fully with your potential customers, readers, visitors, friends, and peeps!

Giveaways

What free product or giveaway will you use to attract people and get them to provide you their email addresses?

Email Marketing

What tools will you use for your newsletter, and how often will you send it out?

Engage Your Audience with Polls

Decide where your customers spend time online, and begin varying your interaction with them by running a poll. What type of information do you want to collect? Will you test this on LinkedIn, Facebook, your website, or your newsletter? How and where will you share the poll results?

Engage with Questions

What questions can you ask that will engage your audience? Post inquiries in LinkedIn groups and try posing your questions on Quora, Twitter, and Facebook to win engagement and get answers to questions.

Promote Events

Use social networks to spread the word and communicate your event.

Being Social After the Sale

Create a thank you page that thanks your customers and tells them more about what to expect from you.

Endorsements, Recommendations, and Testimonials

Ask customers for written feedback to help you grow your business and provide the best service possible.

17 How to Create Buzz for Your Business

I f you thought only celebrities needed to generate online buzz, welcome to your new reality! Even if you manage to capture email addresses from possible clients and build magnetic social media and online profiles, you should always be thinking about how to generate buzz so people will talk about you. Luckily, once you tap into the power of social media marketing, you will have a plethora of choices at your fingertips to help you generate conversations and interest in your business online.

PANERA BREAD EMPLOYEE GARNERS GOOD WILL VIA SOUP

Brandon Cook was caring for his grandmother, who was on her deathbed in the Nashua, New Hampshire area. Her one request was for clam chowder from Panera Bread, a chain soup and sandwich restaurant and bakery. Brandon knew they only made clam chowder on Fridays, but decided to ask, even though it was only Tuesday. He wasn't sure how much longer his grandmother was going to be able to eat soup, so timing was everything.

continued from page 257

The store's manager, Sue Fortier, not only agreed to create a pot of soup for his dying grandmother, she also packaged up some special cookies as a gift. When Brandon shared this story online in a heartfelt thank you on Facebook, the post got over 670,000 "likes."

The Panera story made the television airwaves in many local markets. It's not unusual for online tales to become part of the traditional media's news cycle. Try to pay special attention and notice what types of memes (ideas or concepts that go viral online) spread far and fast. How? Keep an eye on your own social media community. If several people who don't know each other in your Facebook stream are posting the same quote, picture, or video, assume it is probably on its way to going viral. Depending on how plugged in you and your community are, you may even notice new trends before they make their way to your local news broadcast.

Don't just notice these; take note! Think about how you can tap into the power of social networks to share your information. Once you understand what's popular and most likely to be shared, consider how you can incorporate new ideas into your online marketing arsenal to spread the word about your business.

The Panera story illustrates that you can't always plan your buzz. You don't run the Internet, and you can't control what will appeal to people. (Seen a million cute animal videos, anyone?) However, if you pay attention to trends, you'll be able to tap into people's inclinations to share. You do not need to be a huge company to generate big buzz.

Be creative and offer your community new ways to experience you and your brand. Use your online networks to provide an experience your audience will appreciate. You have many choices to help get people talking about you and your business!

Plain Old Blogging

You create the potential for buzz whenever you blog. Consider your blog to be the home base, or the centerpiece, of all of your other activities. What does your blog do for you?

- Showcases your subject matter expertise and displays your specialty knowledge.
- Lets people know you have good ideas.
- Illustrates your passion and commitment to your field or industry.
- Helps you make a name for yourself with the people who have the authority to contract you.
- Creates a network of people who rely on you for information, share what you say, and engage with you when you need to solve problems or land new opportunities.
- Sells you, your products, and your services.

Ultimately, a blog is probably the most cost-effective and efficient way to solicit buzz. When you optimize your blog for the keywords you want to be known for, and write content to help introduce people (and search engines) to your expertise, you are well on your way to creating the type of ongoing buzz you need to sustain your business.

Guest Blogging

One popular strategy to introduce yourself to new audiences is to guest blog for a popular and well-read industry site. You should definitely consider identifying several potential blogs to pitch your guest posts. Be aware that not every blog accepts guest content. Look for submission guidelines on blogs where you'd like to contribute. You should be able to tell if they host guest posts by reading the site, and if they do, it is okay to reach out and ask if they'd be interested in a post you write.

If you're interested in this buzz-creating strategy, follow these steps:

Identify Blogs with Authority

Blogs earn authority online from people and from search engines. One important benchmark is Google PageRank. To find a site for assessing a website's rank, just Google {Google Rank Checker}. When you identify candidates for your guest posts, you should target sites with a Google rank of at least a four, but ranks of five or above are better. (Ranks are 0 to 10, with 10 being the best.) Ideally, once you identify a well-regarded blog, it will have an engaged community of readers who will comment and pass along the link to their communities. Be sure to interact with the blog owner before you ask for an opportunity. Comment regularly on the blog, connect via Twitter and retweet (pass along) content from the site owner, and "like" the site's Facebook page and comment on Facebook. It's helpful to have a relationship with the person who owns the blog before you ask for a favor. With a little effort, it is easy to get to know most blog owners online.

HOW NOT TO ASK FOR A GUEST POST OPPORTUNITY

This actual letter is one of many Miriam receives daily, from people offering to guest blog for her. While she does not accept guest posts, even if she did, this note would not compel her to offer her platform to this stranger, who makes it clear she "stumbled upon" Miriam's blog! We cannot overemphasize how important it is to build a relationship with the blogger before you ask for a favor. Then, make sure your inquiries are personalized and include your credentials for writing about the blog's topic. (This writer's suggestion that she is qualified to write anything isn't particularly compelling.) If your inquiry reads like this note, stop and start over!

continued from page 260

"Dear Mlrlam,

I recently stumbled upon your blog and noticed that you write about many of the things that interest me as a writer. I'm a freelance blogger hoping to expand my portfolio. As a mother, former teacher, boating enthusiast, and consumer electronics junkie, I feel qualified to write about just about anything. I'd be thrilled to write something for you, if you'd be interested in a contribution.

In case you're wondering about my writing chops, here are some of my best clips:

[includes a variety of links unrelated to career or social media topics]

I look forward to hearing back from you about a possible partnership.

Cheers, Susan"

Create Several Blog Topic Ideas

Most blogs will require unique posts, which means you cannot repurpose content from your blog or rehash something you've already written. Send a personalized note with your offer, indicate you understand the blog's guest post guidelines, and wait for a reply.

Write a Bio

Most blogs will allow a short bio with a link back to your site. Be sure to write a mini bio that clearly outlines your value proposition. If the blog allows it, choose a few keywords you want to use as anchor text to link back to your site. For example, if your top keywords are "buy golf clubs," you might write a bio with that phrase linked to your site. You may also invite people to follow you via your favorite social networks.

Prepare a Designated Landing Page to Link Traffic

Once you secure your guest post spots, be sure to prepare a specially designated landing page on your site and provide that link to include in your bio. You may also wish to have people land on a blog post relevant to the most likely audience for the guest post. Include information on the landing page that you want the post's readers to learn about you, and include a specific call to action (something you want readers to do, such as sign up for your newsletter. Read more about calls to action in Chapter 16). Use your Google Analytics (see Chapter 22 for details about Google Analytics) to keep track of how many people visit your designated landing page.

Host a Blog Carnival

Another way to use your blog to get some buzz is to partner with others who write in your niche and host a blog "carnival." There are many ways to organize a blog carnival, which is nothing more than an opportunity for all the designated bloggers to share links to each other's posts. For example, you can invite each blogger to write about a particular topic or answer a question, and then share links to all of the other bloggers' responses (on their own blogs). You can also have one central blog "host" who links and references all of the posts. The goal is to earn a little "link love," or new inbound links from other blogs. This can be a great way for a new blogger to get some traction. The trick is to convince several high-profile, established bloggers to join the group. Don't be bashful!

If you blog regularly, participate in an active online community (a formal or informal group of colleagues), and build relationships online via tweeting and commenting on successful blogs, their authors may be very receptive to joining in your group effort. Build your community first, and then put out feelers to see if people would be interested in participating.

Run an Interview Series on Your Blog, Video Cast, or Podcast

One way to inspire people to point their friends and contacts to your blog is to feature them on your blog! Authors may be willing guests, as most are happy to have new platforms to help get the word out about their books. If there are people in your industry who recently released products or introduced new services, consider inviting them to join you on your podcast. (See Chapter 15 for more suggestions about getting started with podcasts.)

Don't worry about featuring a competitor. You know what they say, "Keep your friends close and your competitors closer!" Another suggestion is to find people to interview whose expertise relates to your audience, but does not compete with you. Potential pairs include: interior designer/real estate agent, vintage clothing dealer/auctioneer, food blogger/new restaurant, website designer/SEO expert, and a golf sales professional/golf club manufacturer.

You could also create a series of tips or information. For example, if you have a productivity business, you could invite people to submit their favorite online application. Your resulting post, "100 Top Productivity Applications," should earn a lot of eyeballs and interest.

Host a Contest or a Giveaway

Who doesn't like to win? Some of the best buzz-getting contests give more chances to win if people pass along the details and inspire their friends to enter. You'll likely need a tracking application to help run the contests. SocialMediaExaminer.com, a useful blog about social networking and social media marketing, published a list of applications that work with Facebook. Many of these require you to pay a fee:

- Fanappz.com
- Vitrue.com

- BuddyMedia.com
- Votigo.com
- BulbStorm.com
- NorthSocial.com
- MomentusMedia.com
- Friend2Friend.com
- Strutta.com
- Offerpop.com
- PromoBoxx.com

Facebook's rules prohibit you from running a contest or sweepstakes on their site without a third-party application. These rules are always subject to change. Be sure you check Facebook's policies before you plan to give anything away through your business page.

Leverage Your Social Networks for Buzz

What information does your community expect from you? Dream up a campaign where you post a little information each day to help generate buzz. For example, if you're a food blogger, launch, "100 Days of Holiday Recipes," leading up to New Year's Day. Post them on Twitter and/or Facebook and link back to your blog. For someone with a golf business, "A Tip a Day" to help people improve their golf swing (including links to video instruction on your blog via YouTube) could generate some buzz.

Another popular buzz-driving idea is to create a "Best of" list. You could create a post listing the "Top 10 Blogs" about your niche topic. You could also be very ambitious and write about 50 or 100 "bests." Best Twitter feed, best LinkedIn group—any best you choose will likely win you traffic, click-throughs, "likes," and possibly new visitors to your business site. Be sure everyone on your "Best of" list knows it so that businesses or individuals can share the news with their networks. Everyone likes to be recognized, which is why this is a good technique.

Alternately, you could consider running a Twitter chat. As mentioned earlier in the book, you can Google {Keppie Careers, Twitter chat} to find a blog about Twitter chats with a link to the list of existing chats. Plan to participate or watch existing chats to learn how they work and decide if starting a new chat is a good idea. Typically, chat leaders pose several questions and invite experts and followers to chime in during the chat, which is usually between 30 minutes to an hour long.

One of Google+'s features is Hangouts, where you can literally "hang out" with up to nine other people via webcam. Consider hosting some informational Hangouts. Advertise them as "don't miss" opportunities for people to learn something new from you or your guests. Find existing public events by Googling {Google shared calendar events}. Consider participating in an event someone else runs before hosting your own online program. You can even consider recording the hangout to post on your site and share with your online community.

Don't forget Google+ Communities. Create a community or join one to engage and interact with new people.

Host an Event or Make News

If you create news, you can create buzz and inspire press coverage. For example, you may commission or conduct your own research about an important topic in your industry. What do people want to know? What would social media outlets covering your niche be interested in picking up? For example, if you're a consultant to small businesses, you could research demographic preferences useful for your audience, create a short research report or press release, and send it to people who may be willing to publish it or post a summary. If you're in the travel industry, you could do a survey of the best places for young single people to travel. At the very least, you should be able to capture some buzz from the winning companies or service providers you feature in your summary!

Another way to get attention is to host an event. Invite a prominent speaker to join you at an event, or tap into a charitable need at a local non-profit. When you connect your business name with something people feel good about, you can garner positive attention. For example, if you run a golf business, consider creating an event for underprivileged children to teach them about the game. Contact the local print, radio, and television media outlets; many of them will happily cover charity events.

BE PR SAVVY

Don't forget, you can actually distribute your own press release, and have it published as "news." Various services help small business owners push their content out. Review Chapter 15 for details.

Plan a Stunt

Creativity-online.com reported about a stunt the pizza chain Mellow Mushroom commissioned. The chain, whose mascot is a big mushroom, invited people to follow @mellowmushroom on Twitter in exchange for a chance to have the mushroom mascot follow them—for real! The site notes, "The brand stalked 20 Mellow Mushroom followers in a week, and recorded the whole thing using hidden cameras." Of course, hilarity ensured, and Mellow Mushroom is using the videos to promote its brand.

How to Incorporate Social Media

No matter how you create buzz, make sure you get the ball rolling by posting about your event, research, list, or other activity via your social media channels. Use the suggestions in Chapter 9 to share news with your Facebook and Twitter communities during the optimum times for the most eyeballs, and include language that inspires others to repost or retweet your content. Don't forget to spread the news on LinkedIn through the Update feature. If you participate in relevant groups, ask your contacts there to get involved.

If you publicize a local event, use hashtags on Twitter to try to reach local people. For example, #ATL tells people the event is in Atlanta. #NYC lets people know something is going on in New York City. Research the typical hashtags for your area on http://tagdef .com or http://www.hashtagdictionary.com.

DON'T IGNORE EMAIL MARKETING

Don't forget email. Especially if you plan a local event with potentially far-reaching appeal, such as a charity program, let everyone in your in-person community know what you are doing. Email your friends, and ask for their support. Make a specific request when you contact the people you know: invite them to involve their contacts, and let them know how (exactly) they can help.

After the event, showcase pictures on your visual feeds (Facebook, Flickr, and Pinterest, for example) and add pictures to your blog. (Make sure everyone agrees to be photographed and captured on video at the event.)

Make a YouTube video of some of the best moments. Did one of the children at the golf charity event make a great shot, even if they never held a golf club before? If you are diligent about getting video of your program, you're likely to get some good footage. Make sure you use and share it on all of your online properties. (Tag and annotate YouTube videos as detailed in Chapter 4.)

Write about your event after it is over, too. Thank people who helped you, and honor any co-sponsors or donors. Tell a story and highlight the event's successes. Consider hiring someone to create a write up for you if writing is not your strong point. A poignant, well-written, and well-photographed story could really help you display your business and win you useful buzz in your immediate and/or online community.

Just For Fun!

Try the following apps to collect and share content you found across the web in one place. They read like mini websites or newspapers, and you can showcase your expertise, industry trends, or almost any other topic you think would benefit your potential clients. These applications will send out great-looking links to content that you generate from Twitter, and you can link these summaries to your main site so people can see the links and information you curated.

- Paper.li
- Storify.com
- Storyful.com
- Twylah.com
- RebelMouse.com

Get It Done

These buzz-generating ideas are only the tip of a wide and deep iceberg of possibilities to consider. Some things to keep in mind before, during, and after your campaigns:

1. Target your audience and structure your plan to appeal to them.
2. Stick with your brand or VIV-id: are you a wild and crazy business? If so, a funny stunt or series of videos could be

just the thing you need. However, if you and your clients are more conservative, aim for a published whitepaper or a news-y press release.

3. Consider all of the options available: writing, video, radio or podcasts, social media tools, and events. There's no limit to what you can do to create buzz.

4. If necessary, hire someone to help you make the most of a big push for buzz. If a photographer, videographer, or writer would help capture the best moments of your event for posterity, it could be worth an investment.

5. Use social media before, during, and after your buzz event to let people know what you're doing.

6. Remember to involve people you know through email and in-person requests whenever appropriate.

18 Referral Partnerships

A sustained, significant business needs more than just good marketing and a lot of buzz to be successful. You need to have people on your side, too! Ultimately, one of the most important reasons to use social media is because it allows you to expand your circle of contacts, colleagues, and potential customers. When you use it well, social media provides the opportunity to meet people who can support your business (even if only virtually). While it's great to network with and get to know new people, it's even more important to rally your contacts and convince them to become your business allies. One way to do this successfully is to create mutually beneficial referral partnerships with other business owners.

We recommend strategically creating these relationships; they are unlikely to come to fruition unless you purposefully nurture them. Let's face it—most people don't stop to think about how they can help you. Even friends who are business owners you know well don't automatically take the time to think about the ways they can

It's important to build relationships before you ask for or offer anything in return. Use the strategies in this chapter to identify good partners, and get to know them as much as possible—either online or in person—before you suggest becoming referral partners.

support you and your business. Similarly, you're probably not doing all you can to lend a helping hand to your networking contacts.

How can you make sure you don't leave any stones unturned, and that your network helps create a steady stream of referrals and clients? The first step is to decide how to best connect with other business owners. Think about what you offer potential partners and make collaborating and referrals a priority for you.

Identify Businesses Whose Clients May Also Need Your Services

Remember when we asked you to envision your ideal clients or customers? What type of professionals do those people regularly hire? Those professionals are the ones you need to engage as your referral partners.

Be creative when you make your list. For example, hairdressers typically have large networks of people, and they spend all day speaking to their clients. Just because they do not specifically attract the types of clients you seek does not mean they can't be good partners for you. If you need to network with parents, perhaps your neighbor or a stay-at-home parent can connect you to the local parenting clubs. Similarly, someone at your gym may be the president of the Parent Teacher Association at the large, local elementary school. Just because these contacts don't own businesses doesn't mean they would not want to network with you. Keep an open mind about how to target your networking efforts, and you'll be more likely to be creative and identify partnerships.

For example, if you are opening a cake baking business, and your target clients are people celebrating special events, like birthday parties, you may try to connect with party venues (for example, bounce houses, bowling alleys, and art specialty stores) that cater to children. Other good partner businesses include specialty toy stores with upper-income customers, schools, and day care centers. Consider pediatric practices such as dentists and pediatricians to be possible referral partners.

Maybe you prefer to bake and design high-end, specialty cakes for weddings. Your referral partners obviously change—you might try to connect with party venues for weddings (including hotels and other special event locations), caterers who don't offer cakes, boutiques where brides and grooms register for gifts, and bridal gown stores.

As a cake baker and designer, your referral partners will probably be other local businesses.

For a freelance graphic designer, referral partners don't need to be local, since work can be shared virtually. This makes it easier to identify partners, since your pool of possibilities is so much larger. Some possible virtual partners include Web designers, copywriters, marketing consultants, and commercial photographers.

Potential local partners include local print shops, and companies that specialize in printing signs.

CONNECT TO CREATE BUSINESS LEADS

Your customer profile will help you identify the people running businesses who already serve your projected customers. Connect with those business owners so you can help each other via referrals. Amy Jane, a certified massage and aromatherapist and owner of Organica Jane, built relationships with chiropractors, alternative medicine practitioners, and the YMCA. These businesses already serve customers who are likely to need her services, too.

continued from page 273

It all started when Amy met with clients who needed specific help and started asking her for recommendations. She had previously visited an acupuncturist in the area for her own personal treatment and naturally thought of that practitioner. Amy contacted him, and brought up the idea of referring clients to each other.

She also knew a lot of her clients were members of the YMCA. She approached the YMCA leaders and proposed they pay her to be an on-site massage therapist. They refused. She went back to them and offered to schedule and collect payment for her massage therapy services on site at the YMCA. She also offered to provide educational information on how massage therapy works and why it is an added benefit to working out. There was no cost to the YMCA. All they had to do was make the space available in order to provide an additional service to their members, so they agreed.

How to Create Partnerships with Local People

First, conduct some research to find the people in your area who have the best professional reputations. Review endorsements, talk to people, and Google business names. You can also check with the Better Business Bureau and various online endorsement sites to make sure there aren't a lot of complaints against the business.

Once you identify target referral partners, identify any networking groups these business owners typically attend. How can you find out? Check local business publications, newspapers, local LinkedIn groups, and chamber of commerce meetings. If your targeted business owners don't attend these meetings or events (or, even if they do), feel free to contact them directly. Ask about the best ways to meet in person to discuss how you can help grow each other's businesses. Maybe you'll meet for coffee or arrange a time to visit the potential partner's store.

TAP SOCIAL MEDIA

Also, don't forget to see if these local businesses are using social networks. You may want to set up a special list on Twitter or a designated circle on Google+ for your local contacts. Monitoring the local scene will keep you up-to-date about area business events and news. You can use social media to build your relationships with local contacts when you share their updates and happenings among your network. They will appreciate your help.

Below are some tools to find and connect with people based on their location on Twitter:

- www.localtweeps.com
- www.nearbytweets.com
- www.twellow.com/twellowhood

To find local restaurants and businesses via Google+, use the "Local" tab. It is located under the "More" section on the left hand sidebar of Google+. You may find businesses that would make good partners for you.

LinkedIn's "Advanced Search" (located on the right from their top toolbar) makes it easy for you to narrow a search to a particular location or zip code.

Facebook's search toolbar will allow you to filter your search once you start it. If you want to find people in Atlanta, you can type "Atlanta" into that top search bar, and then select the "People" filter on the left of the screen. It also allows you to search groups and places.

When you get to know the business owner during your meeting, make sure you ask the following types of questions to learn something about him/her and the business, as well as decide if you will be comfortable referring clients to them:

- Why are you so good at what you do? What differentiates you from your competition?
- What challenges, if any, do you face in getting new clients?

- Who are your ideal customers? How can you help refer business that would be useful?
- What additional services do your customers need?
- Do you have a seasonally busy or slow time?
- What advantages do you want or hope to see should the two of us collaborate?
- What are the best ways for us to help each other?
- How should you plan to communicate and keep in touch to make sure the relationship is meaningful and helpful for each of you?
- What additional networking contacts do you know who could be involved in the partnership?

Referral-Networking Groups

Active networkers who understand how to expand their circle of business owners through research and by taking advantage of online networks can be very successful at generating leads and networking partnerships. However, we would be remiss if we did not include a shout out to referral-networking groups. There are a variety of these types of groups of every ilk around the world. Typically, membership involves a fee and an ongoing (usually weekly) commitment to attend meetings.

Typically, the group's main goal is to help provide referrals to each other. Usually, groups try to include one person to represent each business area. For example, a group might consist of one professional in each of the following businesses: a realtor, an insurance agent, a life coach, someone selling a product (such as makeup, jewelry, or gift items), a banker, a mortgage broker, a housepainter, and an attorney. You can easily see that there are some obvious potential referrals there (for example, between the realtor and the mortgage broker, or the broker and the banker). Meanwhile, the life coach will need to make a very strong pitch for her services and skills to help inspire members to mine their contacts to make referrals.

Many business owners have been successful filling their business funnels in these groups. One such group, BNI, notes on its website that it has *"over 145,000 members worldwide . . . is the largest business networking and referral marketing organization in the world (and) last year alone, generated 6.9 million referrals resulting in $3.1 billion dollars' worth of business for its members."*

You can Google {referral networking group, your city or town} if you are interested in this formal type of referral networking. Alternately, you can find national groups (such as BNI) and look for local chapters. Expect to make a firm calendar commitment to attend weekly meetings, and be prepared to focus on how you can tap into your network to help other members of your group succeed.

THE VALUE OF BNI NETWORKING

Arnie Fertig, MPA, is Head Coach of Jobhuntercoach.com. He writes weekly for the "On Careers" section for *U.S. News & World Report*, and is an approved career expert for Careerealism.com. As a member of BNI, we thought he would be a perfect person to describe the value of a referral-networking group. Arnie explained why he recommends BNI:

"'Givers gain' is the motto of Business Network International (BNI), which is dedicated to helping people gain sales for their businesses through referrals. It has more than 135,000 chapters throughout the U.S., and internationally. The group is built on the general premise that if I refer business to you, in the end you will likely do whatever you can to return the favor.

Chapters typically range from 20 to 50 people. I belong to one of the largest, most active groups just north of Boston, in Wakefield, MA. Even with this number of people, we all get to know each other and each other's businesses quite well over time. Attendance

continued from page 277

is expected (with some 'passes' each year) at each structured 90-minute weekly meeting. The constancy of attendance with our network fosters the creation of trusting relationships. We each become, in effect, a valuable part of each other's sales force. We keep our ears and eyes open to the needs of people outside the group, and make a referral when we learn of a particular need that can be appropriately filled by a member of our group.

The network gains strength through its diversity, and the fact that no two people can market within the chapter the same goods and services. At the same time, interest spheres are effective in sharing business. For example, think about all the people and businesses whenever a person buys a home: real estate broker, home inspector, attorney, mortgage broker, and moving company. And after the sale, the new homeowner may also need a plumber, electrician, interior decorator, and so on. Each one of these kinds of people might be present in any given BNI chapter, and each likely has many opportunities throughout a year to refer business to other members of the same sphere.

In addition to the meetings, members are encouraged to learn more about each other in 'one-on-one' sessions. Over coffee or an early breakfast, I've come to develop personal relationships with many of the members of my group. And, like many in the group, I've 'referred myself' internally to other members. Of course, when another member goes 'above and beyond' to meet my needs, I'm more than happy to recommend that person to someone outside the group.

BNI has made me a 'hero' to my wide circle of friends and acquaintances when I can say to them, 'I know that you are looking for "X." So-and-so and I see each other every week, and I'm certain that s/he will be able to more than meet your needs.' I love it whenever I can help other people by introducing them to each other for their mutual benefit!

continued from page 278

As a coach helping people advance their job hunt process, I've benefited from BNI in multiple ways. In my sphere is the owner of a recruiting company, also dealing with hiring from the standpoint of employers. He and I actively refer each other. Beyond that, most people know someone who is out of work—or recent college graduates, or people who are dissatisfied with their current job for whatever reason. All of these kinds of people make great referrals for me, and the members of my BNI chapter have been able to boost my business by introducing them to me and the services I provide.

There are many avenues by which a client might come to me for my services, but BNI has produced a reliable, steady stream of new clients that have enhanced my business. Like everyone else, I'm a part of many distinct networks, but BNI has become a valuable component contributing to the health of my business."

How to Create Partnerships in the Virtual World

When you're creating online business referral partnerships, start with the same research suggested in the "in-person" relationship section. Be sure you identify people with strong reputations who provide their clients with excellent service.

Once you identify those potential partners, begin to consider how you can network your way into their circles. Social networking offers limitless ways to connect with people. Here are just a few suggestions, but be sure to use other ideas to meet new people listed throughout the book:

Identify active, large groups on LinkedIn frequented by the types of people you want to know. When you click on the group in LinkedIn, scroll down and find the banner message that says, "Group Statistics." Follow through to learn information about the types of people active in the group, how many discussions post weekly, and geographical details about members. When you locate an active group of potential partners, start to contribute and get involved before you start asking for anything. You need to establish yourself as an expert. When you post comments, respond to questions, and share details from things you are reading, the group will start to know you as a strong potential business partner.

Search LinkedIn to find people interested in growing their online networks. Which business owners might be good partners for you? Consider searching LinkedIn to see who is updating their status in relevant topics. It can be helpful to try to meet and engage with people who actively use online tools because, when people turn to social media, it is likely that they are open to meeting new people and could be interested in forging new partnerships.

Become very active on Twitter. Find niches of your target business referral partners online. Where do they spend their time? If you're looking for web designers, there are probably forums of web designers engaging in Twitter chats. Use the advice in Chapter 17 to find Twitter chats, and look to find out if you can identify some people to research and possibly approach as referral partners. Remember, you don't need to jump in and comment in these forums, especially if web design is not your expertise! You can, however, get a bird's eye view by observing online interactions to locate highly qualified professionals.

Use Google+ to find active and involved professionals in the niches you seek. See who is hosting Google chats, who updates their Google+ streams frequently, and who seems to have a lot of conversation and engagement with people via the network. (Look at gphangouts.com to find the public hangouts.)

We actually have a great, personal success story illustrating how you can meet and build relationships with people using social media. We met each other online via Twitter and our blogs. We "ran" in some of the same online circles, and began retweeting each other's tweets and commenting on each other's blogs. When Miriam teamed up with another career professional, Jacqui Barrett-Poindexter, to create a new collaborative of career bloggers, Hannah was one of the people asked to join. To make a long story short, after knowing each other online for some time, we arranged to talk on the phone and eventually met in person at an industry conference. Having partnered on an eBook titled, *You Need a Job: 5 Steps to Get One,* we decided to write this book together! It's hard to believe that we would never have met if it hadn't been for Twitter and blogging. You can see why we're both such big proponents of using social media to expand your circles.

Manage your own online footprint, because anyone you try to approach via virtual networks will visit those same networks to learn more about you. Do you have a supportive online community? How about endorsements and recommendations on LinkedIn? Does your community comment on what you share online and ask you questions? Keep up with the social media activities we suggest in this book, and anyone who researches you will find details that make them want to learn more about you, your business, and how you can work together.

Forging Partnerships

Once you find the people you want in your referral networks and create relationships with them, it's time to make sure you are both on board with how your partnership will work. While it's possible to have informal alliances where you each keep the other in mind when business needs arise, it's better to create more formal agreements so each partner gives the arrangement the focus it needs to succeed.

Be sure to answer these questions:

- What do you each agree to do?
- Will there be a financial incentive? For example, will you provide a referral fee when you close a client your contact sent you? (While this may spur your partners to recommend you, we think it's equally valuable to avoid exchanging money to focus on helping each other find good clients.)

Some suggestions:

- When you send referrals, ask them to tell your referral partner you recommended they get in touch.
- Send your referral partner a quick email with the name and contact information of potential clients. Establish a plan to close the loop when a referral becomes a client. (For example, a quick "thank you" email may be the most appropriate way to touch base.) Even if you are not paying each other for referrals, you want to make sure the partnership stays relevant and top-of-mind, so it's important to keep close track of successful results.
- In some cases, it may be appropriate for one of you to personally introduce a possible client to the other contact instead of just offering your referral partner's name. Be sure you agree to these types of introductions if you're going to incorporate them. You don't want to waste your referral partner's time, so if you follow through with a formal introduction, make sure you find out enough about the potential client to know that he or she is a good contact and open to doing business with your referral partner.
- Think about how you can tap into your partner's email list, if they have one. Perhaps there are opportunities to help

promote an upcoming presentation or eBook with a special referral partner discount. Of course, you would offer to promote their specials, too. Alternately, you and your partner may decide to co-brand an eBook, survey, or other content, which would serve as a win-win for both of you.

- Don't forget about opportunities to cross-promote via social networks! Be sure you are "friends, fans, and followers" with all of your referral partners, and that they follow you, too. Make a point to retweet their content, showcase their posts on your Facebook page, and pass along their content through Google+ and LinkedIn. The more ways you can connect, the stronger and more fruitful your partnership is likely to be.

- If your partner is game, team up and leverage both of your client and customer lists by giving a presentation or webinar together. You could also try recording a YouTube video to cross-promote. This two-for-one approach could be a huge value for your customers.

QUALITY, NOT QUANTITY

Nothing will kill a referral partnership faster than one partner hearing from many possible clients who are not good fits for his or her business. Focus on quality of referrals, not quantity.

Maintaining Referral Partner Networks

Agree to work together consistently. Arrange follow-ups, either in person, on the phone, via social networks, or via email. Make sure you create meaningful opportunities to touch base so they aren't a waste of time. When you communicate, consider asking each other a series of questions, such as:

- Is there anything I need to know about your business plans or goals that will affect my referrals?
- Have you re-envisioned your ideal client since last we spoke?
- How have my referrals worked out?
- Is there anything you would like me to know so I can be as helpful as possible in filling your sales funnel?

Add any other questions and share information that will help you continue to be relevant partners for each other. If you fail to touch base and assess if your referrals are successful, you cannot expect your partnership to blossom.

Get It Done

- This is a recurring theme in this book: before you do anything for your business, identify your goals and incorporate the steps you need to take to achieve them. The same is true for referral partners: decide what you need and how you can help. Then, do your research and identify the right people to help you accomplish your plans.
- Think about businesses that serve your clients. Be creative—do not limit yourself to the obvious.
- Consider both your in-person and online networks, and purposely grow them if necessary in order to connect with potential partners.
- Think of questions you want to ask people as you're learning more about them and their customers. What do you need to know to decide if someone is a good referral partner?
- Research the names of people you'd like to know, and identify who has the best reputation. Consider factors such as generosity, online and in-person identity, and personality. Remember that these are contacts you're going to want to

keep in your close network. Make sure you actually like and can work with the people you identify.

- Consider if formal membership networks suit your schedule, budget, and personality.
- Agree to fully vet possible referrals so you don't send a slew of unqualified leads to your partner.
- Finally, keep in touch and agree to regular updates so you can check in, tweak plans, and keep up-to-date about any changes in your referral partner's business goals that will affect who you send his or her way.

19 Staying Organized via Effective Goal Setting

Even when you have great partners and an effective marketing strategy, it's a challenge for any business owner to get everything finished, especially if you are busy with a full-time job and are creating your business on the side. How can you succeed when you already have a full plate of duties, assignments, excitement, and stress? There's an old saying, "That which gets measured gets done." When you identify and track your goals, it helps you accomplish the tasks you set out to do.

It takes discipline, commitment, and even a sense of humor to piece it all together. Stay focused on what you want to accomplish by setting goals, allocating your time wisely, and creating boundaries for you and your business.

Finding Time to Build a Reputation

As we mentioned earlier in the book, years ago, Hannah was a MOXIE starting her business on the side while working full-time.

When she was invited to speak to a group of eMBA students at a local college, she realized she had very little online clout. Worried that her experiences alone would not provide the credentials she needed to launch as a full-time entrepreneur, she decided to set some specific goals to improve her credibility. Having done her research, she knew blogging would help get her name out as a go-to expert in the career sphere. Her goal became to create a well-known blog.

Working a full-time job, teaching herself to blog, as well as running a family (including two boys under the age of six), meant she needed to find more hours in the day. Hannah snuck downstairs at 4:00 am every morning and diligently created content for her blog. These quiet hours in the morning were all she could steal before the chaos of getting the family ready for school and herself out the door for work.

Two things helped Hannah accomplish her business goals then and now. First, she blocks her time in one-hour increments, which helps her stick to a daily schedule and helps her accomplish her targets. Second, every six months, Hannah formalizes goals for the number of speaking engagements she plans to deliver. Using those targets, she builds an outreach campaign and enlists the help of colleagues and past acquaintances to introduce her to key contacts at local colleges and institutions. Without setting these speaking engagement goals, it would be easy for her to drop the ball or avoid the uncomfortable task of asking people she knows to introduce her to key contacts. Setting goals helps her follow through and translates into speaking gigs.

BUILD OR BORROW A SYSTEM THAT WORKS FOR YOU

Organization requires a system. Just setting goals is not always enough. Keeping your inbox clear and your workspace uncluttered, and knowing where to find files on your computer or in your office makes a world of difference. There is no one system that works for everyone, but there is certainly no shortage of help available online, in books, and from coaches.

Goal Setting

Setting goals for your business may take several attempts. Out of the gate, you may miss something important; that's okay and to be expected. Refine your goals carefully to make sure you can follow through on them.

Write Your Goals Down

Goals floating around in your head or on scraps of paper are useless. When you see your goals in black and white, it reinforces your commitment and reminds you what you are striving for. You are also more likely to hold yourself accountable and stay focused. If you don't believe us, we challenge you to try it. Create and use the social media marketing plan discussed in Chapter 13 to set and act on your marketing goals.

WRITE DOWN YOUR GOALS

Ninety percent of people do not have written goals, according to Ken Cheo, principal at Winfree Business Growth Advisors. Ken suggests the following benefits of writing goals down:

- It reinforces your commitment to them.
- It helps you remember them.
- It makes you accountable.
- It gives you focus.

You know what happens when you go shopping without a list; you will come home with some things you don't need and forget crucial items. Do not let your business plans be as haphazard as shopping without a list.

Besides being specific, measurable, and timely, Ken reminds us, "goals are no good unless you chunk them down into the daily, weekly, and monthly tasks required to accomplish them."

Chunk Your Goals Down

How many times have you started your New Year's Resolution and abandoned it weeks later? Why did the exercise or diet routine not stick? You paid for the gym membership; you would think that would be enough of an incentive to keep you going. However, for so many, it isn't.

Your goals need to be achievable within the timeframe allotted and broken down into bite-sized pieces. If the goal is too aggressive, vague, or large, it becomes unachievable.

For example, if your goal is to develop a blog with 12,000 hits a day, how will you reach that goal? If you developed a marketing plan like we discussed in Chapter 13, you've laid out your quarterly goals. Now chunk these into weekly bits.

These are some smaller, more achievable actions that could contribute to your larger goals:

- Write and post new blog entries five times a week.
- Guest post on other websites two times a month.
- Submit at least one article a week to an article directory (as discussed in Chapter 3).
- Comment on popular industry blogs five times a week.

Here are some measurable goals you will want to put some timeframes on:

- Increase Twitter followers by #_____.
- Increase Facebook likes by #_____.
- Acquire #_____ email subscribers.
- Sell #_____ products.

These specific actions have deadlines and will help drive you forward. Push yourself to do things that are uncomfortable or deliver a product that may not be absolutely "perfect," but good enough.

We encourage you to document goals related to these topics. Unfortunately, for the analytically minded business owner, there isn't one benchmark that guarantees profitability. Focus on quality not quantity. In the long run, it would be better for you to have fewer engaged contacts than more disengaged contacts. For example, you could convince 100 more people to subscribe to your newsletter, but if those 100 people are't that interested in what you have to say, then your open rate (how many people actually read your email) could decrease. Your first goal should always be to increase engagement.

Seth Godin updated and simplified the Zig Ziglar Goals Program in his book *Pick Four*. This is a simple, spiral book used to record your steps for achieving four goals by defining and evaluating daily activities for 12 weeks. This tool is valuable for several reasons. First, it provides a place for you to write down your larger goals and the smaller actions to achieve these goals. Once you write them down, you can share them with advisors, trusted colleagues, or a select group of people you choose to meet with for accountability. As an extra bonus, there is a page for you to write a summary of what worked, what didn't, and why. Godin says in his intro, "Most goal achievement is about figuring out all the ways you're unable to reach your goal. Only by identifying dead ends will you be lighting up the path that gets you where you want to go."

How to Allocate Your Time

Now that you have your goals printed and posted in front of you to see, look at how you can use your time more effectively and efficiently. There are many ways to get more done in less time. Though we can't add extra hours in the day, we can learn to use them well.

Here are some suggestions from Natalie Sisson, founder of The Suitcase Entrepreneur, featured in *Forbes*:

- Stay up an hour later or get up an hour earlier.
- Plan your week on Sunday evening.
- Turn off emails on your phone.
- Limit how often you check your email to twice a day.
- Keep an idea book to dump your spur of the moment thoughts into and revisit once a week.
- Focus on one activity at a time.
- Take breaks throughout the day; listen to your favorite song, take a quick walk, or check your favorite social network for updates.
- Don't answer the phone during scheduled work time. (If it is important, they'll leave a message.)
- Stop procrastinating and just DO it!
- Set a daily routine and communicate to your family.
- Delegate non-essential work and home tasks as much as possible.
- Define the start and end of your workday and work week. Hold tight to those hours.

THE POMODORO TECHNIQUE

Make a list of tasks you need to perform. Choose one. Pomodoro tends to work best when you choose strategic or complicated activities that require your undivided attention. Set a timer for 25 minutes. When the timer goes off, take a five-minute break. Continue this pattern and at the fourth occurrence you earn a longer break. You can learn more about this technique through their website: www.pomodorotechnique.com.

Know where you invest the most time. Keep a weekly journal if necessary and conduct an audit.

Look at the time you spend on small tasks or interruptions. These distractions are not usually real crises, they are just unproductive time; for example, the time you spent on the phone speaking with your website maintenance person about future updates, or the three spam emails you read before deleting. After a week, you should see a pattern of effective and ineffective activities, times during the day when you accomplish most and least, and how you treat high priority versus low priority tasks. Use the results from your audit to implement new behaviors and schedule best practices.

Entrepreneur.com asked several serial entrepreneurs for their top time management tips. Respondents mentioned making to-do lists, setting goals, and waking up early. One important tip not to overlook is scheduling personal time. Alma Steger, owner of Alma & Co., a direct seller of fashion jewelry and an advertising company, recommends you schedule personal time as you would a can't-miss business meeting. She admits that finding time to fit work and family into each day is a constant struggle. Alma says, "It's easy for entrepreneurs to be working 24 hours a day. Oftentimes, the best ideas come during your down time."

Leverage Support Wherever You Can Find It

Sometimes we all need a little help from our friends. Doug McSorely, an IT consultant, explains his family and friends helped him through the hard times. Doug says, "You have to have a support system because you are off on your own, and you're going to have good days and bad days. If you have a great support system, that will really help you keep grounded and focused on the tasks at hand."

If you need someone to bounce ideas off, or a fellow entrepreneur to brainstorm with, you can find an existing group or possibly pull together your own. You could also search for an existing master-mind group. Napoleon Hill's 1937 book, *Think and Grow Rich*, first described the concept of a mastermind group. It's commonly defined as, "a small club of like-minded advanced talents who meet periodically for mutual brainstorming/accountability sessions."

If you go to MeetUp.com and search for "entrepreneur," or "mastermind," you may find a local meeting. Another option is to find your local BNI meetings, which serve as "tip clubs," where business owners meet to share referrals and leads (described in depth in Chapter 18).

Post Across Multiple Social Networks with Ease

These tools make posting and sharing content across different social networks a breeze. From a single app, you can post content to multiple social networks, which is a huge time-saver.

Buffer
http://bufferapp.com/
Buffer works well if you plan to update your social networks several times a day. You can cross post to Twitter, LinkedIn, and Facebook from Buffer, all at the same time. It also auto schedules updates at optimum times based on when you get the most followers online to evenly space out your updates.

G++
http://gplusplus.me/
G^{++} is a browser extension (add-on) for Firefox and Chrome that turns Google+ into an integrated social networking platform. You can post status updates to Twitter directly from Google+. You can even like, comment, and post to Facebook directly from Google+.

IFTTT

https://ifttt.com/

If This Then That (IFTTT) is a tool with many time-saving features. By using a simple formula, IFTTT can carry out many Internet tasks for you, such as send you a text every time someone tags you on Facebook, share your newest blog post on LinkedIn, or call to remind you about a scheduled meeting. You create a "recipe" based on the task you need automated. If you don't want to create your own recipe, you can use one another user created. To find recipes, go to Browse (http://ifttt.com/recipes) and choose from Popular, Hot, What's New, or search for terms to find all recipes that use a certain channel, trigger, or action. For example, you could search "Facebook" to find all IFTTT recipes for Facebook.

TweetDeck

www.tweetdeck.com

TweetDeck lets you monitor all your social networks from a single dashboard. You can collect your Twitter mentions (when someone on Twitter uses your name) in one column, and your favorite Twitter list of experts in another column. Organizing your Twitter interaction ensures you will not miss an important mention or tweet. Add another column for Facebook updates and another for LinkedIn status updates and you are ready to go! TweetDeck also makes it easy to schedule updates and tweets in the future. Currently owned by Twitter, this tool simplifies your social networking efforts and is a favorite of many power Twitter users. (We both use this tool ourselves.) Unfortunately, TweetDeck does not allow you to post to Google+ at this time.

> **⇒ TIP**
>
> Someone who sees your automated tweet may expect that you are at your computer sending it at that moment. While your customers may not mind if you set up some scheduled tweets, be sure to add a personal touch when you can. For example, with a handwritten note, a quick phone call, an email, or a private message on Facebook or Twitter.

While it is easy to cross-post to more than one social network simultaneously, and it seems very productive to plan your social media activity using these tools, every network is different; the way you communicate on the networks should be different, too. For example, on Twitter, you may include a hashtag with your update, but the # looks funny and out-of-place if it cross-posts to Facebook or LinkedIn. Try to avoid regularly cross-posting your social media updates.

HootSuite

www.hootsuite.com

HootSuite is a social networking dashboard that allows you to monitor and share content across many different networks such as Twitter, Facebook, and LinkedIn. A major difference between HootSuite and TweetDeck is that you can update your Google+ and LinkedIn accounts from HootSuite.

Productivity Tools

Experiment with some of these free or almost free tools to help you create to-do lists, schedule meetings, or automate time-consuming tasks.

TeuxDeux—teuxdeux.com: This Web-based app is also available as an iPhone app ($2.99). It allows you to create to-do lists by day and category, and then cross them off when you are done.

Wunderlist 2—www.6wunderkinder.com/wunderlist: No matter what needs to be done, from shopping lists to projects and to-do's, Wunderlist can manage it all. You can share and print your lists or access them via your mobile device.

Astrid—www.astrid.com: Another to-do list manager, Astrid is a super easy way to keep on top of all you have to do and, even better, it is available for both iOS and Android.

WorkFlowy www.workflowy.com: This lets you create lists and take notes. You can even reuse a checklist or list of actions if it worked for you before.

Goal Setting and Planning Tools

These tools (paper and electronic) come recommended by thenextweb.com, a popular online publication providing Internet users with the latest news on technology, business, and culture.

Paper Tools
Dave Seah's Emergent Task Planner—http://davidseah.com/blog/node/the-emergent-task-planner: Learn how to structure your day to make sure you don't try to take on too much, and how to get the most out of your day with the things you want to get done the most.

Productive Flourishing Free Planners—http://www.productive-flourishing.com/free-planners: This site has free paper planning sheets that can help you figure out what method of planning works best for you.

Electronic Tools
Remember the Milk—www.rememberthemilk.com: Create your tasks and check them off, see what events are coming up, and receive reminder emails.

IQTell—http://iqtell.com: This app pulls all your files, favorite sites, online accounts, and email, all together in one place to let you manage and access your business and productivity tools from anywhere. This tool is in beta.

Schedule Clients

The following list of tools comes from two sources, ReadWrite.com, and Freelancefolder.com, providing ideas and support for freelance workers.

Acuity Scheduling—www.acuityscheduling.com: The basic version is free and provides limited personalization. It provides online appointment scheduling for a single calendar.

ClickBook—www.clickbook.com: ClickBook's basic account is free. Additional functionality is available for a fee. This tool targets client-service providers.

Doodle—www.doodle.com: Doodle does not require you to register or sign up. Just email your poll of meeting times to a group (large or small) and easily find a time to meet. There is a BookMe feature, for a monthly fee, that allows your customers to schedule and book services online and syncs with your calendar.

TimeTrade—www.timetrade.com: Email or post your online scheduling link and let people book appointments with you. You can connect to your Outlook, iCal, or Google Calendar so you never have to worry about double-booking.

TimeBridge—www.timebridge.com: TimeBridge is a Web application that makes it incredibly easy to schedule meetings and follow up after you meet. Think of them as your calendar-wrangling, agenda-making, note-taking, team-motivating, secret weapon in the battle against workplace inefficiency.

Congregar—www.congregar.com/create: Congregar lets you create a new event to schedule right from the home page, preview what the emailed poll will look like, and then move immediately to inviting people. Done, end of story.

WhenIsGood—www.whenisgood.net: WhenIsGood is a bare bones app. Like Doodle, there is no sign-up required. It has a highlighted calendar grid for choosing a range of dates, and it works the same whether you're setting up the poll or responding.

Meeting Wizard—www.meetingwizard.com: Meeting Wizard will help organize meetings. You can send online invitations to schedule meetings and events. It lets you propose optional dates, manage responses, and it sends automatic reminders.

SnapAppointments—www.snapappointments.com: SnapAppointments is free for a single user, making it a nice option if you intend to meet with clients. Some of its features include an online calendar that syncs with your mobile devices, and a "book an appointment button" for your website.

Appointy—www.appointy.com: Sole proprietors who use Google Calendar to manage appointments will appreciate the tools offered by Appointy. The online scheduling system is linked to Google Apps and syncs with Google Calendar in real-time.

Get It Done

As you embark on your new journey and juggle your startup with perhaps a full-time job, find a system and tools that work for you. If you decide to use automating systems and processes to save time, be sure to add that personal touch every once in awhile, through a hand written note, a quick phone call, an email, or a private message on Facebook or Twitter.

Set Measurable Goals and Write Them Down

Whether you keep track of your goals on a piece of paper or electronically does not matter. What is important is that you right them down and hold yourself accountable.

Chunk Goals into Manageable Pieces

Make sure your goals are small enough to accomplish. Nothing will overwhelm you faster than a huge task that seems insurmountable. Chunk complex tasks into smaller bits.

Decide How to Allocate Your Time

Know where you invest the most time. Keep a weekly journal if necessary and conduct an audit.

Leverage Support Wherever You Can Find It

Find existing groups of like-minded entrepreneurs for support. Your choices include joining a mastermind group, searching MeetUp.com for local meetings, or investigating BNI meetings. If you come up empty handed, you could always start your own.

Finally, experiment with some of the tools listed in this chapter to improve how you manage your time and activities.

20 Social Sharing— Tools and Applications

I f a tree falls in the forest and nobody hears it, does it make a sound? It is a good question to ask yourself when you think about your business and your social media efforts. Posting tweets, updating your LinkedIn status, and filling your Facebook, Pinterest, and Google+ pages with interesting and informative content won't do much for you unless you have a little help amplifying your message online.

Social sharing is the term for this amplification. It encourages your readers and online community to become allies who spread your content. The result? You can increase your traffic, extend your reach, and improve your search engine optimization results.

Social sharing can include everything including emailing an article to a friend, posting a link to a blog post on Twitter, Facebook, Google+, or LinkedIn, or simply "liking" a story online. When you create content (for example, a blog post, an eBook, or status updates for your social media streams) that helps people and provides valuable resources, they are more likely to pass it along to their communities. When they do, this gives your information even more traction online and can exponentially expand your reach.

> ⇨ **TIP**
>
> If you are giving an important speech in a room full of people, but you have laryngitis, you will ask for a microphone. Similarly, you will want to amplify what you post online via social sharing tools.

What Inspires People to Share?

The New York Times Consumer Insight Group researched why people share content online. Participants in their research acknowledged that social sharing is nothing new—pre-Internet, we would share information at the lunch table or on the phone with our friends. While the mechanisms for sharing have changed, we still have the same urge to let people we know about things we think they will enjoy. The study highlights the following five reasons people share information online:

1. To bring valuable and entertaining content to others—94 percent carefully consider how the information they share will be helpful to others.
2. To define ourselves to others—68 percent share to give people a better sense of who they are and what they care about.
3. To grow and nourish our relationships—78 percent share information because it allows them to stay connected to people.
4. Self-fulfillment—69 percent share information because it allows them to feel more involved in the world.

5. To get the word out about causes or brands—49 percent say sharing allows them to get the word out about products or services, and potentially change opinions or encourage action.

Some additional interesting statistics from the study:

- 85 percent of the people say reading other people's responses helps them understand and process information and events.
- 73 percent say they process information more thoroughly when they share it.

The study suggests the following key factors to keep in mind that influence sharing behavior:

- It's important to appeal to consumers' motivation to connect with each other, not just with your brand. Remember, people want to share useful content and information; they don't want to share a blatant ad for you, your products, or services. When you provide information, advice, and useful news and details, people will want to share it because it helps their friends.
- Trust is a big factor. Make sure you don't do anything that would make your community doubt your motivations. Don't pass along anything unless you're sure it will be useful.
- Keep it simple so you don't muddle the message. This is why photos are great to share; they are simple and speak for themselves.
- Appeal to humor. When you start to notice items that go viral (get shared thousands of times online), you'll see that humor (and the cute factor) often have a lot to do with their success.
- Embrace urgency. When there is up-to-the-minute news, and it's applicable to your community, get on board and share it with them.

What You Should Share

Your creativity is the only thing that limits the types of things you can share online. An article by Ann Handley in *Entrepeneur* says, "Websites that facilitate sharing generate seven times more mentions online than those that don't." The article asks the all-important question: "How do you grease the sharing skids? How do you get folks to share your stuff online?"

Ann suggests, "Create things they'll want to pass around or embed on their own blogs or sites." One very popular form of content people share is *infographics*. An infographic is a visualization depicting some type of information, usually involving statistics or numbers about a particular topic. Infographics are hot today because audiences appreciate visuals that help convert complex information into easy-to-follow images. Other things you may want to consider sharing include:

- eBooks you wrote
- Special reports, or white papers you wrote
- Podcasts or blog talk radio programs
- YouTube videos
- Pictures and other visuals, including charts detailing important statistics and data
- PowerPoint slide decks (you can share these via SlideShare)

Best Ways to Share Information

Make it as easy as possible for other people to pass along your content. The best way to do this is to install applications on your website—buttons that make it easy for people to share your information. When you and your agents create your website, make sure you incorporate these sharing buttons as prominently as possible. As you begin to win increasing numbers of shares, consider using tools that show how many people have shared your content. Sometimes, when people notice that others have shared something (because there is a number right there on the button), they will be convinced to share it as well.

Developers consistently create and launch new sharing tools, so you'll want to keep an eye on what's available so you can stay up to date. One good way to keep up with the latest trends is to read a variety of different blogs, including blogs by thought leaders in the blogging community, such as:

- **ProBlogger:** http://problogger.com
- **Copyblogger:** http://www.copyblogger.com
- **Social Media Examiner:** http://www.socialmediaexaminer.com
- **Chris Brogan's blog:** http://www.chrisbrogan.com
- **Jeff Bullas:** www.jeffbullas.com

You can assume they'll either be sharing information about up-to-date options for your website and blog, or using the best tools themselves.

Tools to Make it Easier for People to Share Your Content

Webpages with buttons inviting you to pass along their content on social media sites such as Twitter, Pinterest, LinkedIn, or Facebook, are engaging in social sharing. Be sure to give your readers the option to easily share your content by including the right technological tools on your blog.

You can use a catchall service, such as:

- **AddThis**—http://www.addthis.com: It works as a popup so it's not overly intrusive
- **ShareThis**—http://sharethis.com
- **Sociable**—http://wordpress.org/extend/plugins/sociable: This is a WordPress plugin
- **Yoast**—http://yoast.com: Includes tracking in Google Analytics

TIP

Make sure you include buttons for Google+ to allow people to +1 your site, which will help with your find-ability on Google.

Invite People to Interact via Other Social Networks

Decide if you want to share your Twitter or Facebook stream on your blog. This is one way to get people who follow you in one place (for example, your blog) to keep in touch on another network, assuming you use the networks for professional posts only (since they will be posted on your business page). You've probably seen this on other blogs. If you want to incorporate these crossover sharing tools, Google {add social widgets} to find ways to include information directly from your Twitter, Facebook, Flickr, and other sites.

Get It Done

Consider it part of your job to incorporate social sharing tools on your website. Use the suggestions in this chapter or see what other websites you like and choose your favorites to incorporate on your site.

TWITTER BUTTONS = SEVENFOLD SHARING

Websites that display Twitter sharing buttons link to Twitter nearly seven times more often than sites that do not display tweet buttons. Among the 10,000 largest websites, those that feature Twitter share buttons are, on average, mentioned in 27 tweets that contain a link back to the site. In comparison, those not featuring tweet buttons are mentioned, on average, in only four tweets that contain a link back to the site.

21 Word of Mouth on the Web

Since it's likely you're not only just a business owner (or prospective business owner), but also a consumer, it's no surprise that people don't trust advertising as much as recommendations from people they know. That is why social sharing is so important—when you convince people to share your information via their networks, you begin to infiltrate their networks, too! The numerous sites to rank and rate businesses and products wouldn't exist if people didn't turn to those online recommendations and reviews for information before making purchasing decisions.

The online journal *Social Commerce Today* highlighted a Nielsen Global Trust in Advertising report, which surveyed more than 28,000 Internet respondents in 56 countries. According to the study:

> *"92 percent of consumers say they trust recommendations from friends and family above all other forms of advertising—an increase of 18 percent since 2007. Online consumer reviews rank as the second most trusted source, with*

70 percent of global consumers surveyed online indicating they trust messages on this platform, an increase of 15 percent in four years. Ranking third, fourth and fifth are editorial content (58%), branded websites (58%), and opt-in emails (50%) respectively. Traditional forms of advertising using media such as television, print, and radio rank lower, and have seen a significant drop—as much as 24%—since 2009."

With so many people relying on word-of-mouth, you don't want to ignore this aspect of your social media strategy. The *Social Commerce Today* article notes, "What is of greatest importance is that your social media engagement be marked by authenticity and transparency. People want to be told the truth. They want their interactions with you to be validated by a genuine personal response. And they want the acknowledgement that what they have to say matters."

This brings up two important points: One, you need to monitor what people say about you and your business online, and two, you need to respond when people comment or ask questions about your business, products, or services. Be sure to check Chapter 22 for information about how to track what people say about you online.

Buzz vs. Word of Mouth

In Chapter 17, which is about how to solicit buzz for your business, we encouraged you to provide content people will want to discuss and pass around. While it shares some qualities with buzz, word-of-mouth is more about interacting with customers so they are willing to go the extra mile to help you succeed. While buzz can be incidental—someone sharing something because they felt good about it or because they think it's cute—you will succeed at word-of-mouth when you can convince people to go out of their way to recommend you. It is the difference between someone sharing a blog you wrote (a simple, one-click act) because they thought it was helpful and provided good content, and someone making a concerted effort to post a review or otherwise recommend you to their contacts.

Consider word-of-mouth to be a two-way conversation. Your goal is to attract allies who will spread the word about you and your business via their networks, even if it requires more than just a click.

HOW TO GENERATE WORD-OF-MOUTH SUPPORT

How can you co-opt this kind of support? We believe the best way to solicit positive word-of-mouth is by being the best at what you do, and by listening and talking to people online so they are compelled to go out of their way for you. Entrepreneur.com excerpted these ideas from Gail Goodman's book, *Engagement Marketing: How Small Business Wins in a Socially Connected World* (Wiley, 2012).

DO SOMETHING SPECIAL

Just as Panera Bread engaged a large audience when the story about the soup they made for a dying grandmother went viral, consider how you can provide outrageously great customer service that provides a personal touch. Gail offers these suggestions:

> **Consulting practice:** *"Send clients small gifts, such as cookies or gift cards, once in a while, as a thank you for their business."*

> **Bank:** *"Offer biscuits to customers' dogs in cars at the driver-up teller window."*

> **Retail shop:** *"Personally deliver goods during special circumstances, such as an illness, birth of a new baby, or death of a family member."*

ENCOURAGE CUSTOMERS TO STAY IN TOUCH

Encourage your customers to stay in touch with you. Ask them to join your mailing list (see Chapter 16 for ideas to convince them to join),

continued from page 309

incite them to engage via your Facebook page by posting useful data, and prompt them to add you to their Google+ circles and to follow you closely on Twitter. Good marketing and customer service always translate into positive word-of-mouth. Gail suggests trying these types of enticements to maintain continued engagement:

Free information: Provide ongoing reports, newsletters, expert tips, tele-classes, and to-do checklists.

Special events: Nonprofits or associations can invite people to members-only events, as can businesses with retail or office space.

Birthday cards: Offer people discounts during their birthday month in exchange for their contact information.

Discounts: Many people will give their emails in exchange for the promise of ongoing discounts or coupons.

CREATE RAVING FANS

Once they like (or even love) you and your business, keep your customers engaged so they will rave about you and your business (If this sounds a lot like "buzz," it is similar. The difference is that, in this chapter, we will give you specific ideas for things to ask your audience to do once they are raving fans, beyond simply sharing, or buzzing, about you and your business.) Gail offers the following suggestions for ideas and content to share to create raving fans:

Question and Answer: Ask a question (or answer one) and invite people to weigh in on the subject. (This is a great idea, which is why it comes up in so many different chapters!)

Sharing Information: Provide original content through blogs, whitepapers, case studies, and infographics. Also, share other people's content, such as a news item, article, or blog post, and add your expert analysis or feedback.

Discussion: Gail says, *"Fill in the blank discussion starters are a great way to get people to participate."* For example, "I spent Small Business Saturday shopping at _____."

continued from page 310

Promotions and Announcements: Share offers and company news. Give samples, trial offers, coupons, special sales, eBooks, reports, and free consultations as part of special promotions.

Events: Deliver workshops or training classes, seminars, user groups or conferences, private sales, parties and open houses, trade shows, sidewalk sales, or demonstrations. You name it, you can create it.

Online Endorsement Sites

Do you make a big purchase before reading reviews? If you're buying an expensive item (such as a refrigerator) or an inexpensive one (such as a book), it's likely you check online to see what people say about the product. You might look at Yelp before you take your in-laws to a new restaurant, or you might read Amazon reviews about any item you may want to purchase.

Identify the places where it makes most sense for people to review your business, and then create profiles on those platforms. Depending on what you do, you may want to seek local business write-ups, using services such as the ones listed here. (If your business is not geographically bound, or if you are only selling services and not products, you'll gravitate to different options.) Consider the following review services and investigate if you should encourage your customers to write reviews for you.

Google Places for Business

This is a free service. Although there are locally targeted advertisements available, Google Places for Business allows you to literally put your business on the map by showing your location. Their materials indicate that you can choose a "service area" instead of a specific address when you list yourself, so you'll use one listing per physical location, even if you cover multiple locations. (Remember, a map comes up with these listings.)

Yahoo! Local

Listings here are similar to Google Places for Business. They have a map, landing page, and reviews. You can include information about your business in the profile. Just because Google is the most popular for search isn't a reason to totally ignore Yahoo!

Local.com

You can get a free listing on this site that aims to help "your business get found."

Yelp.com

You can consider this not only a review site, but also a social community. You can add friends, gain a reputation, comment, and display profile pictures. As a popular and visited site, it is probably one of the better sites for you to use due to how well it ranks in Google and search engines. While some online forums and business owners complain about Yelp because the site sometimes removes suspicious-seeming reviews that may be legitimate, it is one of the better-known review sites, so it is worth investigating.

Citysearch.com

With a format similar to Yelp!, this site includes reviews, compiles "best of" lists, and votes for favorite businesses by category.

MerchantCircle.com

MerchantCircle incorporates deals and coupons from its members.

InsiderPages.com

This site categorizes reviews by city, including a special category for top doctors.

Angie's List

Founded in 1995 as a printed publication, Angie's List has been online since 1999. It charges a membership fee for consumers seeking to read and post reviews. (Listings are free for companies, though.) Even with the fees, they have over 1 million members, with over 40,000 reviews posted each month.

Third-Party Sellers

Don't forget, it will be important to have high rankings and reviews on the sites that sell your products. For example, if you're an author, Amazon reviews are most important. If you sell on eBay or Etsy, make sure you pay attention to your reviews there. When you ship products, make sure you set realistic expectations. For example, unless you have the resources necessary to follow through, don't promise same-day shipping.

Soliciting Reviews

If you choose to put your hat in the ring for some of these review sites, how can you convince your customers to help you out by word-of-mouth? Remember, you want to be so remarkable that clients and customers want to stand on rooftops to tell everyone about you and your business. However, there is another factor to word-of-mouth: telling people exactly what you want them to do. If you want reviews, you're probably going to have to solicit them.

Here are some ideas to help move your best customers from fans to allies:

Ask for Reviews

Depending on the nature of your business, you can consider different options. Remember, even if they love you, your customers are busy and unlikely to consider how they can help you unless you make it as easy as possible for them. If you sell merchandise, include a note with deliveries letting customers know how helpful reviews are for your small business and ask them to take their valuable time to help. List the review sites you hope they visit, which should be prominently linked from your website. Another suggestion: set up an email to automatically contact a customer after a purchase to request a review. Include a link to your preferred review sites.

Guide the Customer

We are big fans of helping people help you, and one way you can garner the types of reviews that will make you proud is by giving your customers guidance regarding what to say in the review. For example, consider providing a list of questions for them to address in their reviews:

- How did our customer service go above and beyond your expectations?
- What are the best qualities of the products you purchased?
- Why would you recommend others become our customers?
- If you have experience with other service/product providers in our field or industry, please comment on how working with/purchasing from us was better.

Writing questions to guide your clients who may write reviews should help solidify in your mind how you want customers to think about you and your business.

Give Incentives

Some may consider this a bribe, but there is no rule against providing a reward to inspire people to give you good online word-of-mouth. Some companies offer a small discount on the next order in exchange for proof of an online review. If you are not successful at winning reviews when you ask for them, consider sweetening the pot a bit by offering a discount or bonus.

What NOT to Do

No matter how easy it may seem, we do not recommend that you purchase or pay for reviews under any circumstances. There are people who solicit businesses and offer to write rave reviews for as little as a few dollars each. While it may be tempting, review sites are getting better at identifying people who indiscriminately seem to post reviews for companies they are unlikely to have patronized. In fact, these scam artists are actually causing some sites to remove reviews written by honest reviewers because they arouse suspicion—that is how vigilant online review sites have become in order to maintain their credibility as go-to sites for customers to evaluate potential purchases.

While purchasing reviews may seem like a quick fix, the ethical implications and the possibility of having your reviews (or even your listings) removed from the sites you need to help promote your credibility should be enough to deter you from accepting fake review services.

Hopefully, it goes without saying that you should not create your own reviews, either.

What About Bad Reviews?

First, don't freak out if someone provided a less than positive review. Use this as an opportunity to improve your services or products, and go out of your way to try to improve that customer's experience. Even if someone posts something that isn't fair or does not characterize the experience in an accurate description, you have an opportunity to learn something. Post a reply, and try to make amends with the client. Hopefully, you can fix things in a way that will inspire him or her to become a fan.

How to Get "Social" Word-of-Mouth

While the online sites dedicated to reviews will benefit many small business owners, for people with non-local, service, or consulting businesses, those sites may not be the best way to garner online word-of-mouth support. Use the following social media tools to promote specific positive word-of-mouth for your business.

LinkedIn Recommendations

While often considered the purview of people looking for traditional jobs, strong LinkedIn recommendations are helpful for any professional or business owner, especially for someone who provides consulting or other services. When you have recommendations on LinkedIn, it will help possible customers recognize your strengths. The fact that LinkedIn ties recommendations directly to the recommender's profile helps legitimize the reviews—the chances of scamming reviews is low. Customers can also recommend your products or services via your LinkedIn company profile.

There are a few best practices when it comes to asking for recommendations on LinkedIn:

- It is not necessarily better to have many endorsements. You do not need 65 recommendations. In fact, some people say that they are suspicious when people have what they consider to be an excessive number of endorsements.
- Reciprocal recommendations ("I'll recommend you if you recommend me") are not as valuable as when someone writes about you without expecting you to return the favor. Miriam was once conducting a workshop, and a participant found a colleague who had many recommendations. She said, "Wow, that's impressive." Upon further investigation, each recommendation was reciprocal. All of a sudden, it seemed less impressive.

Asking for recommendations on LinkedIn is easy. (Maybe a little too easy!) All you need to do is follow "Profile" from your LinkedIn toolbar and select "Recommendations." Then, you can choose the job (or business) you want a recommendation for and select people to ask for the endorsement.

Here are some tips to get the best recommendations possible:

- NEVER ask more than one person per message. Each recommendation request should be personalized and specific to the endorser.
- Recognize that most people have no idea what to say and can use some guidance. It is your job to help steer your recommenders along the right path. For example:

> *"I am updating my LinkedIn profile, and since you're a repeat customer, I'd be honored if you would write a recommendation for me. As you may guess, in this business, potential customers are looking for a few things: top-notch customer service, on-time delivery and quality products."*

You can also request recommendations for your business if you have a product.

When you provide information that helps your recommender know what you want him or her to say, it goes a long way to ensuring he or she actually writes out a reply, and that the recommendation has information that is actually useful to you.

LinkedIn Skills

In addition to recommendations on LinkedIn, there is another option for you to solicit endorsements. If you spend any time on LinkedIn, you probably already noticed you can endorse people for their skills simply by clicking the skill on their profile.

If you haven't already updated your profile to include skills, just edit your profile and click on the bar that asks you to add skills. Add at least five skills to make sure you'll have a complete profile, and add them in the order that you would like people to endorse you. If you're lucky, your top selections will show up for people who visit your profile and are inclined to endorse your skills.

People are likely to notice if you tout yourself as an expert in certain areas, yet have no one endorsing you via the one-click option. In addition to the obvious benefit of potential clients seeing many endorsements, LinkedIn's search algorithm will include these third-party endorsers as a factor in determining how to rank keyword and other searches on LinkedIn.

Unlike recommendations, where you want to avoid reciprocal endorsements, it would be difficult for the casual observer to notice if the skill and expertise endorsements were two-way, so feel free to reciprocate if you can. As a business owner, it is likely you will be receiving endorsements from people whose skills you cannot reciprocate anyway.

While LinkedIn has been aggressive about informing people about this feature, you may need to ask people if they can endorse skills on your profile. Send a specific note to individuals asking for their assistance. For example:

"I really appreciate you attending my recent presentation at the Athens Chamber of Commerce. Thanks for your kind note afterwards, and invitation to connect on LinkedIn. I'd be so honored if you'd consider endorsing my 'public speaking' skill on LinkedIn. All you need to do is visit my profile (include the link) and scroll down to where I list skills. Click on the blue plus sign next to the skill. This would really mean a lot to me. Thank you for your consideration, and please don't hesitate to get in touch if I can do anything for you."

LinkedIn Company Pages

The LinkedIn recommendations and skills endorsements boost your personal LinkedIn cache, but you can also solicit recommendations on your LinkedIn business page. LinkedIn allows you to add "Products" on your business page, and then you can easily request a recommendation from that page. All you need to do is send a link to the customer you'd like to recommend you. Use some of the same techniques suggested for requesting personal recommendations when you ask; suggest some topics for clients to write about when they recommend your product.

Crossover Buzz and Word-of-Mouth Endorsements on Social Media

Some people believe having more contacts, followers, and people in your circles (in the case of Google+) are akin to tacit endorsements. It is a bit of a stretch to label the "get more followers" strategy as a word-of-mouth approach, but don't forget that you have a better chance to get both buzz and word-of-mouth when people are connected and engaged with you.

For example, if you have an expanded LinkedIn community, and you post updates, you are more likely to capture some word-of-mouth when your community shares your information. Similarly, when you have active Twitter, Facebook, and Google+ communities, you can mine those connections for word-of-mouth shares.

Posting Reviews on Your Own Site

Another option to consider is soliciting and posting endorsements on your own site. When you receive emails from satisfied customers, be sure to ask if they would mind if you post their praise on your site, and suggest they share their endorsements on LinkedIn or any other site you use to collect recommendations.

Go High Tech

Howard Stephen Berg, of SpeedReadingUniversity.com, wrote a post for DotComSecrets.com where he suggested a unique approach to soliciting testimonials. He uses www.SimpleVoiceBox.com, which he says, "*At first glance . . . seems like a program that will just take phone messages.*" However, he uses it to capture verbal endorsements. In follow-up communication with customers (you can use an autoresponder tool or, depending on your business, actually contact customers individually), he sends customers the phone number to one of his SimpleVoiceBox.com accounts. Howard notes,

> "*This enables me to record, and download their testimonials. I can then upload these recordings to my cloud, and link them to my products page to play for new prospective customers. It is a powerful way to get audio testimonials on auto pilot for your products and services.*"

Get It Done

- Designate time to purposefully thinking about how you can provide products or services that will generate positive word-of-mouth. How can you go above and beyond what most people would expect? Use the suggestions included in this chapter and your own ideas. Set high goals for customer service and you'll be well on your way to getting great word-of-mouth.
- If applicable, choose the online review sites you want to join, and make sure to follow through on each site by creating a

complete profile. Then, make sure to be specific when you direct your customers to the sites. Consider offering incentives for reviews, but never purchase reviews from anyone.

- Create a list of questions you'd like clients and customers to answer or consider when they write a review for you. Doing this exercise will help you clarify what you hope to offer, and should help drive your business model.

- Don't forget about social media reviews, especially via LinkedIn. Many people believe having followers and many community members in your social media sites represents a little piece of word-of-mouth.

22 Monitoring Your Activity—Tools and Tips

For any business using social media, it's vital to measure engagement. What's the point of soliciting positive buzz and word of mouth unless you monitor what people say? However, you don't need to track and monitor everything you are doing every minute of every day to succeed with your social media plans. Have you ever been on a diet and tried weighing yourself every day? All of your careful eating and exercise can feel like a waste if you don't see results immediately. Similarly, if you do not see immediate increases in subscribers, purchases, or new followers once you start your social media campaign, do not get discouraged. It will take time to realize your efforts and the results fluctuate from day to day. Monitor weekly trends, monthly new subscribers, or event specific outcomes, rather than hourly or daily results.

⇨ TIP

Some of the most important engagement measurements include the open rate for your e-newsetter, time spent on your website, number of blog comments, and number of retweets or shares via social media.

One Must-Have Tool: Google Analytics

Google Analytics is one tool you MUST set up and use. It is robust and has features to track almost all of your online efforts. Either you or the person who created your website can learn how to set up Google Analytics by reading the guide available on Google's page at http://www.google.com/analytics. While Bing also has a set of analytic tools, Google Analytics is the go-to tool.

> ⇨ **TIP**
>
> To keep up with the latest and greatest features of Google Analytics, follow their blog at http://analytics.blogspot.com/.

Google Analytics will track all of the following:

Number of Unique Visitors

The best indication of your site's overall traffic is unique visitors, which refers to the number of individuals who visit your website. (This is different from the total number of page views, as one person can visit many pages during a visit on your site. Additionally, you may have some fans who visit your site multiple times a day, which might bring up your page views, but not your unique visitors.)

Page Views

The cumulative number of individual pages your visitors click. If your page views are higher than your unique visitors, that indicates your audience finds your content engaging and visits multiple pages.

Search Engine Traffic

The amount of traffic referred to your site through search engines, such as Google or Bing. This number will give you a good indication of whether you're capturing the right keywords and tapping into useful SEO strategies.

Bounce Rate

This term represents the visitors who come to your site, but then immediately leave before clicking on any other pages. Some say an average bounce rate is between 40 and 50 percent. A higher bounce rate may indicate visitors reached your site expecting to find something they didn't see.

Conversion Rate

This is the percentage of visitors to your site who take an action you encouraged them to take, such as signing up for your newsletter, going to a sales page, or clicking through to an older post. Not all of your visitors will convert (an average conversion rate is two to three percent), so if you find this number is low, evaluate the wording on your sales page or your call to action. This will only work if you set up "goals" within your Google Analytics account, which we talk about later in this chapter.

Review your Google Analytics weekly, and look for upward trends like more conversions, unique visitors, and page views. Notice what search terms bring the most traffic to your site and which posts are most popular. However, don't be overly concerned about achieving a specific number of visitors, for example. Measure success not by numbers on your blog, but by engagement (how many people are interested in what you are doing and willing to forward your content) and sales. Remember, you do not necessarily need more visitors; you just need the ones who will buy what you are selling!

What Do You Know About Your Social Networking Traffic?

Do you get more traffic from Twitter, Facebook, LinkedIn, or one of the other networks? When you know the answer to this question, you can invest more time and attention to the networks on which you are more popular. Most social networks do not provide a lot of cumulative data or analytics for you to see how much traffic they refer to your site. This is where Google Analytics comes in. From your Google Analytics account, look at the report options on the left sidebar. Find "Traffic Sources," and under that, click on "Social." When you click on this button, you will see the option for "Sources." This report shows you how much traffic each social network sent to your site. You can even see which website pages visitors clicked most often.

When you know which social networks send the most visitors to your site, you can decide how to spend your time online. Let's say you've been spending a lot of time on Facebook posting new content and having conversations there, but Google Analytics shows you're not getting much traffic from Facebook. Conversely, you spent little time on Twitter, yet you've been getting a good amount of visitors from there. You could decide to change your Facebook strategies and tactics to try to get more traffic. Alternatively, you could decide to spend more time on Twitter because you are seeing results from your efforts there.

Setting Goals

Google Analytics allows you to set up and measure certain goals. Do you want to know how many visitors make it to your Contact Me page (also known as conversion rate)? Maybe you want to see, at a glance, how many people went to a specific sales page, but didn't buy anything. Google Analytics provides this type of conversion analysis and reporting if you've set up goals. From your Google Analytics page, you will have to create the goal. You may want to track how many people get to your sales page or contact form, or track e-commerce transactions. Within your Google Analytics goal setting page, enter the URL of the page on which you want to track conversion data. Creating goals can get a bit more complicated, so we recommend you follow the in-depth instructions provided by Google to ensure you set up your goals correctly. You can start here for more details: https://www.google.com/analytics/features/conversion-suite.html.

Is Your Traffic Coming From Mobile Devices?

Google's 2012 "Our Mobile Planet" report found that 80 percent of Smartphone users in the United States access social networks from their phones, and 55 percent visit more than once a day. Do you know how this applies to the people visiting your site?

Google Analytics clearly tells you what percentage of your traffic is coming from mobile devices. Use these data to evaluate your mobile traffic. If you see a significant number of visitors from mobile devices, you'll want to see how your site shows up on mobile devices and perhaps consider reformatting for mobile consumption.

GOOGLE WEBMASTER TOOLS

Visit www.google.com/webmasters/tools to sign up for Google's Webmaster tools, which will provide you extra insights and information about your website. To use these tools, Google requires you to add some code to your website, so you may want to ask your website developer to handle this when your site is created. Google Webmaster Tools are a great addition to Google Analytics and will help you monitor your site.

Using Social Sharing Tool Analytics

If you use social sharing buttons such as AddThis, ShareThis, Shareaholic, or other third-party sharing tools on your website (read all about social sharing tools in Chapter 5), they each come with built-in analytics, which show how many shares and clicks a post received. When you know what topics are shared the most, you can develop more of that content in future blog posts and discussions.

Track Your Twitter Successes

Steady follower growth and interactions are important, but are hard to track through Twitter. Crowdbooster (www.crowdbooster.com) provides details about your Twitter activity at a glance.

Crowdbooster's easy-to-view dashboard reports how many potential people were reached by your tweets, follower growth, number of retweets, number of mentions, new influential followers, and the best times to send tweets. It prompts you to respond to people who have mentioned you, too. Crowdbooster will even send you weekly email updates, prompting you to review and assess your performance. All this comes at a price of $9 per month. SocialBro (www.socialbro.com) is $6.95 per month. You can manage your Twitter lists, follow and unfollow accounts, and receive helpful analytics. Similar to Crowdbooster, SocialBro shows you the evolution of your number of followers, the number of tweets and retweets, and the best time to tweet.

Twitter Performance

TweetReach—www.tweetreach.com: Who is reading your tweets? How many people are retweeting? What is the measured impact of what you're putting out there? TweetReach shows you a breakdown of how your tweets perform (one retweet, two retweets, etc.), the percentage of tweets retweeted, and total replies.

FollowerWonk—www.followerwonk.com: We mentioned that this is a good tool for searching Twitter bios. However, it also can search users' Twitter account activities. You can learn more about your followers, and analyze and compare your own account against the competition.

Monitoring Yourself, Your Brand, and the Competition

Topsy

We've mentioned Topsy (topsy.com) before. Their free analytics show how the content you shared across Twitter and Google+ performed in two ways. Topsy shows a "mentions" graph so you can see, day by day, the number of times your Twitter name is mentioned in a tweet. You can also see a grid that lists your top-shared articles and the number of times each article was shared. It is helpful to see how your social sharing is doing, but it is also helpful for finding opportunities to connect and engage with people sharing your content.

In a post for SocialMediaExaminer.com, Laura Roeder, founder of LKR Social Media (a company that creates training courses for small businesses to learn how to leverage social media and online marketing), suggested the following topics business owners should track on Topsy:

- Your name
- Your company/brand name
- Your product name(s)
- Your competition
- Your industry
- Your website URL(s) (leave off the "www")
- Your email address

⤳ TIP

Set up Topsy alerts to receive summary emails showing when someone mentions you or your company on Twitter and Google+.

It is difficult to quantify the actual number of people who mention you just by skimming through the mentions in your Twitter stream. When you view the Topsy alert you set up with your name or company name, you can see the number of people who shared your tweet, and how many people shared that tweet. You can even dig deeper and see everyone who shared it. Topsy's reports demonstrate the power of social sharing, but more importantly, they show who has an influential network, and what updates are popular with your social network on a particular day.

WORDING, TIMING, AND LUCK

Several factors determine whether content goes "viral." These factors include the way the tweet or update is worded (does it grab the audience?), the time of day the update is sent (do enough people see it?), and luck. If you monitor the tweets and most-shared content, look for recurring patterns. Was it sent at the same time of day? Maybe you used a popular hashtag. Perhaps, by luck, an influential person with a vast network caught wind of your update and shared it with their network. (Be sure to publically thank them for their help and support!)

Google Alerts

Google does it again. They provide one of the best free tools around to monitor what is being said about you across the Web. All you need to do is set the right set of keywords (we suggest the same ones recommended by Laura Roeder) and identify what you want searched (websites, blogs, pictures, etc.), and Google will collect references to those keywords across the Web. You can either have the results fed to your RSS reader of choice or sent to you via email.

CREATING A SPECIAL URL TO TRACK CAMPAIGNS WITH GOOGLE

The Google URL Builder makes it simple to create custom links. Let's say you want to compare the traffic your email newsletter sends to your new eBook sales page, versus the traffic Twitter sends to your new eBook sales page. You can create a different URL for the different marketing campaigns and compare results.

First, access your website's Google Analytics page, then copy and paste the website URL you will be linking to in your social media promotion into Google Analytics URL Builder.

Remember to fill in the campaign information so you will know what it is later. These are three important parts of the section to complete: Campaign Source (where are you hosting the link—email, blog, etc.),

continued from page 330

Campaign Medium (the method you are using to share the link, such as email), and Campaign Name (what are you promoting—product or promo code). The rest you can leave blank.

Monitor Yourself and Others

Any of these tools can provide you with data and information so you can keep an eye on your business's online reputation. It is more important what you do with the information. If someone has mentioned your name, product, or business online, you want to know what he or she is saying. We hope you choose to respond, in a non-defensive way, to the bad as well as the good comments. When you apologize publically for mistakes made, you just might gain a new customer, or win back the trust of an old customer.

SocialMention—www.socialmention.com: Track and measure who is talking about you, your company, your product, or any topic related to your industry. SocialMention pulls data from hundreds of social media services to give you real-time information.

TwentyFeet—www.twentyfeet.com: TwentyFeet aggregates your activity from various social media platforms so you can get the full picture of your online presence. Then, you can determine which of your activities are most valuable.

WhosTalkin?—www.whostalkin.com: Similar to SocialMention, you can search for your own name or check out who is saying what across blogs, news feeds, social networks, videos, images, and forums.

Facebook's Built-In Analytics

Is one of your goals to gain new "likes" on your Facebook page? If you want to track and measure how many new "likes" you've acquired, and the demographics of your new likes, Facebook's analytics (https://www.facebook.com/insights) can do this. You can assess where the bulk of your readers are geographically located, especially if you are a local business. If you want to plan an in-person event, knowing where your audience resides will result in better planning and attendance. Maybe you are more interested in tracking which posts to your timeline receive the most hits. When you understand your network's needs, you can give them more of what they want! If you designate a specific month or week to try new "engagement tactics," like the ones we mention in Chapter 21, use Facebook's "people talking about this" numbers to compare against previous weeks.

Google+ Ripple

Google+ Ripple is an interactive diagram that shows which users share a Google+ post. You can find the Ripple of any public Google+ post by clicking on the small down arrow on the upper right corner of the post. Ripple shows how far your shares have gone, and how long they've lasted. Ripple provides a nice visual interpretation of the impact and reach of your content. This could identify future partners, collaborators, or allies. For example, if you notice someone has shared your content among others who also are within the same circles, this could be a niche community to interact with and learn more about. You may also want to research where these contributors share outside of Google+.

Additional Tools to Test Drive

While Google Analytics can track and measure almost everything you need, the following tools are all free, and have some interesting functionality to help shed more light on your online and social media accomplishments.

⤳ **TIP**

Mashable.com and SocialMediaExaminer.com are two helpful sources for keeping up with trends. Authoritative guest bloggers regularly contribute to these sites. When new tools hit the market, these sites are among the first to bring you the news.

Social Networking All in One

Buffer—www.bufferapp.com: When you use Buffer, you can set the tool to automatically send your status updates at the optimal time based on past performance or during times you specify. It also shows basic analytics on how your shares performed. The app connects to Twitter, Facebook, and LinkedIn, making it another good option to try. You may also want to try the Buffer app for Firefox, which allows you to simply click on the Buffer icon while you are on any website to set up a tweet or Facebook share.

Measure, Rate, or Compare Your Socialness

These tools help you see how your online presence is doing, compared to others. They also identify influencers you may want to interact with or at least follow. These measure overall impact and, over time, you should expect to see your score improve:

HowSociable—www.howsociable.com: Measure your impact online using their magnitude score. The score analyzes your level of activity online so that you can determine whether you have enough of a presence.

PeerIndex—www.peerindex.com: Determine your online authority and who your online brand advocates are. Learn which topics are best for you to focus on, and who to connect with to spread the word.

Klout—klout.com: Klout provides an influencer score based on your social media activity. You can look at your influencers and whom you influence to regularly share content that is of the highest quality from trusted sources. Klout is one of the more influential and important tracking tools. Generally, a score of 60 or above is considered influential.

Kred—kred.com: Similar to Klout, Kred mines social data to give you a Kred score. The score is a combination of your influence and your outreach activity. Kred measures how often you tweet or post, how people interact with you, and the growth of your audience. The site gives you a detailed breakdown of your score so that you know exactly where you should improve, and the areas that are working well for your company.

Track and Compare Web Traffic

It may feel a bit sneaky, but you can learn which keywords send the most traffic to your competitors and get a sense of how much traffic they have. Why would this be useful to know? With this information, you can indentify new keywords and find your online business rivals. Don't put too much stock into the traffic data (how many visitors they receive). The accuracy varies, especially when these tools measure less-visited sites. Use data from these tools for your own site as a benchmark. If the numbers misrepresent your traffic, assume a similar discrepancy for the sites you're researching.

- Compete.com
- Alexa.com
- Semrush.com

Get It Done

Must-Use Tool: Google Analytics

To keep up with the latest and greatest features of Google Analytics, follow their blog at http://analytics.blogspot.com.

Google Analytics will track all of the following, plus the results from your social networking activities:

- Unique visitors
- Page views
- Search engine traffic
- Bounce rate
- Conversion rate

What Do You Know About Your Social Networking Traffic?

Google Analytics helps you understand which social networks refer the most traffic to your site.

Setting Goals

Google Analytics allows you to set up and measure goals and conversion rates to measure the success of your marketing efforts.

Is Your Traffic Coming From Mobile Devices?

Google Analytics clearly tells you the percentage of traffic coming to your site from mobile devices.

Using Social Sharing Tool Analytics

If you use social sharing buttons such as AddThis, ShareThis, and Shareaholic, each come with built-in analytics.

Track Your Twitter Successes

Crowdbooster (www.crowdbooster.com) or SocialBro (www.social bro.com) will show you, at a glance, how your Twitter activity is going.

Monitoring Yourself, Your Brand, and the Competition

Topsy

Their free analytics show how the content you shared across Twitter and Google+ performed.

Google Alerts

Keep up-to-date on news and new web content mentioning you and your business, plus any other important keywords.

Monitor Yourself and Others

These tools help you monitor your company and social interactions across multiple social networks: SocialMention (www.socialmention.com), TwentyFeet (www.twentyfeet.com), and WhosTalkin (www.whostalkin.com).

Facebook Built-In Analytics

Facebook's analytics (https://www.facebook.com/insights) provide robust reporting about engagement on your Facebook page and the demographics of people who "like" your page.

Google+ Ripple

Google+ Ripple is an interactive diagram that shows which users share a Google+ post. Use this to track the reach of your post and find new people to engage with.

Additional Tools to Test Drive

Every day, it seems as if new tools enter the scene. Keep you finger on the social pulse by subscribing to these blogs: Mashable.com and SocialMediaExaminer.com.

Measure, Rate, or Compare Your Socialness

These tools help you determine how your online presence is doing, compared to others: HowSociable (www.howsociable.com), PeerIndex (www.peerindex.com), Klout (klout.com), and Kred (kred.com).

Conclusion

Keep in mind: while there are many tools, tips, and tricks to know when it comes to using social media, we hope you'll keep focused on the big picture. Use LinkedIn, Twitter, Google+, Facebook, and your own website to demonstrate your expertise, grow your networks, and learn new things. The most successful business owners who use social media recognize that it is not about how many followers you have, or how many people +1 or retweet your updates or blog posts. The most important factor that influences your success is how well you build, develop, and maintain relationships with your customers and clients, and also with the larger community, including your competitors.

We hope this message was clear throughout the book, but in case you missed it, we saved the most important "Get It Done" for the end.

Get It Done

Help other people. When you generously extend yourself and your expertise online, your business can only benefit from warm referrals from satisfied customers and your supportive social network.

Ask your network for help. Luckily, social media makes this easy. Don't be shy! Once you join or create a community, you will have a ready resource to get your questions answered. (Sometimes, even at two in the morning!)

Do one thing at a time. Don't be overwhelmed. Try to maintain a healthy work/life balance. (We know it's tough.) While at work, keep your focus on your audience of clients and customers, and keep moving ahead, one step at a time. When you do, your credibility, business, and income can exceed your expectations.

Be flexible. The only constant in life (and business) is change! Go with your gut—when something doesn't feel right, make a change. Things will probably turn out even better than you expected.

Keep in Touch!

Please let us know what was helpful in the book, and if there is anything else you need to know. Both of us blog frequently, so we may be able to answer your questions online! Find us on Twitter @Keppie_Careers (Miriam) and @CareerSherpa (Hannah), or via our websites: www.keppiecareers.com and www.careersherpa.com.

Appendix

We created these bonus chapters with tips and advice for people who are just starting new businesses, as well as for experienced entrepreneurs who are facing new challenges growing their businesses via social media. If you are exploring the idea of starting a business, but haven't settled on a specific idea, Bonus Chapter 1 is perfect for you. It provides ideas based on experiences of successful entrepreneurs, and includes resources and suggestions to help you identify a side gig. (Even if you already run a business, you could find some ideas there to expand your offerings.) If you have a business and anticipate growing pains as you try out these new and unfamiliar tools to attract clients and customers, the financial and legal information in Bonus Chapters 2 and 3 will be invaluable references.

We know first-hand that when you wear many hats it is easy to overlook some important operating details, especially those that seem overly academic or administrative. We hope these chapters help you along your journey, whether you are just starting out or taking the next logical steps for your business.

Selected Businesses That Fit the Second Income Model

You can monetize almost anything today. As the saying goes, "Necessity is the mother of invention," and every good business fills a specific need. These are some of the many businesses people leverage to earn money in unexpected ways:

- Miso Media, featured on the ABC television show *Shark Tank*, created a free app to teach users to play instruments. They actually make their money selling customers sheet music!
- Did you hear about the nine-year-old boy who built replicas of arcade machines out of old cardboard boxes and ended up with over $152,000 for his college fund? This heartwarming story of a young entrepreneur went viral, which sent people to his website. The website featured a short film about his arcade and asked people for a $1 donation for his college fund.
- Many people earn a living customizing wine labels for weddings and special events.
- Pet sitting is a big business now, as is home organizing. (Who would have thought you could earn money offering to rearrange someone's closet?)

To succeed, you need to position yourself and your services to solve a specific or unanswered need for a business or individual.

Whether your question is, "I've got an idea, but how do I get started?" or "What could I do?," in this chapter, we suggest business ideas to provide an extra income stream—a stream that may become successful enough to support you and your family.

Ask yourself these questions:

- What problems can I solve?
- Are there unfilled needs for a product or service I could provide?
- What outside interests do I have?

Only your creativity should limit your ideas! We'll outline some options that other budding entrepreneurs have chosen to get started, but you don't have to stop there. Think outside of the box.

Keep in mind: if possible, try to combine what you love to do with what you are great at doing. You will invest a lot of sweat equity into your business, so you really have to love what you are doing to help make it successful.

Skills That Fill a Need or Solve a Problem

These are some categories of skills and interests that people like you have turned into revenue-generating businesses:

Writing

Are you a strong writer? You don't need to write a book, though that is an option. Businesses you could consider include freelance technical writer, copy editor, review writer, blogger, ghostwriter, or even grant writer. If you have some technical skills, you could create newsletters, brochures and marketing materials, website copy and content, proposals, business plans, college essays, or speeches. Writing assignments typically don't require you to work normal business hours, or work from an office. This means you'll have flexibility to schedule your writing during convenient times for you.

If you want to investigate options to earn money as a writer, you can see short-term assignments on sites like oDesk.com, Sologig.com,

Elance.com, Guru.com, and GetAFreelancer.com. Guru.com lists these categories of writing jobs available:

- Writing, Editing, and Translation
- Creative Writing
- Web Content
- Articles and Press Releases
- Copywriting
- Ghost Writing and Books
- Editing and Proofreading
- Academic Writing
- Blogs
- eBooks
- Technical Writing
- Reports
- Sales Materials
- Screen and Script Writing
- User Guides and Manuals
- Grants and Proposals
- Newsletters
- Other—Translation
- Speeches
- Resumes and Cover Letters
- Children's Writing
- Songs and Poems
- Foreign Language Translation

If you visit Guru.com, you will see jobs available for creating sales pages, reports, translations, scripts, and many other types of writing projects. The budgets range anywhere from $250 or less, up to a potential of $25,000 (though we didn't see any of those high-budget projects listed when we looked).

Getting work from sources like these may not pay as much as acquiring your own customers, but if you can land these gigs without expending a lot of time and effort with a marketing campaign for your own business, it may be worth the lower payout. These assignments also benefit you because they allow you to build a portfolio of work to share with future clients, and you gain experience and familiarity doing this type of subcontracted work. You may decide that taking on some of these gigs when you have free time could be the easiest solution, especially if you don't like selling yourself or your skills, which you will probably eventually need to do if you want to make a real go of your side business.

EVELYN BOURNE, PRODUCTIVE PEN— WWW.PRODUCTIVEPEN.COM

Writing was Evelyn's passion. However, the opportunity to be a professional writer didn't present itself until she was laid off. She found it difficult to secure a new nine-to-five job, so she decided to seize the chance to tap into her entrepreneurial heritage and create a living doing something she was deeply passionate about—writing. Evelyn writes articles, web content, and other specialized online content. The biggest challenge she had when initially branching off on her own was landing new clients. Evelyn credits her presence on Twitter and Facebook with helping her network, generating traffic, and marketing her business. In essence, social media tools provided exposure to a larger audience of potential clients than she would have been able to gain any other way. There were free marketing platforms and word-of-mouth endorsements for her work. Due to Evelyn's smart keyword selections in her bios and on her site, she increased her ranking in search engines as well.

In the beginning, Evelyn's biggest challenge was doing it all. Marketing her business and producing content for clients required her to invest every waking hour she could to get her business off the ground. Luckily for her, that has changed. Her business has evolved and grown to the point where she now she has several blogs and traffic to generate a steady income. Today, she has found a better work-life balance.

HEADS UP—BLOGGING DOES NOT PRODUCE INSTANT MONEY

Let's debunk a myth right now. You will not become rich overnight starting your own blog. The people who make money blogging either have huge lists, extensive traffic, great sponsors, or all of these!

So how do bloggers make their money? Usually, it's via a combination of ads and paid links on their sites, a mega list of subscribers to market and sell products to, affiliate links to Amazon or other products, or writing paid reviews. If you are seriously considering starting a blog as a source of income, we recommend reading Problogger.net. Darren Rowse of Problogger.net earns his living with his blog. He recommends these options to generate income:

- Advertising and sponsorship programs
- Affiliate programs (where you earn money selling someone else's products or services)
- Donations (tip jars)
- Selling items

We write about affiliate programs, advertising, and more ways to generate income in the body of the book.

Keep in mind, if you want to earn money using your blog, you'll need to expand your network and demonstrate your expertise. When you do so, you may earn the opportunity to consult, speak, or write (a book or articles) and generate income by selling your products and services.

Be aware, it is difficult to find paid opportunities to blog for other sites, especially at first. You may be surprised by how many blogs for major organizations, such as *Harvard Business Review* and *Forbes*, are actually authored by a network of people providing insights in exchange for exposure to large audiences. There is nothing wrong with writing for free; in fact, both of us have blogged in exchange for visibility. The key is to make sure you have a specific strategy and goal for how your volunteer writing will help you. Is your goal to bring new visitors to your site? Be sure the site features links to your page. Is your goal to gain credibility as a recognized expert? If you choose prominent sites, you could easily earn this distinction. Sometimes, adding a "big name" to your bio will help you win other paid opportunities down the road.

Technical Services

Do you love tinkering with the latest gadgets or software? Maybe you are a whiz at setting up networks or developing code or websites. You can offer your expertise to help others who are technically challenged. If you like public speaking, your services could even include training (either in person or virtually). Here are some of the related available job categories on Elance.com:

- Web Programming
- Website Design
- Mobile Applications
- Software Application
- Other IT and Programming
- Database Development
- Search Engine Optimization
- Blog Programming
- System Administration
- Technical Support
- User Experience Design
- Networking and Security
- Flash and Flex Animation
- Project Management
- Testing and Q&A

Consulting

Fixing other people's problems as a consultant is a go-to business idea for many people. From personal organizing to coaching, there are few barriers to entry; all you need is a good idea and a way to collect money! The hardest part is finding people willing to pay you to help them. IBISWorld, a market research firm, created a report in January 2012 titled, "Hot Industries for Start-Ups," which ranked consulting highly as a potential business concept. Some suggestions on their list included:

- IT Consulting
- Management Consulting

- HR Consulting
- Environmental Consulting
- Scientific and Economic Consulting—Noted by IBISWorld-wide as a hot sector. (According to IBISWorldwide: In November 2011, National Public Radio (NPR) featured a story highlighting a strong and growing demand for analysts to make sense of "big data"—the troves of data companies keep about their customers and financial transactions.)

How to Find Consulting Opportunities

Your network and word-of-mouth referrals will make or break your consulting business. This is why personal branding, reputation management, and social networking are so important. They provide a platform for you to demonstrate your expertise online to people who may want to hire you, and, if you are lucky (and good at what you do), to publicly praise your work and share it with others who need to know about you.

Coaching

If you enjoy helping people succeed, coaching may be a good profession for you. Life coaching is a relatively new and rapidly growing field, largely in response to the stress and pressures of balancing work and personal life. (We've all seen how stressed people are at work. Especially after a layoff, the remaining employees take on the workload of those that were let go.) These are some of the areas of coaching to explore:

- Personal coaching
- Career coaching
- Executive coaching
- Business coaching
  - Management development training
  - Professional development training
  - Quality assurance training

ROSA SMITH-MONTANARO, MIND OVER PLATTER

Rosa loved reading self-help books and attending personal development seminars. This led to her becoming an active alumnus and coach with the local Anthony Robbins franchise. She found helping and teaching so rewarding! When she thought about what she wanted to do for the rest of her life, it became obvious. She turned her hobby into a business and started a private practice in 1996. Her coaching practice, called Mind Over Platter, focuses on wellness and weight loss. Having recently lost 30 pounds of her own, she was able to duplicate these results with her clients in both one-on-one sessions and in groups. Rosa's clients kept telling her that they wished she could work with their out-of-state friends. This led her to record sessions and write a book as a way of touching more people. In 2002, Rosa launched www.MindOverPlatter.com to support the online products and education she provides for clients across the world.

How to Find Coaching Opportunities

Joining professional associations can add to your credibility, and the people you meet can help you make connections by referring clients or contacts. Many professional associations have searchable directories. Learn what certifications or training you can acquire to make yourself more marketable.

When you join groups dedicated to your specific consulting practice, you'll learn what fellow experts talk about and the issues they face, and begin to understand your competition. Here is a list of coaching associations to start your exploration process:

- Association for Coaching (AC)
- Association for Professional Executive Coaching and Supervision (APECS)
- Institute of Coaching Professional Association (ICPA)
- International Association of Coaching (IAC)
- International Business Coach Institute (IBCI)

- International Coach Federation (ICF)
- The International Consortium for Coaching in Organizations (ICCO)
- Institute for Professional Excellence in Coaching (iPEC)
- The American Coaching Association (ACA)
- Worldwide Association of Business Coaches (WABC)

Crafts and Hobbies

You may be an avid artist, photographer, stamp collector, or guitar enthusiast. Believe it or not, you can convert all of these interests into an income-generating business. We talk about the different platforms you can use to promote your business idea in Chapter 13, but for now, start thinking about how to make money doing what you enjoy.

You may consider:

- Selling the result or product of your work, such as your recorded songs or art.
- Selling instructions about how to do what you do.
- Offering classes online or in-person.

When you have a specific interest, you know there is a group of people who love it, too. Find them! Chances are, there are groups of people on Facebook talking about your interest. Search the groups from the search bar in Facebook and see what groups exist. You can see who is on Twitter by searching for the specific interest using WeFollow.com or Twellow.com. You can also search Google+ for people and communities who share your interest. Joining these groups allows you to be part of a community who most likely will be interested in what you sell in the future. You can also research the competition by noting what other group members are selling. You may decide to compete or partner with some of these fellow entrepreneurs.

Consider Any Service a Good Opportunity

Any service you provide may have great potential. Many of the businesses mentioned in *55 Surefire Homebased Businesses You Can Start for Under $5,000* (Entrepreneur Press, 2009) by Cheryl Kimball are service based:

- Bicycle Repair
- Boat Cleaning
- Chimney Sweep
- Cleaning Service
- Computer Repair
- Editorial Services
- Electronics Repair
- Golf Coach
- Home Energy Auditor
- Household Organizer
- Private Cook
- Personal Concierge
- Property Management
- Solar Energy Consultant
- Taxidermist

- Used Book Sales
- Computer Training
- Desktop Publisher
- Music Lessons

Areas Ripe for Growth

Staying up on trends might allow you to seize the moment and build a business where there is growth potential. Businesses in a healthy growth mode make ideal targets for MOXIEs. IBISWorld's report of 11 top start-up industries for 2012 suggests "hot fields" for starting a new business. The following list identifies potential opportunities due to increased customer desires (or unfulfilled needs.) Some of the fields mentioned include:

- Corporate Wellness Services: Chair massages, yoga, and workout programs.
- Human Resources and Benefits Administration: Outsourced administrative HR functions and tasks.
- Scientific and Economic Consulting: Analyzing global economic data and trends in growing markets.
- Relaxation Beverages: Energy drinks, specialty water, and teas.
- Street Vendors: Specialty food carts.
- Ethnic Supermarkets: Primarily Asian and Hispanic ingredients.
- Wineries and Craft Beers: Microbrews, craft beers, and wines.
- Social Network Game Development: Blending two hot trends—gaming with social networking—spurs innovation and new business.
- Internet Publishing and Broadcasting: Online books, eBooks, and music publication and distribution.

- Online Survey Software: Easy-to-use and interpret tools to capture customer satisfaction.
- E-Commerce and Online Auctions: New aggregators and online tools for buying and selling.

How to Monitor Growing Trends with Social Media

Monitor questions people ask on Quora.com and LinkedIn groups to provide a taste of what is new and upcoming. You could also check trending topics from the Twitter interface. Twitter highlights high-frequency tweets mentioning the same keywords or hashtags—the # sign you see on Twitter—that give you insight into what people are talking about on a day-to-day basis.

Checking LinkedIn for the news of the day will also keep you up-to-date. For example, if you are in Human Resources and follow other HR experts, you may notice upcoming conferences or events, in-person meet-ups, or even the just-announced merger of two major software providers.

A quick scan of Pinterest's main feed may reveal new or popular infographics or visual statistics.

You may decide to seize a hot, or trending, topic. For example, you could write a blog post to take advantage of people's interests in these trends. If you are a marketing consultant, you could convert the reference to a controversial movie star into an article on what mistakes not to make when branding your business.

Riding the Wave of Hot Trends

Is it possible for you to run an ancillary business related to a hot field? For example, what if you created billing systems for corporate wellness services, or even website development targeted to this group? How about creating a newsletter for a hot new local winery? Maybe you can offer to take photographs for any of the above businesses? You might want to consider expanding your business idea to collaborate with one of the hot fields as they are positioned to grow. These new businesses run lean and mean, and may not have all the necessary skill sets required to get the job done. They will most likely try to do some of these things themselves or ignore them. This is where you come in.

Accounting and Bookkeeping Support

Small companies with one or two employees may not want to invest their precious time in bookkeeping. This is a prime opportunity to introduce your services. Watch newspapers and chamber of commerce meetings for new business announcements or new contracts awarded.

Keep a lookout for new consultants or coaches who will need an accounting system set up or perhaps refined or fixed. You may even consider offering them a group discount if they all agree to use your services together.

Marketing, Event Planning, and Electronic Newsletters

Almost all new businesses need help with marketing and communications. You could pitch your services to a new local cupcake shop or microbrewery to help them promote, coordinate, and/or organize events at their facilities. You could recommend and maintain a monthly electronic newsletter to help keep current and potential customers up-to-date on their businesses. You may even offer to solicit advertisers for the newsletter to help offset the cost of your services.

Website Development, Social Media Strategists, and Community Managers

Reach out to new businesses and send them tips about how to build and design better websites. If they see the need to improve their sites' designs, they may select you when they are ready.

It is important for all businesses to be visible online. You could present yourself as a social media expert to new and existing businesses who do not yet have an online presence. Business owners often believe they don't have the staff to handle this extra set of duties. You can position yourself as a company's "community manager," a role that oversees and manages the social media platforms for companies. A community manager's mission is to engage the company's followers in dialogue, elicit feedback, and create an overall sense of community.

Offer your services as a social media contractor to manage the development of presence and create a loyal community, launch a Facebook campaign, or teach customer service reps how to respond to issues raised on Twitter and Facebook.

Technical Support and Implementing New Technologies

One suggestion is to approach IT solutions providers to discuss the possibility of being a contract employee—perhaps they could refer smaller, less desirable projects over to you.

Industries that are less technically savvy need your help. For example, not-for-profits may need help streamlining processes and implementing new technology to improve their operations.

For any business that collects payments, propose to help them implement mobile payment options to decrease bad debt or late payments.

Lead Generation and Proposal Development

You could offer to make phone calls or send emails to prospective customers to build a lead pipeline for a business, which helps it focus its attention on hot prospects. Offer to write proposals for businesses. As an add-on service, you could also search for other opportunities to submit requests for proposals.

New Business Development and Sales

Present your ability to open up a business to new channels and industries by leveraging your industry contacts. You could also suggest serving as a contract salesperson for their business.

Entering Unchartered Waters: Products or Services With Potential

If you are bound and determined to do this MOXIE thing, think about creating products or services that don't yet exist; products or services that have not moved into new markets or industries; or those that do exist, but need major improving. You probably stumble across problems and wish there was a better way of doing things. This is how it starts. The key is putting this wish into action.

Brainstorming new products or services starts by identifying problems that exist. One example is Zipcar (recently purchased by Avis). The company's mission is to change how people think about transportation, which they do through car sharing. The basic idea is to provide access to cars, either by the hour or day, to their members. They use the latest and greatest technology to make renting a car fast, easy, and convenient. It started as an improvement to the standard car rental, moved into the U.S. market after success in Europe, and then constantly continues to improve upon its own services by additions like a mobile device application, which simplified the process for the end-user.

A couple of Syracuse University graduates founded BrandYourself.com. It got its start because Pete Kistler discovered he shared his name with a drug dealer, which was hurting his job search. He and his technically savvy friends began building a website that could help an individual become digitally distinct. The Internet-based software tool guides individuals through steps, and suggests actions they can take to improve how their name ranks online. This is a great example of meeting a need and solving a problem. The only competition was from corporate branding tools, which are too expensive for the average person. At the time, BrandYourself was a new answer to the problem in the growing field of online personal reputation management.

Another example of someone with MOXIE is Anne Osovski, a

certified fitness trainer. One of the complaints she heard frequently from her clients was that they missed her workouts while they were traveling. After hearing this repeatedly, Anne began thinking about creating an iPhone app her clients could take with them on the go. She contacted a mobile application developer and began working on her specifications and marketing and pricing strategies. Now, less than a year after her initial contact with the app developer, she has launched Workout in a Bag for iPhone.

Get It Done

First, ask yourself these three questions:

- What problems can I solve?
- Are there unfilled needs for a product or service I could provide?
- What outside interests do I have?

Remember, brainstorming means writing down every idea. Do not filter or block ideas that may initially seem crazy! Follow your passion!

Decide what skill set you will use to base your business around. A reminder of some examples:

- **Writing:** Can you write? Do you like writing? Are you any good at it?
- **Technical:** Many people may not be as technically inclined as you are. Who would benefit from your expertise?
- **Consulting:** Do you feel you have the authority and ability to advise others?
- **Coaching:** Do you gravitate towards problem solving?
- **Crafts and Hobbies:** When you consider monetizing your interests, you can be sure you will enjoy your MOXIE work.

Create a list of the products and services you will offer. Can you see an opportunity to tap into the areas that are ripe for growth? Could you propose any of these services?

- Accounting and bookkeeping support
- Marketing, event planning, and electronic newsletters
- Website development, social media strategy, and community management
- Technical support and implementing new technologies
- Lead generation and proposal development
- New business development and sales

Remember, some of your ideas may be for products or services that don't yet exist!

Identify resources to stay on top of what is happening within your chosen industry. You will also want to look for thought leaders, movers and shakers, and other potential like-minded thinkers. Find them using the following resources:

- Online resources (blogs, newsletters)
- Professional associations
- LinkedIn, Facebook, Twitter, Google+, or Pinterest

What Business Model is Right for You?

There is a lot to decide when you start out as a business owner! You need to know whether you will go solo, partner, contract, or invest in someone else's business. The answer depends a lot on your tolerance for personal and financial risk. Those who are risk averse will make different choices from those who love the rush of adrenaline that comes from taking a chance. The key to building a successful business is to understand how you feel about taking risks, and determine a setup that feels right for you. Here are four different structures or models to consider.

Solopreneur

Going solo requires you to wear every hat imaginable. You are in charge of managing administrative tasks, strategic planning, accounting, marketing, sales, product development, IT, contract development and negotiations, scheduling, and almost every other job—even if you have no experience with that type of work. The benefit of doing this alone is that you don't have salaries to pay, and all the income and profit belongs to you. Need and greed can be very powerful motivators.

Partnerships/Joint Ventures

Joining forces with other business owners can feel less risky, especially if you join an existing business. As the saying goes, "two heads are better than one." Partnering with someone helps you leverage your joint strengths. Consider partnering with someone within the same line of work, or maybe with a professional whose clients would be interested in your products or services. One example of this complementary partnership is a nutritionist and a personal trainer. This symbiotic relationship creates instant referrals and a potential pipeline of business. If someone is trying to lose weight or get healthy, they may visit a nutritionist who specializes in food intake and diet. If the nutritionist recommends adding exercise and can also refer their client to a personal trainer, it is a strong endorsement for the client.

When two or more independent businesses come together to work on a specific project, it's called a *joint venture.* Both parties agree to develop, for a finite period, a new entity in which they both have input into the direction of the business and share revenues, expenses, and assets. When the project or time period ends, these partners are free to go their separate ways or, if successful, they may choose to work together again.

One such notable joint venture includes Sony and Ericsson. They partnered to combine Sony's consumer electronics expertise with Ericsson's technological leadership. As a result, they no longer compete. They make phones as partners.

There are many ways both parties can benefit from entering into joint ventures. Joint ventures can cross promote to one another's customers either by sharing lists, or advertising on websites. They can build a product or service together. They could share resources such as technology or meeting space. They can also write new content for each other's sites.

Contract/Freelance

An organization may hire a contract worker when it needs someone to do a particular job or project. The organization provides the project's description, and a person or company may apply for it. The organization reviews all the applications, chooses the best-qualified candidate, and then offers him or her the job. The major difference between a contract job and regular employment is the duration of the job. Once the project is complete, the contract ends. The titles "consultant" and "freelancer" fall under contract work. They are both free agents brought in for a specific project, and when that project is over, they move on to other projects. Contracting can be a full-time job, or it could be fewer than 40 hours a week. Sometimes you have to visit the client site, and other times you can work virtually. Savvy contractors always have a pipeline of projects queued up.

If you contract your services, the organization with the project typically establishes the hourly wage. However, sometimes this is negotiable, and you should do your research to determine the going rate for the type of work you will be performing. You can use a job board such as Indeed.com to search for job titles similar to the one you are considering. Fewer and fewer employers list their pay or salary information, but you should be able to find some. You can also solicit information from other contractors.

Calculating Your Rate

One way to establish an hourly rate is to use the average prevailing annual salary and divide it by 2,000, which assumes a 40-hour work week. However, you have other costs to cover, such as Social Security contributions, so your hourly rate needs to be higher. Salary.com suggests adding 30 percent to the regular hourly wage to convert an hourly wage to a contract employee rate.

SOMETHING TO CONSIDER: HOW MUCH DO YOU NEED TO EARN?

There are many tax implications you'll need to consider when you earn independent income. Alexis Grant, an entrepreneurial writer, digital strategist, and author of *How to Create a Freakin' Fabulous Social*

continued from page 359

Media Strategy, listed these considerations on her website, http://alexisgrant.com:

"As a sole proprietor (and that's an important distinction because taxes will affect you differently if you're incorporated or have some other fancy title), here are two places you'll get hit harder than if you worked for a company:

1. **Social Security tax.** *It's 10.4 percent. If you work for yourself, you pay it all. If you work for a company, you pay 4.2 percent and your employer pays 6.2 percent.*

2. **Medicare tax.** *It's 2.9 percent. If you work for yourself, you pay it all. If you work for a company, you pay 1.45 percent and your employer pays 1.45 percent. Social Security plus Medicare is often referred to as the self-employment tax. It's a total of 13.3 percent (on income up to $110,100).*

Keep in mind, you will have some opportunities to write off business expenses, including supplies, networking expense, mileage to work-related events, and other things you buy for your business. You may even be able to write off a percentage of the expenses for a home office you use exclusively for work. However, depending on how much you earn, it's unlikely your expenses will offset a significant amount of your income and taxes."

Additionally, there are online tools you can experiment with to help you determine how to calculate a profitable rate. These are some helpful rate calculators to help you pin down an hourly rate:

- FreelanceSwitch.com: http://freelanceswitch.com/rates/
- Modernfreelance.com: http://www.modernfreelance.com/freelance-calculator/

Finding Freelance and Contract Opportunities

There are many sites dedicated to contract work. The sites below list opportunities and allow the freelancer to post their expertise and rates of pay:

- Elance.com
- Ether.com
- LiveAdvice.com
- Ingenio.com
- FreelanceSwitch.com

Franchise and Direct Sales Businesses

Many big names fall under this category, for example, McDonalds and Mary Kay. They all require up-front financial investments from you.

Franchise

This is not an ideal MOXIE business, unless you can hire people to run it right away, but we thought we should include it for your reference. By definition, a franchise is a successful, proven business model. In a franchise, you not only purchase the business model, but also the rights to sell particular goods and/or services. The franchisee must follow the business model exactly. If franchisees want to deviate, they need the prior approval from the main office.

> **⇨ TIP**
>
> This is a partial list of Entrepreneur.com's "Top 50 Franchises to Buy in 2012." The investment ranges from $31,000 to over $1 million:
>
> - Anytime Fitness
> - Dunkin Donuts
> - H&R Block
> - ServePro
> - Subway
> - Supercuts

Although this type of venture is a bit more expensive and time consuming than other opportunities, there are benefits to getting involved with an established name, including: brand recognition, and receiving pre-established and proven delivery and service models, infrastructure, support, and technology.

There are many franchising opportunities available. You can research franchises independently or use a service like FranNet.com, which provides a type of matchmaking service and business consulting to help you select the correct opportunity.

Direct Sales Business Opportunities

Instead of starting from scratch, you may be interested in opting into a direct sales business like Mary Kay, Silpata, Pampered Chef, or Tastefully Simple. Independent representatives market and sell a variety of products to consumers through direct selling or home parties. Some of the products commonly associated with direct sales include jewelry, cosmetics, kitchen supplies, spa items, home décor, and health and wellness products. Representatives work on full-commission compensation structures, and often need creative marketing ideas to entice their customer base and keep revenues flowing. According to the Direct Selling Association, approximately 90 percent of direct sales business owners operate their businesses part time.

A spinoff of this is network marketing, also known as multi-level marketing (MLM). With multi-level marketing, you make money by selling products or services and building representatives under you who, in turn, sell the products or services and you get a commission from their sales. Ambit Energy for example, enables you to earn a commission on the energy people you sign up and are billed for. Not only does the customer save money, but the salesperson earns a commission from each monthly invoice. Does it sound iffy? Don't turn your nose up yet. You may have heard unsavory things about companies like Amway, or other multi-level marketing pitches and offers. In 1988, the FTC ruled that Amway was not a pyramid scheme or scam. This reduced the negative stigma of MLM businesses a bit. What really determines the legitimacy of a MLM business is the fact that a product or service is involved in the exchange of money. All the structures and systems are in place, which makes these a nice option for those without a lot of entrepreneurial or business experience. The lower cost of entry (compared to franchises or direct sales) also makes these opportunities attractive. Beware: while some savvy MLMers will earn big money, most (90 percent) will drop out within two years.

If you want to learn more, you can go to the Direct Selling Association website for a listing of their members. This national association has set a code of conduct, which states in part that "It ensures that member companies will make no statements or promises that might mislead either consumers or prospective sales people. Pyramid schemes are illegal and companies operating pyramids are not permitted to be members of the DSA."

These business opportunities are legitimate and will send you a 1099 at the end of the year to track income. Additionally, most of these businesses offer "turn-key systems"; that is, they provide tools to track sales, produce billing statements or invoicing, and have systems in place to make the business run efficiently.

Evaluating MLM Opportunities

These are some questions you should consider when you evaluate MLM opportunities:

- Are the products/services offered unique?
- Is there a genuine need for the product/service and one that is of great value so the customer comes out feeling like a winner?
- Do their marketing and sales systems leverage current technology?
- Has the company been in business for more than five years?
- Is the company private or public?

At the height of frustration with his job, Dan Howard learned of a business plan from an acquaintance. This business plan laid out how Dan could leverage his talent for developing relationships, and his numerous contacts, into a financially rewarding business. The business was ACN, a direct-selling telecommunications company. When you sign people up to use the ACN phone service, you make a commission based on the minutes used. Dan learned he could make even more money by becoming a group leader, and approached a top performer to ask for mentoring. Dan invested 15–20 hours a week while employed, and reached a point where he could quit his day job and focus entirely on building his ACN business.

The key to success in selecting the right option is understanding your buyers' values, says Dean LoBrutto of BestFitBiz. Buyer values include your skills, income and lifestyle goals, attributes (aligning your values and attitudes with those of the product/service), type of business model, and level of structure and support needed.

- What is the long-term residual income from the product/service? Is it a short-term fad?
- Will you be able to generate immediate income?
- How much time will you need to invest in order to generate the income you desire?
- Will you have FUN?

Your level of success will be directly proportionate to the money you earn.

Level of Investment

Each business model requires different levels of investment on your behalf. This chart helps illustrate these differences.

BUSINESS MODEL	TIME	FINANCIAL INVESTMENT	OPERATIONS	MARKETING/ SALES	SUPPORT	EMOTIONAL	INCOME OPPORTUNITY
Solo	High	Varies	High	High	Low	High	Slow
Partnership	Medium	Medium	Medium	Medium	Low to Medium	Medium	Faster
Contract/ Freelance	Low None	None	Low	None	High	Low Med	Immediate
Direct Sales	Low to High	Low	Low	Medium	High	Medium	Faster

Time is the amount of your time it will take to get the business up and keep it running. When there are no systems, processes, or procedures in place, setting up your business can consume a lot of your time, not to mention the marketing and sales, new product development, invoicing, collections, and myriad of other time-consuming activities. We talk about managing your time in Chapter 22.

Financial Investment is the amount of money it will take you to get your idea started. We believe it is possible, and even doable, to start a business without breaking the bank.

Operations refers to the activities related to keeping your business operating: creating systems, implementing processes, managing accounting, and resolving IT issues, to name a few. When you are part of a larger organization, many times you don't need to get involved with these details. They are the backbone and infrastructure of your business.

Support refers to the tools and resources available to you to run your business. Who will answer the phone and take orders, or answer customer questions? Who will manage the calendar and schedule?

Emotional Investment is high when you have your own business. There is the risk factor and the pressure to succeed. There is a lot riding on your success, and often you feel the pressure.

Income Opportunities means measuring/assessing the stability of income. The faster the right business model is established, then, conceivably, the faster the income will come pouring in. This chart assumes there is greater income stability within established businesses.

Get It Done

Decide which of these models sounds most attractive to you based on your ability and willingness to invest time, money, and free time:

- Solopreneur
- Partnership/Joint Venture
- Contract/Freelance
- Franchise
- Direct Selling

Your decision to structure and invest in your business depends on how you perceive risk, and your needs and wants around these issues:

- **Time:** How much time can you realistically invest?
- **Financial Investment:** How much money do you want to invest?
- **Operations:** Do you have enough experience and resources to put processes and procedures in place?
- **Support:** Are you organized and disciplined enough to follow through on all the parts of the business that need to be managed?
- **Emotional Investment:** How do you feel about risk? What if you start your business and it fails? Are you motivated by the prospect of working tirelessly to build something and see it grow and become profitable?
- **Income Opportunities:** How much does money motivate you?

The Legal and Financial Stuff

There are all types of legal matters and financial decisions you need to think about as you start and grow your business. We can't possibly cover them all, but this chapter highlights some key legal and financial issues and decisions we believe new business owners face. Be sure to speak with the right attorneys, accountants, and other professionals who have experience advising small businesses like yours for answers to your specific business questions. We do not intend this chapter to provide specific legal, financial, or insurance advice for you or your business; we are not experts in any of those areas. Please consider this information as a guide to help determine some questions to ask the appropriate professionals who are qualified to advise you about your legal and financial concerns. Every business and business owner is different, so never rely on general information for these crucial decisions.

The Cost of Expert Advice

If you are creating a side business as a MOXIE, you probably have an income and benefits from your full-time work. Be sure to invest it wisely! Expert advice comes with a price tag. Be prepared to dole out cash to get the best advice possible. Ask for recommendations from small business owners you know to find the best professional resources. Other good resources are available via professional groups on LinkedIn and through industry associations. Don't overlook the opportunity to network and share resources and referrals with local groups of budding entrepreneurs—consider visiting your local co-working space to find people to share ideas.

If possible, select advisors with experience in your start-up niche who have small business expertise. Make the most effective use of their time and yours by having all your information and questions prepared in advance of your meetings. You may decide to put together a business plan. It is a helpful document to have, and creating it forces you to think about details you may have missed. Additionally, the advisors you meet with will probably ask you about it. There are many different business plan templates out there, but our recommendation is to keep it simple to start. Honestly, neither one of us had a written business plan when we first started. It was only after we started to grow a little that we saw how a plan would help guide our business. However, if you are looking for any kind of funding, funders will most likely want to see a business plan.

SIMPLE BUSINESS PLAN

Business Name: It's I low I Roll

Value Proposition: I work with busy professionals to organize their homes for a less chaotic, more peaceful life.

Goals & Purpose

1. By consulting and learning about their lifestyle patterns and needs, co-create a system that fits and de-clutters.
2. Provide structure and organizational discipline to simplify the fast-paced lives of professionals.
3. Create an ongoing system for adjusting and modifying changes in schedules and life events.

Social Media Strategies

4. Create corporate blog, updated weekly, to provide tips, advice, recommendations, and case studies.
5. Seek guest blog opportunities on 3rings, Design*Sponge, Houzz, and decor8.
6. Find, follow, and engage with real estate agents, wedding planners, professional associations, corporate wellness groups, executive coaches, personal trainers, moving companies, and chambers of commerce.

369

continued from page 369

7. Share pictures on Facebook, Pinterest, and Google+.
8. Join and participate in online forums and groups: Quora; on Facebook: Organizing Homelife, Organizing Made Fun; on LinkedIn: Timely Time Management Tips.
9. Start group on LinkedIn.
10. Obtain column in local newspaper for weekly article on organization.
11. Build list of potential clients and create bi-weekly newsletter.

Financial Targets

Revenue: $10,000 annually
Minus $1,500 expenses
Profit: $8,500

Products and Services to Reach Your Goals and Targets

6 workshops at professional associations, libraries, and colleges ($2,000)

2 eBooks on organizing and tools and resources ($2,000)

15 clients ($6,000)

What Kind of Business Structure Do You Need?

What's the difference between a sole proprietorship and an LLC? Read the summary below, but be sure to talk to your personal accountant who can explain the tax implications of each with you. If you already have an attorney, you may want to see what he or she advises based on your personal situation.

You may decide to go with the easier and less expensive DBA sole proprietorship, with the intent of forming a corporation when your business grows. Whichever way you do it, there is something psychologically motivating when you invest in your business for the long-term. It makes you feel like you are more committed to your businesses.

Sole Proprietorship vs. Incorporating

A sole proprietorship indicates an individual owns and operates the business. If your business is responsible for damage to a customer or client's health, business, or property, it becomes your sole liability. For example, if a client visiting your home office gets hurt, or if you make any type of error that could potentially cause damages, then your home, vehicle, and other assets could be seized if the client files a lawsuit against your company. We don't want to scare you, but there are many people willing to sue you at the drop of a hat.

Sole Proprietorship: DBA

DBA stands for "Doing Business As." When you file a DBA, you can then use your business name for transactions. As a sole proprietor, you must file a DBA. During the filing process, you will find out if another business already uses your name. You then have the choice to change your trade name in order to prevent customer confusion and protect the reputation of both businesses.

DBA/Sole Proprietorship may be the path for you if you do not have valuable assets (for example, a car, home, or other property) and if your business is unlikely to face civil or financial liability. You can always change your business's structure in the future if your company changes directions or your assets grow.

LLC

LLC means "Limited Liability Corporation." It structures your business as a separate entity from you, the business owner, and protects you by separating your personal and business assets. With an LLC, your assets remain protected if someone files a civil or financial lawsuit against your business. You remain responsible for paying taxes on the business's income. The main reason some people avoid using this business structure is that it involves fees and paperwork.

The initial paperwork is more complicated than a simple DBA; however, this business structure makes sense if you have assets you don't want to risk losing.

An LLC also protects your name. When you file a DBA, you register your business's trade name, but this does not prevent other companies from using it. If you anticipate building a brand and creating an empire (which we hope you are), an LLC ensures your name remains legally protected. FYI: the Federal government does not tax an LLC. You will owe income tax on your business's profits when you file your personal taxes. If you start your business with a partner, you both share the tax liabilities.

How to File and How Much to Pay

Once you determine which type of business structure works best for you, you are ready to take action. If you want to file a DBA, contact your county clerk's office or your state government. The cost varies by state and county, and the forms are relatively easy to complete. Expect to pay less than $100.

An LLC normally costs more to file than a DBA. With limited funds, starting as a sole proprietor is an affordable option, but if you own assets, the extra start-up cost of an LLC is worthwhile. The cost to file varies by state, but is usually from $50 to 800. Check with your state's Secretary of State office for exact costs. (For some states with a complicated process requiring legal help, add the cost of legal fees you will incur to the price.) You will also need to register and pay annual fees to maintain your LLC, which range from $20 to 200.

Banking and Accounting

Once you formalize your business entity, you need a separate bank account and system for tracking income and costs. Many local banks and credit unions try to attract new business customers by offering free business checking accounts. Check around and see what deals they offer. Most banks include online banking services, which will make your life easier. Read the fine print and see what service charges you may incur and if there are any minimum requirements.

LEGAL ASSISTANCE ALTERNATIVE

If you find your state's process too complex, you may want to ask for legal assistance. Besides hiring an attorney, another resource you may want to consider is LegalZoom.com. LegalZoom's pricing packages vary based on the type of legal assistance you ask for, but it is considerably less than what a standard attorney would charge. You would be wise to check with a small business attorney before doing this to make sure you know what information is required and that you have the appropriate information to complete the online forms.

A simple Excel spreadsheet may be enough to get you started tracking your income and expenditures. Ask your accountant for recommendations to facilitate your end-of-the-year tax preparation. Solutions that many business owners use, and you may want to consider, are Quickbooks, Quicken, or Peachtree. Here are just some of the things you will need to keep track of for tax purposes:

- Advertising costs
- Unpaid invoices/outstanding client bills
- Car expenses (mileage and gas)
- Commissions and fees
- Depreciation of assets (for example, your computer)
- Insurance
- Interest
- Legal and professional services (including coaching, web development, etc.)
- Office expenses and supplies
- Postage
- Printing
- Seminars and training you take to improve your business
- Taxes and licenses
- Travel, meals, entertainment
- Utilities

Hannah has found that accounting is not her strong suit. What she realizes now is that it would have been wise to have a bookkeeper help her set up the accounting software for her business. As her business grows, she will give serious thought to farming out her bookkeeping to a professional to save her the anxiety and have more timely and accurate records.

We highly recommend you start tracking where your money is going from the beginning. If you aren't tracking your expenses and income, chances are, you will lose opportunities for tax deductions and will limit your business's ability to be profitable.

Insurance Types

Protecting yourself and your assets is important; that is one reason for incorporating. You may also consider purchasing insurance for you and your business. You will want to review your homeowner's insurance policy to see what, if any, part of your business is covered. You probably don't want to stop there. Set up a meeting with your insurance agent and discuss your specific business needs. These are some types of insurance you will want to investigate before you meet with your agent.

⇨ TIP

If you do not have employees, the law generally does not require business insurance.

Business Insurance

Your state determines insurance requirements for businesses; do research to find out what, if anything, is required. Some states may mandate insurance for specific business activities. For example, if you use a car or truck for business purposes (do you transport people or things?), the state may require you to purchase commercial auto insurance. If you are reselling goods or services offered by someone else, you will want to find out how much your vendor's insurance policy covers. In other words, determine your liability if a customer has an issue.

General Liability Insurance

General liability insurance covers legal issues due to accident, injury, and negligence claims. These policies kick into gear if someone makes a claim against your business because of bodily injury, property damage, medical expenses, libel, or slander. Liability insurance would also cover the cost of defending you in lawsuits or other legal procedures.

Product Liability Insurance

Product liability insurance protects your business against financial loss because of a defective product that causes injury or bodily harm. If your business manufactures, wholesales, distributes, or retails a product, you could be liable if it causes an injury. The amount of insurance you should purchase depends on the products you sell or manufacture.

Professional Liability Insurance

This type of liability coverage protects your business against malpractice, errors, and negligence for the services provided to your customers. If you provide services, you should consider having professional liability insurance (also known as errors and omissions insurance). Depending on your profession, your state government may require you to carry coverage.

Home-Based Business Insurance

Homeowners' insurance policies do not generally cover home-based business losses. Depending on risks to your business, you may add riders to your homeowners' policy to cover normal business risks, such as property damage. (For example, fire damage to business products you store in your home.) However, homeowners' policies only go so far in covering home-based businesses, and you may need to purchase additional policies to cover other risks, such as general and professional liability.

Do You Need a Business Owner's Policy?

You may purchase insurance separately or as a bundle, which is called a business owner's policy (BOP). Purchasing separate policies from different insurers may result in higher total premiums. A BOP combines typical coverage options into a standard package, and some insurers offer this at a savings compared to buying each type of coverage separately. Typically, BOPs cover property, general liability, vehicles, business interruption, and other types of coverage common to most types of businesses. BOPs simplify the insurance buying process and may save you money. However, make sure you understand the extent of coverage in any BOP you are considering. Not every type of insurance is included in a BOP. If your business has unique risks, you may require additional coverage.

Buying Insurance

Business insurance costs work the same way as individual coverage. Generally, the higher deductible you agree to pay, the lower your premium will be. Obviously, when you agree to take on a high deductible, you take on additional financial risk.

Research Different Insurance Companies

The Small Business Administration recommends using The National Federation of Independent Businesses to help you assess your risks and to make sure you have insured every aspect of your business. The costs for coverage vary from one insurance company to another. Some brokers specialize in insuring specific types of business, while others can connect you with policies specific to your business activities. Often, specialist brokers can offer the best coverage and the best rates. Don't forget to use your in-person and virtual network to source the most appropriate insurance provider.

Find a Reputable, Licensed Agent

Finding a good insurance agent is as important as finding a good lawyer or accountant. You should always work with someone who is licensed to sell in your state. Many states provide a directory of licensed agents.

Annual Check Up

As your business grows, so may your liabilities. You don't want to be caught underinsured after the fact. If you have purchased or replaced equipment, or had other major changes, you should contact your insurance broker to discuss your coverage.

Protecting Your Ideas: Trademark vs. Copyright

If you create presentations, or write papers, eBooks, or other intellectual property, you should investigate if you should protect your content. The choice between registering a trademark and a copyright can be a bit confusing. There are important differences between trademark and copyright protection, but they are both means of protecting your intellectual property rights.

Copyright

A copyright protects your ideas. It essentially lays claim to your work and says that no one can copy it without your permission. You've seen this before: ©2013 John Smith. This means that John Smith copyrighted the work in 2013, and it cannot be copied or used without his permission. To acquire a copyright, complete an application on the U.S. Copyright Website: www.copyright.gov. The online registration fee is $35. Check with an attorney or someone who has already successfully filed one to make sure you complete it correctly.

Whenever you create material (eBooks, presentations, whitepapers, reports, or other intellectual property), you will want to claim ownership and indicate it is not acceptable to copy your work without your permission. Note: a copyright does not cover titles, names, short phrases and slogans, familiar symbols or designs, or unique lettering styles or coloring. You will need a trademark to protect these things.

Trademark

A trademark protects a word, phrase, symbol, or design (or a combination of these) that identifies and distinguishes the goods or services from those of others. You delineate a trademark by the recognizable symbols TM, SM, or ®. Think of memorable advertising slogans, such as "It's everywhere you want to be®" or "Melts in your mouth, not in your hand®." These are registered trademarks. The Nike swoosh, M&M's®, and the Coca-Cola® logo are trademarked, as is Coke's contour bottle.

If you want to register your trademark, you will need to file a trademark application with the U.S. Patent and Trademark Office (USPTO). Also note: there are additional steps and costs involved in filing for a trademark. Our advice is to check with your attorney and follow his or her recommendations.

Get It Done

Address these questions and issues:

- Does sole proprietorship (DBA) or incorporating (LLC) make the most sense for your situation?
- Don't ignore your banking and accounting. Start tracking your expenses and income.

- Determine what type of business insurance you'll need:
  - General Liability Insurance
  - Product Liability Insurance
  - Professional Liability Insurance
  - Home-Based Business Insurance
  - Business Owner's Policy
- Will you need a trademark or copyright to protect your business and ideas?

Resources

Blogs Covering Social Media and/or Small Business Topics

Alexis Grant—http://alexisgrant.com

Alicia Arenas—http://saneracamp.com

Brian Solis—http://www.briansolis.com

Boom Social, Kim Garst—http://kimgarst.com/blog

Chris Brogan—http://www.chrisbrogan.com

Danny Brown—http://dannybrown.me

Escape from Cubicle Nation, Pamela Slim—http://www. escapefromcubiclenation.com/pamela-slims-blog/

Heidi Cohen—http://heidicohen.com

Inside Facebook—http://www.insidefacebook.com

Intrepid Group, LLC; Todd Schnick—http://intrepid-llc.com

Jeff Bullas—http://www.jeffbullas.com

Jenny Blake—http://www.lifeaftercollege.org/

John Jantsch; Duct Tape Marketing—http://ducttapemarketing.com

Jon Loomer—http://www.jonloomer.com/blog

Lighthouse Insights—http://lighthouseinsights.in

Liz Strauss—http://www.successful-blog.com

Mari Smith (special focus on Facebook)—http://www.marismith.com

Pushing Social—http://pushingsocial.com

Razor Social—http://www.razorsocial.com

Schaeffer Marketing Solutions: http://www.businessesgrow.com

60 Second Marketer—http://60secondmarketer.com/blog

Social Fresh—http://socialfresh.com/blog

Social Media Examiner—http://www.socialmediaexaminer.com

Windmill Networking, Neal Schaeffer—http://windmillnetworking.com

Keep Up with Social Media News

TechCrunch (social media news)—http://techcrunch.com

Mashable—http://mashable.com/

SmartBrief—http://www.smartbrief.com/ (search for SmartBrief on Social Media and Small Business)

Alltop—http://social-media.alltop.com/ (a list of social media blogs covering a variety of topics) and http://small-business.alltop.com (a list of small business-focused blogs)

Search Engine Optimization (SEO)

Search Engine Land—http://searchengineland.com

Search Engine Watch—http://searchenginewatch.com

SEO Journal—http://www.searchenginejournal.com

The Daily SEO Blog—http://www.seomoz.org/blog

Marketing and Branding

Fix, Build & Drive—http://fixbuildanddrive.com/blog

Kissmetrics—http://blog.kissmetrics.com

Personal Branding Blog, Dan Schawbel—
   http://personalbrandingblog.com

Schaeffer Marketing Solutions—http://www.businessesgrow.com

Seth Godin—sethgodin.typepad.com

Small Business

Business 2 Community—http://www.business2community.com

Small Biz Trends—http://smallbiztrends.com

Online Marketing Blog—http://www.toprankblog.com

Blogs Targeted to Bloggers

Copyblogger—http://www.copyblogger.com

Problogger—http://www.problogger.net

Our Blogs

Hannah Morgan, Career Sherpa—www.careersherpa.net

Miriam Salpeter, Keppie Careers—www.keppiecareers.com

Books

Brogan, Chris and Smith, Julien. *Trust Agents: Using the Web to Build Influence, Improve Reputation, and Earn Trust* (Wiley, 2010).

Brossman, Martin and Mcgaha, Anora. *Social Media for Business: The Small Business Guide to Online Marketing* (Outer Banks Publishing Group, 2011).

Godin, Seth. *The Dip: A Little Book That Teaches You When to Quit* (and When to Stick) (Portfolio Hardcover, 2007).

Godin, Seth. *Purple Cow, New Edition: Transform Your Business by Being Remarkable* (Portfolio Hardcover, 2009).

Godin, Seth. *Poke the Box* (The Domino Project, 2011).

Guillebeau, Chris. *The $100 Startup: Reinvent the Way You Make a Living, Do What You Love, and Create a New Future* (Crown Business, 2012).

Hadley, Ann and Chapman, C.C. *Content Rules: How to Create Killer Blogs, Podcasts, Videos, Ebooks, Webinars (and More) That Engage Customers and Ignite Your Business (New Rules Social Media Series)* (Wiley, 2012).

Hayzlett, Jeffrey W and Eber, Jim. *The Mirror Test: Is Your Business Really Breathing?* (Business Plus, 2011).

Jantsch, John. *The Referral Engine: Teaching Your Business to Market Itself* (Portfolio Trade, 2012).

Jantsch, John. *Duct Tape Marketing Revised & Updated: The World's Most Practical Small Business Marketing Guide* (Thomas Nelson, 2011).

Jantsch, John. *The Commitment Engine: Making Work Worth It* (Portfolio Hardcover, 2012).

Kawasaki, Guy. *Enchantment: The Art of Changing Hearts, Minds, and Actions* (Portfolio Trade, 2012).

Kawasaki, Guy and Welch, Shawn. *APE: Author, Publisher, Entrepreneur—How to Publish a Book* (Nononina Press, Jan, 2013).

Kerpen, Dave. *Likeable Social Media: How to Delight Your Customers, Create an Irresistible Brand, and Be Generally Amazing on Facebook (And Other Social Networks),* (McGraw-Hill, 2011).

Labovich, Laura and Salpeter, Miriam. *100 Conversations for Career Success: Learn to Network, Cold Call, and Tweet Your Way to Your Dream Job* (LearningExpress, LLC, 2012).

Levinson, Jay Conrad. *Guerrilla Marketing, 4th edition: Easy and Inexpensive Strategies for Making Big Profits from Your Small Business* (Houghton Mifflin, May, 2007).

Pool, Jeanna. *Marketing for Solos: THE Ultimate How-To Guide For Marketing Your One Person Small Business Successfully* (3 Bar Press, 2011).

Ries, Eric. *The Lean Startup: How Today's Entrepreneurs Use Continuous Innovation to Create Radically Successful Businesses* (Crown Business, 2011).

Salpeter, Miriam. *Social Networking for Career Success: Using Online Tools to Create a Personal Brand* (LearningExpress, LLC, 2011).

Schawbel, Dan. *Me 2.0, Revised and Updated Edition: 4 Steps to Building Your Future* (Kaplan Publishing, 2010).

Scott, David Meerman. *The New Rules of Marketing and PR: How to Use Social Media, Blogs, News Releases, Online Video, and Viral Marketing to Reach Buyers Directly.* (John Wiley, 2010).

Sernovitz, Andy. *Word of Mouth Marketing: How Smart Companies Get People Talking, Revised Edition* (Greenleaf Book Group Press, 2012).

Schwerdtfeger, Patrick. *Marketing Shortcuts for the Self-Employed: Leverage Resources, Establish Online Credibility and Crush Your Competition* (Wiley, 2011).

Slim, Pamela. *Escape from Cubicle Nation: From Corporate Prisoner to Thriving Entrepreneur* (Portfolio Hardcover, 2009).

Stratten, Scott. *UnMarketing: Stop Marketing. Start Engaging* (John Wiley and Sons, 2010).

Strauss, Steven D. *The Small Business Bible: Everything You Need to Know to Succeed in Your Small Business* (Wiley, 2012).

Vaynerchuk, Gary. *The Thank You Economy* (HarperBusiness, 2011).

Vaynerchuk, Gary. *Crush It!: Why NOW Is the Time to Cash In on Your Passion* (Harper Studio, 2009).

NOTES